For Mark —

May God bless you
every day —

Ralph K. Clark

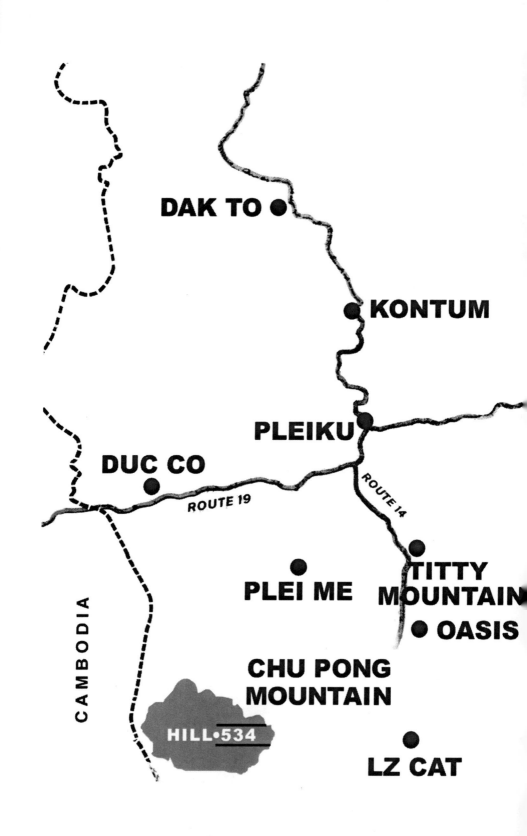

JUST LET ME WALK AWAY

RAY KENNETH CLARK

AN AMERICAN COMBAT
HELICOPTER PILOT IN VIETNAM

Edited by Terri Clark Beckham

VIRGINIA PRESS

Published by
VIRGINIA PRESS
112 Cumberland Trace
Nashville, TN 37214

First Edition
Photograph Enhancement, Maps by Dennis Carney
Jacket Art by Ed Breeding
Jacket Design by Terri Clark Beckham
ISBN: 0615546706
ISBN-13: 9780615546704
2011944182 CIP

Contents

II

Foreword

EVERY VETERAN OF Vietnam who was ever under enemy fire has a fond remembrance of a helicopter approaching his position. To those of us on the ground, the helicopter pilots and crews were a lifeline for fire support and resupply. Most importantly, they carried us out of danger. Ray Kenneth Clark, one of those brave pilots, has written a passionate, personal story of the war in Vietnam.

Whether a Vietnam veteran, a history buff, or a novice on the subject of this polarizing war, you will be impacted by this story. You will see the war, in combat and day-to-day life, through Ray's eyes. You will see what he saw, feel what he felt, and experience what he experienced. You will feel the emotions of love, fear, pain, anger, and, yes, even humor. You will witness the courage, bravery, and leadership that were the heart of the Vietnam helicopter pilot and crew. You will understand how ordinary people, when called upon by their country, were able to achieve extraordinary feats. You will also gain an insight into the horrible homecoming most of us experienced when we returned to the United States. Unlike any American war veteran of the past, the Vietnam veteran came home to a country torn by apathy and disdain for the war. Those private homecomings, while emotionally difficult, made Vietnam veterans' compassion and respect for each other profoundly strong.

While Ray and I never met "in country," we both served in the Central Highlands, an area particularly challenging to helicopter pilots because of its difficult, mountainous terrain and thick, triple-canopy jungle. Many, many vets are alive today because of brave men like Ray and his crew members. If only we could get our wounded on a chopper, we knew that within 20 minutes or so they could be in a hospital, receiving care. Each of those wounded soldiers would love to show his appreciation today, if he only knew who to thank. Although highly decorated, Ray would tell you in his soft-spoken, Oklahoma manner, "I was only doing my job."

The title of this book is intimately appropriate and is every soldier's personal prayer: Just let me walk away. I have read many books on this subject, but this one is the best, told from this immensely personal perspective.

To all who seek to understand the war in Vietnam and the men who fought there, *Just Let Me Walk Away* is a must-read. After reading this book, veterans will thank Ray for giving them a voice. Their families will thank Ray for giving them an insightful appreciation of how their loved ones served. When you finish this book, you will understand the statement, "We went as strangers but came home as brothers."

I am proud to call Ray Clark my brother and my friend.

Thomas H. Coffey
Former U. S. Army Captain
4th Infantry Division, 4th MID
Pleiku, Kontum City and Dak To
July 1967–July 1968

Preface

MY FATHER WAS leaving to fight with the 4th Infantry Division in World War II.

He was wearing that dark, olive-drab uniform of the time, the one with the waist-fitting "Ike" jacket. Only four years old, I had no thought that he might not come back: I knew he would be away a long time; and I knew it was serious.

Mom and Dad, the four of us kids, and Mom's mother all piled into her 1935 Chevrolet. From our town of Jenks, Oklahoma, we headed north to Tulsa. When we reached the outskirts of the city, my grandmother stopped the car on the side of the two-lane cement highway, and Daddy got out.

I don't remember saying goodbye. The last time I saw him that day he was settled in an easy crouch by the side of the highway, beginning his hitchhike back to his Army camp. His weight was on his right leg, his left foot in front. His olive-drab cap was cocked at a jaunty angle, as was every hat I ever saw him wear.

We turned the car around in the middle of the highway and drove away. I stood in the back seat and watched out the back window as the image of my 29-year-old father became smaller and smaller until, finally, he was out of sight.

Several months later, I received my very own letter from Dad as he fought across France and Germany in that last, fierce drive of the war in the winter and spring of 1944 and 1945. In his handwriting, the return address read simply, "Somewhere in France."

I still have that letter. I think of my dad, there on the side of that road, as I read the last line.

"Don't forget me, son."

ℭℨ

Physically imposing, my dad seemed fearless. A number of times I heard his friends discuss the probability of Dad beating world heavyweight champion Joe Lewis in the ring. When I was a boy, my father often took me with him on his daily travels, telling his friends and others we met that I was his bodyguard. I swelled with pride every time he made that comment. I was so proud of my dad. He was the most important figure in my life.

Occasionally he would talk about his combat experiences as an infantryman in France and Germany. I often asked, "Daddy, how did you keep from getting killed?"

Although not a churchgoing man, he would reply, "The Good Lord had both arms around me, son."

He talked to me continually as I was growing up, teaching me simple but powerful lessons which would guide me through life. He would say, "Always take care of your feet. They are the only ones you will ever have." And, "Always listen to what another man has to say. Then you will know what you know, and what he knows too."

When I was leaving for my first year in Vietnam, I went to say goodbye. After some small talk, Daddy spoke quietly in that deep, gruff voice of his.

"You're a professional. You'll be okay. You've always been able to take care of yourself. Keep your head down. Don't volunteer."

It was reassuring and important to hear this affirmation of his confidence in me as we discussed the deadly business I was headed into. These words were not only from father to son, but seasoned warrior to a young, unproven one.

"Okay, Dad."

Acknowledgements

I WISH TO recognize Harold Jones, my civilian flight instructor at the U.S. Army Primary Helicopter School at Fort Wolters, Texas, in 1965. As I advanced through flight school a number of instructors showed me what to do. Harold Jones taught me to fly. Had it not been for certain techniques he insisted I learn, I would not have survived flying in Vietnam.

Others who strongly influenced my development as a soldier and young officer were MSG Charles J. Hurley, my platoon sergeant when I was just a kid of 18 to 19 years of age in the 82nd Airborne Division, and LTG (Ret) Charles W. Dyke, who as a captain was the first officer I worked for after being commissioned a second lieutenant.

The three warrant officers assigned to me when I first arrived in Vietnam, CW3 Norman G. "Norm" Taylor, WO1 George Rose, and WO1 Parry Etheridge, deserve special recognition. As an aviator I was not good enough to shine their boots during the few short weeks I was with them. They saved my life countless times and, more importantly, taught me how to survive in the insane conditions we flew in.

Much appreciation goes to Kyle Maus of Chicago. His assistance in editing and research and contribution as final arbiter in all things unknown was unique and special. I also wish to thank John Phipps and Jan Polak for their many hours spent scrutinizing and improving the manuscript. Dennis Carney was especially helpful with photograph retouching, spending hours with me poring over my photographs and slides and preparing them for publication. His superior knowledge and guidance in this area were incredibly helpful.

ACKNOWLEDGEMENTS

I owe more than I can say to my editor and daughter, Terri Clark Beckham. She went beyond what anyone could expect in keeping her corrections and changes within the special context of the subject matter. Correct English is not always spoken in the heat of battle and the camaraderie of young soldiers. She tolerated my insistence on exact wording of thoughts and conversations and still was able to ensure that prose was correct. Her ideas in shaping the narrative and her insistence that what I wrote was understandable by civilian and military readers alike were invaluable.

Ray Kenneth Clark
Nashville, Tennessee

Introduction

VIETNAM WAS A strange war. The incredible restrictions in combat, and the ill treatment of America's warriors by their own government and populace, had never been experienced by the American soldier. I was a young Army lieutenant who, filled with a sense of duty and adventure, traveled to a little-known land to fight my country's war. The story is mine, built around my experiences as a helicopter pilot and troop commander. Mostly it's about flying helicopters in combat.

It is my intent that, as you read the story that follows, you will come to know in a new and personal way some of what went on in that ancient land where America broke tradition; where, sadly, without the will to win, she sent her youth to fight and die; and those who returned home, she did not welcome. It is not my purpose to examine why the American government conducted the war as it did. I will, however, point out some of the unusual policies and their effects on the soldiers doing battle.

I have endeavored to write everything exactly as it occurred, including my thoughts and key conversations. I have not attempted to impugn anyone, although there is criticism. In those instances I have changed names so as not to offend the parties concerned. None of us was perfect. All who did their best deserve high praise.

In writing this story I do not mean to imply that I was special in my performance by any means. There were plenty of men braver than I, tougher than I, men who were better pilots and leaders than I. This isn't about who was toughest or bravest. This is about the times that we performed well and therefore survived, and the times that we did not perform well and survived anyway. It's a story of how our actions determined whether others—friend and foe alike—would live or die.

This is about what the American combat helicopter pilot experienced every day—the continual, crucial takeoffs with falling engine and rotor speed, the critical landings, the shoot-downs, the engine failures, the minefields, the crashes, the near-crashes, the split-second decisions of combat flying—with the constant awareness that death rode his shoulder. This book is about the heroism and magnificence of spirit displayed by our young men when they were put to the ultimate test.

Over the years what has bothered me most about Vietnam is that no one knows what we did. Ultimately, this is about that. In a way the story is *not* mine; it is the story of all of the American helicopter pilots and crewmen who were there.

This book is about—and for—the unknown heroes of Vietnam.

For Pamela, Terri, and Kenneth

Prologue

BAMMM!

The noise was loud and sharp. The nose jerked hard to the right and the aircraft began plunging downward.

The engine had failed.

Four hundred feet above the ground with no power, we were falling from the sky.

Beep! Beep! Beep! Beep!

The low-RPM warning was screaming in my ears, and the red warning light was flashing with a will of its own. I was on the controls in a flash to get the pitch out of the blades and enter autorotation. Even so, the split second it took to get my left hand from the overhead strap to the pitch control cost us valuable altitude and rotor speed. We were heavily loaded, over trees, at very low altitude, and headed downwind. My pilot, who had the controls when the engine failed, had frozen. He neither moved nor said a word when the engine quit or during what was to follow.

Our situation was critical. We had only seconds left in the air. I had to get airspeed to 60 knots to maintain optimum rotor speed, turn 180 degrees to land into the wind, find a clearing in the trees big enough for my helicopter, and land in that precise spot—all without engine power.

I would get one attempt at landing.

I glanced at the instrument panel to check the airspeed. The sun cast a glare on the gauge—I couldn't read the numbers.

Dammit!

I looked ahead to check the helicopter's attitude against the horizon for an estimate of airspeed.

The nose is too high.

I pushed the nose down and keyed the mike.

"MaydayMaydayMaydayThisisYellow3Ihaveanenginefailure I'm goingdown!"

Dammit! I'm on intercom!

With my left hand on the pitch control, I held the cyclic between my knees, freeing my right hand to reach for the radio switch on the console. I turned the switch from intercom to UHF, took the cyclic back with my right hand, keyed the mike and made the emergency call again.

"MaydayMaydayMaydayThisisYellow3Ihaveanenginefailure I'm goingdown!"

We were falling so fast.

Just let me walk away from this one. Just let me walk away.

I

A ship is safe in the harbor.
But that is not what ships are made for.

—John Augustus Shedd
Salt from My Attic

Chapter 1

In the Beginning

I WAS A young infantry officer, experienced paratrooper, and newly trained helicopter pilot when I finished the Army's rotary wing flight training program the first of March 1966. I was assigned to the 1st Air Cavalry Division, which was operating in the Central Highlands of Vietnam.

My departure date was April 14. I went home to Oklahoma to get my wife, Ann, and our three children situated for the year I would be gone. I rented a little, white house in Brookside, a suburb of south Tulsa that lay just a few miles north of Jenks, the small town where I grew up. The house was directly across the street from an elementary school where I had played summer baseball as a 12-year-old.

We didn't take the children to the airport. Ann and I said our goodbyes in the terminal and I boarded the airplane, feeling somewhat strange. I was headed for combat—the greatest adventure of my life—and who knew what. I never had the idea that I couldn't be killed. Shoot, they killed Christ. I figured I could get it too. But I didn't think about it enough to let the idea be real. I just knew I had to stay alert and do my best.

The plane stopped at Will Rogers Airport in Oklahoma City, where I had taken my first plane ride after leaving home to enter the Army. I was 17 then, with a semester of college under my belt and my father's words that I was a grown man.

There was a big crowd at the airport. Someone said the commotion was because John Wayne was there. That was exciting to me for I respected him a great deal, and I had never seen a movie star in person. I hoped to see him, if only for a moment, but did not. And then we were gone, headed for California.

Hours later we landed in San Francisco. I was to take a bus 75 miles north to Travis Air Force Base where I would board a chartered jet to Saigon, South Vietnam. I retrieved my bags and struggled out the front door to the sidewalk by the circular drive. Those bags of mine were really heavy. I thought of all the movies I had seen with heroes and heroines carrying suitcases and bags. None of them ever struggled or stooped under the weight.

I was looking for the bus stop when I realized that Carl Wesley Coltrane was standing next to me, looking like a lost dog. Wesley and I had just finished nine months of flight school together and were both assigned to the 1st Cav. Everyone knew that, for a helicopter pilot, the 1st Cav was the place to go. It was the first unit of its kind, an infantry division with 434 helicopters and the new airmobile tactics.

I nudged Wesley. "Boy, where you going?"

He grinned widely. "Same place you are, smart ass. Boy, am I glad to see you!"

"Well, let's find the bus and get on that beast. They won't let us stay here."

LT Wes Coltrane at 1st Cav Division Hq. An Khe 1966.

We stayed at Travis two days, waiting on a flight. Wesley and I had dinner at the officers club the night before we left. I ordered steak, thinking it would be my last good meal for a long time.

On a clear and beautiful day we left on a chartered commercial jetliner with 196 troops on board, sitting three abreast on each side of the aisle. Wesley and I sat beside each other during the entire 20-hour journey. We stopped in Seattle to refuel. I was enthralled by the snowcapped beauty of Mount Rainier as we flew into Seattle that morning. I had never seen a mountain like that. After a short delay, we were airborne again and on our way. Soon we were over the Aleutians. The view was breathtaking, the snow-covered islands like white rocks pushing up from the sea.

I punched Wesley. "Hey, I want you to notice the exact direction this plane is flying."

"Why?"

"So, by god, we'll know which way to swim in case this big mother goes down—toward the tail."

"Clark, you're sick."

There were several flight attendants on the plane. They served us sandwiches and fruit about every four hours. We read and dozed and talked.

After many dull hours we landed in Kyoto, Japan. We were on the ground 2 1/2 hours and were not allowed off the plane. That didn't sit well. We were tired and cramped and bored after the long flight from Seattle, but all we could do was sit and wait to take off again on the final leg of our journey.

At last we were airborne again. We would fly down the Asian coast, past Japan, Hong Kong, Taiwan, China, North Vietnam, and finally to Saigon. There we would report to a replacement center for processing and assignment to our units.

It was dark when we left Kyoto and would be near midnight when we made Saigon. As the end of the trip grew closer, the mood on the plane began to change. There were fewer jokes, more nervous laughs. Voices, already low, faded. Conversation melted away. Then all was quiet. As I sat in the darkness, the silence was so heavy I could almost feel it. Finally it was time, and we began to descend. It was evening, April 14, 1966.

We saw the lights of Saigon's Tan Son Nhut Airport as the huge plane eased onto the runway. The plane was taxiing unusually fast toward the terminal. I looked out the window and saw two jeeps of military police with weapons, escorting us down the runway.

Someone shouted, "Hey, there's shooting on the edge of the airport!"

Wes turned to me and said, "Listen to that rookie. Hell, they aren't going to land us in the middle of a fight."

I had been looking past the MPs at what lay beyond.

"Wes, I hate to tell you this, but that building over there is on fire. And so are those storage tanks. I don't think it's a fireworks display put on for our benefit."

In perfect Hollywood style, the replacement center and airport were under attack. Small arms fire was reported off the end of the runway, and there were numerous fires throughout the area. We had just landed, and already we were in harm's way.

God Almighty, this is war.

Chapter 2

On to An Khe

WE SPENT THREE uneventful and boring days at the replacement center in Saigon. Then it was time to go. Wesley and I boarded an Air Force C-130 and flew north to An Khe and the base camp of the 1st Air Cavalry Division. I had spent a lot of time riding in the back of C-130s because of my years of jumping with the 82nd and 101st airborne divisions. When you board an airplane knowing you will leave it by jumping feet first into a blast of wind 1200 feet up in the air, it affects your attitude toward it. I loved jumping in the early years. It was fun and I couldn't wait to do it again. Later I viewed it as simply the no-nonsense endeavor that it was and had always been. Boarding a C-130 usually meant there was serious business at hand. Riding to An Khe, the term "serious business" seemed to be an understatement.

It was a clear April morning when we landed in An Khe. We walked down the ramp at the rear of the C-130 carrying our bags and looking for someone to tell us what to do and where to go. At home in Oklahoma it was my favorite month of the year, all fresh rain, new green, and spring sunshine. As I stepped out on the sparse landscape, struggling to maintain my bearing under the weight of my bags, it was as if I had landed on another planet. Red clay and a few scraggly, stunted trees surrounded the runway, its pristine asphalt surface in stark contrast to everything else we could see. We stood around for a while, then rode trucks a short distance into the base camp in An Khe for administrative processing and assignment to our units. "Camp Radcliff" was the name of the 1st Cav base camp, but to us, it was simply "An Khe." The village of An Khe was "the village." "Camp Radcliff" sounded like a nice place in the Adirondacks. We never used the name.

The village was located on Highway 19, the main east-west artery in that part of the country. It was thought that North Vietnamese Army (NVA) forces intended to split the country of South Vietnam along Highway 19, from Cambodia to the coast at Qui Nhon. The mission of the 1st Cav was to prevent that from happening.

There wasn't much to the camp in An Khe in early 1966. The size of a small town, it consisted of dirt roads, a zillion tents, lots of construction, and a well-defined perimeter defense line encircling the camp. It was dirty, dusty, and hot. The camp area was basically flat, with a small winding river between it and the village. The dominant feature of the area was a cone-shaped mountain west of the camp. Hon Cong Mountain was a perfect spot for communications facilities.

Top: Village of An Khe. 1966.
Bottom: Westward aerial view of Camp Radcliff, the 1st Air Cavalry Division base camp in An Khe. The Golf Course is the organized-looking area on the right. Hon Cong Mountain is in the background. The village of An Khe, not captured in the photo, is to the left. 1966.

In August of 1965 an advance party of the 1st Air Cavalry Division arrived in An Khe to prepare for the main body's arrival in September. Brigadier General John Wright, the assistant division commander, led officers and enlisted men alike into the scrub jungle to clear a landing field and parking area roughly a quarter-mile wide and a half-mile long. The general is reported to have said that when they finished, the area would be clean as a golf course. Thus the famous "Golf Course" came into being.

GIs have a wonderful way of naming everything. At the southern end of the camp, the side nearest the village, was "Texaco," the refueling area for the division's helicopters. Get on the radio any day and you would hear "An Khe, this is Gunslinger Yellow One, half a mile west with a flight of 12, coming into Texaco."

Division headquarters was a long, double row of the Army's General Purpose (GP) tents. The soldiers at headquarters took our records, processed forms, and did all the administrative things they do in the military to assure you are properly paid, assigned to a unit and, if you die, you are shipped home to the proper address, in the proper box, with the proper letter of condolence from the senior officer who never saw your face, let alone knew your name.

While in the finance section that day, I ran into Tyler Tugwell, a classmate from Officer Candidate School (OCS) at Fort Benning, Georgia. Tyler had transferred from infantry to finance and was a finance officer at division level. I hadn't seen Tyler since OCS. It was good to see him and a stroke of luck to have a friend in division finance—any financial snafus I might have would be short-lived.

Every new helicopter pilot arriving in Vietnam was anxious to fly gunships. I was no different. At that time it seemed that anything else was just...well, flying. But flying guns, that was exciting and macho. That was what we had come for, to shoot and kill the bad guys, whoever those guys were. Problem was, there weren't that many slots to fly guns.

I was assigned to the 227th Assault Aviation Battalion. The 227th and her sister battalion, the 229th, made up the primary transport force for the division's infantry units. Each battalion consisted of three helicopter assault companies, one gun company, and a head-quarters company. Each assault company had 20 UH-1D Hueys, Bell Helicopter's finest. An assault company's mission was to fly the troops in on combat assaults, take them out, resupply them, medevac them—whatever was needed. These D model Hueys were called "slicks." In comparison to the B and C model Hueys with machine guns and rocket pods hanging off the sides, the D models, with only two side-mounted machine guns, were relatively slick in appearance.

D Company had 12 UH-1B and UH-1C helicopter gunships, each armed with varying arrangements of machine guns, rockets, and grenade launchers. D Company's job was to protect and support the lift companies and provide ground troops with fire support from the air.

I badly wanted to fly guns, but B Company needed pilots the day I arrived, so I was assigned there. I was disappointed. I wanted to mix it up. I thought there were better ways to do that—with the infantry, where most of my training and experience lay, or flying gunships. But at least I wasn't flying administrative flights and VIPs out of division headquarters like Wesley. I was thankful for that. I couldn't fathom training all the years I had, coming to the combat zone, and then doing nothing but flying generals and VIPs around.

I would later find these thoughts about our assignments not altogether accurate assessments, as would be proven by one of Wesley's routine administrative flights a few months later. One night about 10 p.m. a young soldier had to be immediately taken to Qui Nhon. Chosen to make the trip were Wesley and CPT Jerry Watson, a good friend of Wesley's and mine. They were to fly eastward at about 6000 feet altitude over mountains and land on the coast at Qui Nhon. If they somehow missed Qui Nhon and continued flying eastward, it would be all ocean.

The weather conditions that night required instrument flying. Though inexperienced, most of us new aviators were fairly competent at keeping the aircraft upright in the clouds. We had received instrument training in flight school, but we were not fully instrument-qualified. The Army called ours a "tactical instrument rating." It meant that in Vietnam (but nowhere else in the world) we were allowed to fly in instrument-flight conditions—that is, limited or no visibility. The problem was that there were almost no navigational aids that we could use in our Hueys. There were a few Air Force bases scattered around the country that had electronic navigational aids, but we rarely landed at an Air Force base. Our primary tool for navigating was a 1:50000-scale topographical map, practically useless at night when you couldn't see.

At least there were city lights in Qui Nhon. Except for a few of the larger cities, there were no ground lights in Vietnam—no streetlights, no yard lights—nothing to offer any relief to the all-encompassing, velvet blackness of night. Wesley and Jerry had been to Qui Nhon many times and hoped they could find the city by its lights. If clouds covered the lights, there was a radio beacon that might assist them, although radio beacons were notoriously

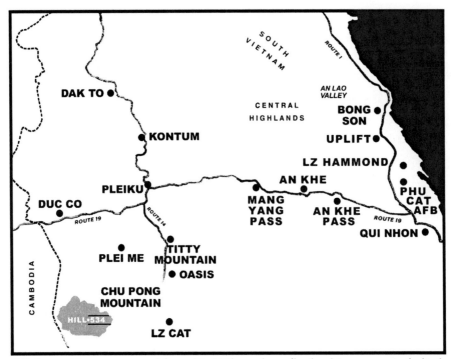

Highway 19 ran westward from Qui Nhon along flat land into a vertical climb called An Khe Pass. The road through the pass ascended the plateau on which An Khe sat. Just west of An Khe the road went through Mang Yang Pass where the French Mobile Group 100 was ambushed and annihilated by the Viet Minh in 1954. From there Highway 19 went down off the plateau and on to Pleiku and continued westward to the Cambodian border.

unreliable in Vietnam. When Wesley and Jerry took off in the darkness, they were aware that if they flew past Qui Nhon, they would be flying out to sea with limited fuel. It was a simple administrative mission that could kill them.

They didn't like the conditions, but the mission was not extraordinary. What *was* extraordinary was their engine failure at 6000 feet over the mountains. When an engine quits in a helicopter, there is a sudden lack of noise and loss of momentum as the bottom falls out from under you. The saving grace is that a safe landing is possible. With the pitch angle of the rotor blades flattened, the helicopter will glide to the ground, provided the maneuver is done with skill.

When the engine quit, Wesley and Jerry got the pitch out of the blades immediately and went into the glide to the ground called "autorotation." They talked. Because of the flight time that had elapsed, they knew they were closer to An Khe than Qui Nhon. They were sure to crash if they landed in the mountains, because they would be unable to see the ground in time to react. They turned back toward An Khe, hoping to clear the mountains, break out of the clouds, and glide to a landing. They held the helicopter on course at 60 knots, and let it fall.

Imagine falling from a mile high in the sky, with no power, and in total darkness. They had no automatic pilot, no navigation aid, no air-traffic controller, no outside help or contact of any kind. It was the two of them, and their knowledge, skill, and poise—two young Americans from North Carolina and Arkansas, holding themselves together.

They landed inside the perimeter defense of An Khe. Damage? A broken skid.

It was an awesome feat. We who knew the story marveled at their poise and courage under such pressure. Of course, we told them they were just lucky and too eaten up with the dumb-ass to die, and that the machine alone had saved their sorry asses.

But at the present moment I had to get by my disappointment and get ready for the assignment I had. I threw my bags into the back of a jeep at the administration center for the ride down to B Company.

We drove down the dusty, winding dirt road toward the southern end of the Golf Course, to the living area of B Company of the 227th. The roads were dirt. The air was full of dirt. Construction was going on everywhere, and everywhere were bulldozed mounds of dirt. And it was plenty hot. I didn't mind the heat. I had grown up in Tulsa County hauling hay and throwing 30-foot joints of three-inch pipe onto flatbed trailers in 105-degree heat while working for my dad. I thought it was supposed to be hot. But back home the heat was simply part of the day. Here it was superimposed on a danger that I could already feel.

I was a little anxious as we drove to B Company. I knew I'd be all right, but I felt like a rookie. I was more experienced than most Army lieutenants because of my five years as an enlisted man in the 82nd and 101st airborne divisions before I was commissioned a lieutenant. But I was a novice flyer about to join a company of seasoned professionals. I steadied myself for my introduction to the company.

It turned out to be a non-event. The company was out flying somewhere and wouldn't be back for two or three days. A senior warrant officer who worked in operations met me as I got out of the jeep. He looked to be in his late 40s. I thought he was pretty old to be in a place like that.

The B Company area ran north from the road up a slight incline and ended at the edge of the Golf Course. The operations building, at the top of the hill and adjacent to the Golf Course, was a small, simple structure of new two-by-fours, a corrugated metal roof, and cement floor. The company commander lived in a similar one-room structure a few feet away. About halfway down the hill was a mess hall with a metal roof. Everything else was under a tent.

The GP tent, olive drab in color and made of water-resistant canvas, was the standard living quarters for most of us. It was about 20-feet-by-40-feet and 12 feet high at its highest point. The tent sloped from the center down to about six feet. Flaps on each end served as entry and exit ways. The sides were rolled up when it was dry to facilitate light and circulation. When it rained, which was about every day, the sides were let down to keep the rain out, but the tent leaked through the top. When the top sagged under the weight of pooled water, we would take an extra tent pole and push up from the inside to spill the water down the side. A new leak was created due to wicking action, a process set off by the simple contact of the pole. GP tents were better than no protection, but they left a lot to be desired as permanent living quarters.

I was told to move into the officers tent next to the operations building. It was the only tent in the company area that had a wooden floor—that was luxury. There were rows of folding canvas cots down each side and stacks of personal gear around them.

I found an empty cot and put my gear down. The place was filthy, the wooden floor covered with dirt. I figured the officers who lived there would appreciate having a clean place when they returned. I got a broom and went to work.

As I was sweeping dirt out the door, I felt a twinge in my neck, a remnant of an injury suffered in OCS for which I had been in traction a solid week. It had hardly bothered me since. Now, the day before the company was to return and I would meet everyone and begin flying, I had this near-paralyzing pain. I couldn't believe it. I lay flat on my back all day and all night. Fortunately the pain was gone the next day.

I was introduced to my platoon leader, Major Hylwa, that morning. He didn't say much but seemed a decent sort. About half an hour later I walked into the tent to find several officers standing about. If anyone noticed the tent had been cleaned, they didn't let on.

My new leader spoke to me rather curtly. "Lieutenant Clark, you're in the wrong tent. You get your bags and get down there to the FNG tent."

"What's the FNG tent, sir?"

"The fucking new guy tent, Lieutenant. That's it down there by the mess hall."

A voice came from the back of the tent. "And when you learn to fly, Lieutenant, *if* you learn to fly, maybe you can move back in here."

They were all captains and majors, great pilots, combat-experienced. I was a green lieutenant—and worse, an FNG. I would not—could not—be one of them until I had proven myself under fire and through hundreds of hours of combat flight time.

It wasn't the reception I had envisioned. I was humiliated and angry, but it was no time to retaliate. I stood up straight and turned toward the anonymous voice. Saying nothing, I stared at those closest to me for a moment, then picked up my gear and left.

Chapter 3

Breaking In

THE ORIGINAL MEMBERS of the 1st Air Cavalry Division must have been the greatest ever to fly helicopters. They were pioneers in airmobile warfare, flying in the first unit of its kind ever assembled. No one had their experience. When I arrived they had been in Vietnam about nine months. Before Vietnam, the original 1st Cav pilots had flown together for more than two years, testing and refining the new airmobile techniques. Furthermore, they flew the D model Huey in the Central Highlands, a mountainous region where flying was vastly more difficult. Later versions of the Huey were much more powerful and easier to fly than the D models we and the old guys flew.

One would have thought the old guys would have been glad to see us. After all, they couldn't go home until they were replaced. But most of the original pilots in B Company were downright snobbish with anyone who wasn't as good as they were at flying the machine. They didn't care for us FNGs.

First Lieutenant Charles "Chuck" Evans was the first aviator replacement in B Company. He arrived in February 1966. Second Lieutenant Robert S. Lawson was second, coming in March. Arriving in April, I was third.

Chuck was about six feet tall and solidly built. His hair was dark and his gaze straight in your eye. He was from Sylvania, Georgia, a small town north of Savannah. He had a wife and small children at home whom he loved and spoke of often. You couldn't ask for a better friend. And he was a worker. He put hammers and tools in the hands of us all whenever he had an idea. When the going was tough, he was always right in the middle of it. Going into an alley fight, I'd take him with me.

Bob Lawson grew up on a farm near Niles, Michigan. He was

commissioned through the Reserve Officers Training Program at Western Michigan and had been in the flight class ahead of me at Fort Rucker, Alabama. I had seen him there but we had not met. When I moved into the FNG tent with Bob, Chuck, and the others, I found

LT Chuck Evans (2nd from right) and LT Bob Lawson (far right). From left (foreground): MAJ Coburn and CPT Foster. From left (background): WO1 Willis, WO1 George Wallace, WO1 Marrott, LT Harrison. An Khe 1966.

Bob reserved but not shy. I noticed that while he didn't say much, he stood his ground. Strangely, his quietness made him stand out. I began to notice how solid he was. The guy was a rock. When something important was going on, he was always there. He was logical, his opinions made sense, and he would not back down from anything. One could not help but respect his character. I began to like this man who never pushed but was himself resolute. He would become my best friend.

Bob was a top pilot. While the rest of us were certified to fly instruments only in Vietnam, Bob was good enough to earn a standard instrument rating. We all got the same amount of instruction; he was just better than the rest of us. I saw him get in trouble only once.

We were near the coast picking up troops and flying them northward toward Bong Son. The pickup zone was flat, with a lot of small trees and large bushes. The rough, hilly terrain of the LZ made it the most difficult to land in I had seen.

Bob was just ahead of us as we returned to the pickup zone, touched down, and loaded six troopers. We took off right behind him. We had cleared the trees and were beginning to climb when Bob's helicopter began to wobble and then sink rapidly. As we flew over him, he sank out of sight. Being in formation, there was nothing we could do but continue. We heard nothing on the radio. All we knew was Bob's helicopter had gone down. Finally, word came: He'd had some sort of mechanical failure and lost power, but had managed to land safely.

The next day Bob stormed into our tent so angry he could barely speak. As it turned out, a few days before the

Hueys on the Golf Course, B Company, 227th Avn Bn, 1st Air Cav. 1966.

incident he had told maintenance that that particular helicopter was weak, that something was wrong with it. The maintenance warrant officer told him his trouble was probably pilot error, Bob being an FNG. When the engine was examined after Bob's power loss, it was discovered that some portion of the engine packing had been left in the engine when it was installed. This had caused the weakness Bob had reported, and ultimately the power loss.

Our FNG gave that maintenance warrant pure hell.

I SOON FOUND that graduating from flight school was merely a license to kill myself or learn to fly, whichever came first. I had 212 hours' flight time when I graduated from flight school. I was qualified in the Hiller H-23, a small two-seater, the H-19, an ancient albatross, and the Bell UH-1—the Huey.

I came to love the Huey, but the first time I stepped into one I found it tough to handle. I couldn't "feel" it. I didn't trust it. Even though I was manipulating the controls, I didn't have it—it had me. Later I would strap it on my rear end and away we would go, body and soul as one. But that was a long time coming.

My first flight in Vietnam was with the company instructor pilot (IP). The operations officer didn't put my name on the schedule board. The flight was listed simply:

IP—Capt. Olsen   Pilot—FNG

In our unit, even after being signed off as qualified by an IP, all pilots new to Vietnam had to fly with someone experienced at flying in country. Had that not been the policy, I would have killed myself and my crew numerous times during the first several weeks. Despite my excellent training in flight school, I simply was not equipped to handle the difficult flying conditions in Vietnam.

I was a section leader with three warrant officers reporting to me, CW3 Norm Taylor, WO1 George Rose, and WO1 Parry Etheridge. They were good men and simply outstanding pilots. I, for the most part, was simply trying not to crash.

At first they were a little ugly with me, so I had a meeting right off. "Look, I don't know much about flying, but I do know the Army. I can read a map, and I can run a unit. You are going to have to teach me how to fly. That may not be the best situation for you, but that's the way it is. You'll teach me, or I'll have your ass!"

They looked at each other, saying nothing. They would be going home soon, and I had a year of combat flying ahead. I tolerated their lack of patience, and they tolerated my ineptness in the Huey. There was a certain respect for military ability, but full respect never came until there was flying proficiency. The proficiency I sought came at its own pace, as if it made its own decision.

I was scheduled for my first flight since being checked and cleared to fly by Captain Olsen. Chief Warrant Officer Taylor was the aircraft commander. I got in the right seat and adjusted the seat up as high as it would go.

"Lieutenant, put that seat on the floor."

"On the floor?" I asked. "What do you mean 'on the floor'?"

"Sir, put the seat all the way down to the floor. Put it down as far as it will go."

"No, I don't want it that low. I like it up high like this, so I can rest my arm on my leg. It makes it a lot easier to hold the cyclic steady."

"Damn it, sir. You see that flimsy little side shield between you and the door? That little shield is the only piece of anything on this goddamn helicopter that will stop a bullet. Now, with your seat up high like that, your head and neck stick up four or five inches more above that shield than they do when the seat is on the floor. This helicopter is made mostly out of magnesium, Lieutenant. It's maybe one-tenth of an inch thick. That little shield is all you got. Put the seat on the floor, sir."

I put the seat on the floor. It felt awful at first, but soon I preferred it that way. I would learn that when one of my warrant officers told me something about flying, like it or not, he was right.

Later, as an aircraft commander, I trained a number of lieutenants and warrant officers. Invariably, every time a new pilot got in with me, he jacked the seat up high, and the conversation went something like this:

"Put the seat all the way to the floor, Lieutenant."

"But, sir, I like it up high—"

"Damn it, Lieutenant, you see that side shield...."

Every vehicle I have operated since—helicopter, airplane, rental car, truck, whatever—the first thing I do is adjust the seat all the way to the floor.

ONE DAY IN May the company was at Mang Yang Pass with 16 Hueys, waiting to be called to pick up troops. Somebody had to go back to An Khe to pick up lunch for the company. Because it was a short flight and there was a road to follow, two rookies were selected to make the flight. Chuck was given the mission, and I was to go with him. This was to be a small step in the maturation process of two of the three new lieutenants. Chuck and I knew everyone would be watching us.

The big Huey sat on the north side of the road atop the mountain pass, facing westward toward Cambodia. The small mountain dropped four or five hundred feet off a sheer cliff no more than twenty feet in front of us. We would take off over the cliff, turn 180 degrees, and fly eastward along the road to An Khe.

"You wanna fly this thing?" Chuck asked as we walked to the helicopter. "Why don't you fly and I'll sit in the left seat?"

The helicopters had dual controls and could be flown from either the left or right seat, but the pilot on the right had the better view of the instrument panel and usually did most of the flying.

"Hell, no, I'm not gonna fly this goddamn thing. Hell, no. It's your mission. You fly it."

Neither of us wanted to take off in front of this group of the best helicopter pilots the world had ever seen. I crawled into the left seat.

The Huey engine needs 6600 RPM at takeoff. After starting the engine, the pilot rolls the throttle on full, which takes the RPM up to 6000. The remaining 600 RPM is gained by pushing a switch on the throttle with the thumb, a process we called "beeping it up." When the RPM is at 6600, the aircraft is ready for takeoff.

Chuck finished the start and run-up procedures and lifted off. We were quickly over the edge of the cliff with an instant four to five hundred feet altitude, but instead of climbing we were descending! There were no warning lights. I could see nothing wrong, but the aircraft was floundering and continuing to lose altitude.

"Chuck! What are you doing? What's wrong?"

"I don't know! I got no power! I got no power!"

Fuck this!

"I got it," I said, taking the controls. "Let me try it."

"You got it," Chuck answered, acknowledging that he had given up control of the aircraft.

My mind was racing. *What the hell?*

I rolled the throttle to make sure it was all the way on. It was tight against the stop, so that was okay. I had *some* control, but we were continuing to fall, and the ground was coming up fast. Suddenly it hit me.

The beeper! Try the beeper!

I hit the beeper with my thumb. The aircraft responded with an immediate surge of power as the RPM climbed to 6600. We were not more than a hundred feet off the ground when we leveled off and began to climb.

Two rookies. Our stature in the company did not rise that day.

I WENT ON my first combat assault (CA) my second week in An Khe. Aviators were not issued rifles at that time. Most of the old guys had rifles they had brought from home or had somehow acquired after arriving in Vietnam. All I had was my Army-issue .38 caliber pistol, a large pocketknife I kept in my pants pocket, and a heavy, 10-inch-blade Bowie knife Dad had given me when I believed I would be jumping into Cuba with the 101st Airborne Division in 1963.

The crew chiefs and door gunners were already at their helicopters as I walked with my aircraft commander, a captain, up the road to the helicopter we were assigned to that day. Were it not for our holstered pistols and flight helmets in their brown woolen bags, one might have thought we were out for a casual evening stroll.

In our unit the aircraft commander flew in the left seat, so I put my helmet in the right seat and began the customary walk-around inspection of the aircraft. The inspection always ended with a climb on top of the fuselage to check the "Jesus nut," the large nut that secured the rotor blades to the rotor shaft.

We slipped the heavy bulletproof vests over our heads, fastened the Velcro flaps in back, then got in and fastened our shoulder harnesses and seat belts. The crew chief sat behind his .30 caliber machine gun on the left side at the rear of the cargo compartment. The door gunner took his position on the right side.

We started our engines. All down the line the big turbine engines of 16 Hueys began their familiar, deep whine as they slowly started to turn. As they began to run faster, the labored, low whine of the start-up became a high-pitched scream, soon joined by the spinning rotor blades' deep-throated roar.

The noise was deafening. The temperature was above 90 degrees. Sweat was already dripping off my nose and running down the back of my neck when the first radio communication came, a check by the flight leader to see that all the helicopters' radios were working. "Brave Flight, this is Brave Yellow One, commo check, UHF, Fox Mike."

Members of the flight replied in turn, first on their UHF radios, and then FM. "Yellow Two, UHF, Fox Mike." "Yellow Three, UHF, Fox Mike," and so on until all had reported in. Then, with no further conversation, Yellow One picked up to a low hover, eased backward off his parking pad, turned slowly in the direction of takeoff, and began to move forward. We followed in turn.

That first CA involved more than 60 helicopters, the largest number of helicopters on a combat assault I ever saw. Luckily, I was just along for the ride and had no decisions to make. I was in awe of the entire process; it seemed to me there were helicopters everywhere.

By late May I was being trained to lead CAs. By July all the old guys had gone home, and I led regularly from that point on. Some units kept the same flight leader every day. In our company, flight leader responsibility rotated daily among the platoon leaders and one or two other commissioned officers.

While flying CAs was our main objective, a close second was logistic support, resupplying the troops on the ground, what we called a "log mission." Log missions were always two ships flying together.

While there are flat areas with rice paddies in the Central Highlands, most of the time we were flying over mountains or high, rugged, jungle terrain. Flying over the jungle wasn't so tough. It was the takeoffs and landings that tested your mettle. There were often impossibly tight places to get in and out of—a pinnacle, a mountain ridge, a hole in the jungle with tall trees all around, the steep side of a mountain, a bomb crater, a stump for one skid and a tree root for the other. If we thought we could get into a jungle clearing, we went in. Getting out was something else.

The D model Huey was a big hunk of nuts and bolts put together by some utter genius. But like all machines, it had its limitations. Like the pilots who flew them, some Hueys were strong, and some were weak. Some were beat-up old dogs, and some were sleek and fit.

The most sensitive of the Huey's flight controls is the cyclic, a stick-like control that protrudes up from the floor between the pilot's knees. It provides directional control. On one of those steep and demanding takeoffs, rookie pilots would often try to coax the aircraft to fly higher by pulling upward on the cyclic. That did not help, of course, but somehow it made you feel better. Maybe it was a form of prayer. I don't know that I ever completely stopped doing it.

Two things will help the Huey fly: more airspeed and less weight. In flight school the helicopters carried only an instructor and a student. In Vietnam they held a crew of four. There were usually 1200 pounds of JP-4 fuel and up to six combat-loaded soldiers rated at 250 pounds each. Every bit of added weight mattered. All pilots, even experienced ones, had to be trained to make precarious takeoffs and landings in grossly overloaded aircraft. If the helicopter was loaded too heavily at takeoff, the engine and main rotor blades would not turn fast enough. RPM might decline from the needed 6600, to 5800 or 5700 or less. The helicopter's ability to fly would decrease accordingly.

Typically, as we landed on a combat assault, the troops were out and gone in a flash. They did not like being on that helicopter when landing under enemy fire or the threat of it. But they took a little time when they had to jump from a 10-foot hover. In those instances rotor speed often declined dramatically. Then it was get the troops out right now or crash. Thus was born the cry of the aircraft commander, "Kick 'em out! Kick 'em out!"

The green square with the lightning bolt on the door signified B Company, 227th Avn Bn. 1966.

Involuntarily, the phrase always came out twice, as if they couldn't hear the first time. And each time the pilot said it, his voice went up an octave. The crewmen knew exactly what that high-pitched voice meant. They would grab the troops and literally throw them out the doors. You didn't want to be hanging around those doors in back when "Kick 'em out! Kick 'em out!" came back to that crew chief and door gunner in soprano.

One steamy afternoon, my fatigues soaked with perspiration and sweat running down my nose, I was hovering over bushes on level ground while troops jumped out one by one. Rotor speed was down to 6000 RPM. I had the left pedal all the way in against the stop, trying to keep the aircraft pointed straight ahead.

I called over the intercom, "Kick 'em out! Kick 'em out!"

I was anticipating and dreading that uncontrollable, slow turn to the right which surely was about to begin. But somehow, even though I had the pedal against the stop and 6000 RPM, I wasn't spinning.

Jesus! I can't believe this! That's the nth degree! Is this possible?

My wonderment quickly shifted to the pressing danger of the tail rotor dipping into the bushes.

The tail rotor has to stay clear. Don't let me settle. Don't let me settle.

The last troop jumped off and RPM rose back to normal. I had full control again.

The next day I had to drop troops on the side of a steep, grass-covered mountain. On terrain like that the grass could be five or ten feet high, making hover flight difficult and causing RPM to decline much faster. The slope was too severe to land on; I had no

Troop billets at the southern end of the Golf Course. 1966.

choice but to hover as the troops got off. I pointed the nose of the helicopter straight in to the mountain and rested the toes of the skids against the mountainside. That bit of contact with the earth gave us a measure of support as we hovered, although it put the tips of the rotor blades dangerously close to the side of the mountain.

The troops had to jump 10 to 15 feet into the tall grass hiding the ground, and they were slow getting off. Engine and rotor speed were bleeding off fast.

I barked to the crew, "Kick 'em out! Kick 'em out!"

RPM was still falling. The blades were no more than 12 inches from the mountainside.

Holy shit!

"Kick 'em out! Kick 'em out!"

The troops flew out the side doors. RPM immediately stabilized, and we recovered. We flew off to get another load of troops and do it again.

ONE DAY IN August we were sitting at Mang Yang Pass waiting to be called for a mission. When the call came, the flight leader brought us together for a briefing.

"Okay, we're going into a hot LZ to pick up some troops from B Company, Second of the Fifth. It's down near Plei Me. It's a four-ship LZ, so we'll go in platoons. We'll pick them up and take them back to the Oasis. When we are through," he continued, "we'll spend the night at the Turkey Farm. Takeoff is in 10 minutes."

We had 12 Hueys that day, so we took off in three platoons (groups of four), 60 seconds between each group. The flight took about 25 minutes. As we neared the pickup area we saw that the trees surrounding the LZ were tall, 100 to 120 feet. Already tense and senses heightened, we roared below the treetops and down into the LZ, noses high, slowing as we descended. Fires in the LZ added to our concern as we landed.

As we waited for the troops I held the aircraft steady and light on the skids, flames just feet in front of us and on either side of us. We were taking fire, but I had not felt or heard the "thunk" of the helicopter being hit.

Damn, let's go! Let's get out of here!

Six troops scrambled on board and I heard the crew chief and door gunner call out.

"Clear left!"

"Clear right!"

I pulled in power and lifted off to clear the trees directly in front of us. Once we left the clearing we would be above the treetops or in the treetops. I could not let the blades get into the trees—that could take us down.

I felt the helicopter shudder as it overcame the drag of the lift-off and began its steep climb. The square-shaped RPM warning light on the instrument panel began flashing bright red, and a constant *beep! beep! beep!* was screaming in my ears that the engine and rotor blades were losing speed. I had to retain enough power to keep climbing. The more power you pull in, the more the RPM decreases. If I let that RPM continue to decline, at some point the aircraft would cease to fly.

I glanced at the RPM. 5700. *Dammit.* Way too low.

With gritted teeth I applied just enough power to get the blades above the trees, which caused the fuselage to fly into the treetops. Leaves and small limbs poked through the windows and doors. I could hear and feel foliage and branches brush against the helicopter as the lower part of the machine struggled to pass through the trees. We were going to make it or not, right here. I was barely breathing....

We passed on through the treetops and into the clear. On top of the trees now, I was able to reduce power a bit. RPM stabilized and began to creep back up. Blessed airspeed began to increase.

As I felt her begin to fly smoothly, I released some of the tension in my body and began to breathe a little easier. I said a silent thanks to the old guys who had taken me through this same type takeoff in earlier days.

D model with 227th Avn Bn logo on the nose. 1966.

We gained airspeed and closed on the rest of our flight just ahead. As I moved in to the prescribed 45-degree angle and one-rotor-blade distance from the helicopter in front of us, I realized it was quiet again, with only the familiar dull roar of the rotor blades in my ears.

"Chief, everybody all right back there?"

"No sweat, sir."

"All right," I said. "Good job."

Chapter 4

The Day I Made It

I WAS APPOINTED aircraft commander in June of 1966. That meant I could fly with a less experienced pilot and that I had responsibility for the aircraft. I had the rating, but I wasn't yet solid.

It didn't take long for me to make my first mistake. We were working south of An Khe and west of the coastal city of Tuy Hoa. The mission was to pick up an infantry company and insert it onto a mountainside a few kilometers away. It was all pretty simple—pick 'em up, drop 'em off.

With a D model lift ship. 1966.

Pinnacle (mountain peak) landings and takeoffs in high winds became second nature for us, but they were dangerous. Judgment and feel for a loaded aircraft were senses that had to be highly developed. Pilot mistakes manifested themselves instantly. At a critical moment, the slightest error in judgment could result in crisis or calamity.

Pinnacle takeoffs had lives of their own—unpredictable, and at times, downright thrilling. If the helicopter was empty or light, a normal takeoff was no problem. But when loaded too heavily for a normal takeoff, you could jump off a mountain, point the nose downward, reduce power to allow engine and rotor speed to build, and free-fall down the side of that mountain until airspeed increased enough to allow engine and rotor speed to return to normal, giving you full control of the ship again. The experience was exhilarating—unless you misjudged.

The aircraft I drew that day was one of the beat-up old dogs among our Hueys. It did not have the power it should have had, so I knew I would have to be careful. The pickup zone oddly resembled a sombrero. The troops were on top of a tiny, bald, mountain peak which sat atop a skinny mountain that jutted straight upward. The mountainsides dropped sharply from the small top some seven or eight hundred feet to the flat valley floor.

There was room for just two ships on the mountaintop, so we landed in groups of two. As I touched down on the mountain peak, six troopers climbed on. I picked up to a low hover to see if the RPM would hold. If it did not come off more than 200, we could fly with the load we had. It dropped from 6600 to 6400 and held. I reasoned that with all that airspace between us and the valley floor, there would be plenty of altitude under us if we needed it to regain lost RPM. Even so, the weakness of the ship made me uneasy. I would learn to listen to that uneasiness.

I set the helicopter down, then pulled in power and began moving forward about 18 inches off the ground. She settled to the ground and bounced off the edge of the peak in labored flight. RPM began to dive. No big deal, I told myself. I had done this before. I pointed the nose down the mountain, reduced power as much as I could to build RPM as quickly as possible, and let her fall, holding a certain amount of power so that we would not collide with the mountainside. But the RPM was not building.

Holy shit! What is this? Man, this son-of-a-bitch is weak!

This had not happened to me before. The Huey always responded by gaining RPM in that situation, but we were just too heavy for that particular engine. I had misjudged, and we were screaming down that mountainside with a full load of troops.

Damn! What if this son-of-a-bitch doesn't gain full RPM?

At last the RPM needle ticked higher, creeping upward ever so slowly. When it reached 6600 we rounded out not more than 50 feet off the valley floor. We began to climb laboriously back to the mountaintops to join the flight. It was slow going, but we caught up in time to land in proper position in the formation. I did not carry six troops in that helicopter again.

WE WERE PICKING up troops one day at Hotel 12, a landing zone within An Khe, and dropping them a few miles north. The area where we sat was open with a three-foot-high wire fence about 30 yards in front of us that had to be cleared. I was surrounded by 11 other helicopters, some no more than 25 or 30 feet away. All were running at full RPM and loading troops. The noise was deafening. The temperature was near 100 degrees, and the rotor wash from the adjacent aircraft made the air unstable and hover flight exceedingly difficult.

When the troops got on board, the center of gravity and balance of the aircraft shifted. I rolled the throttle on full and started to pick up to a hover to see if I could hold 6600 RPM. Before we even broke ground, the aircraft began to bounce and slide around. Shaken, I set the helicopter back down. I was about to take off in formation with 11 other helicopters in rough, unstable air with a full load of troops—and I was having trouble handling the aircraft.

Being the aircraft commander, I had no one to turn to, and only a minute or two until takeoff. I was sweating profusely, my body tightly strung. I could not fail here. I gathered myself and began to analyze my problem.

That rotor wash is pure hell. The weight shift—it's the weight shift. Go slow, now.

I started again. As I slowly increased power, I felt the helicopter trying to move to the right. I stopped the power increase and corrected left until the machine was steady again. I slowly added power, then stopped when I felt the nose try to come up. I pushed the nose down until the aircraft was steady again.

Easy…easy…more power…light on the skids…a shift to the left…correct it. Off the ground now…steady at an 18-inch hover…RPM holding 6600…okay…I got it.

I eased the power off and set it back down. The fence was in front of me, but the real barrier had been crossed.

The aircraft in front of me lifted off, and it was my turn. I brought the power in slowly, lifting the aircraft smoothly a foot or so above the ground, and began to ease forward, attempting to gain airspeed as quickly as possible. There was the fence. The aircraft settled toward the earth, bounced off the ground once as we left hover, and began to fly. I pulled the nose up slightly and hopped over the fence, sacrificing airspeed for the four to five feet of altitude needed to clear it. RPM dropped slightly. I lowered the nose to gain airspeed. We were flying now, picking up momentum and airspeed. RPM was back to 6600 and the aircraft felt good. I broke to the left and joined the formation.

I didn't realize it then, but fighting through that takeoff had significantly advanced my maturity as a pilot. I was a rookie aircraft commander and still not as good as the worst of the old guys. But, under extreme pressure, I had faced failure in the helicopter head-on and won.

A FEW DAYS later we were again working an operation west of Tuy Hoa. Late one morning we were picking up troops from a clearing in the rainforest. I was to pick up the last six. Sometimes enemy forces would hide while the main body of a group loaded and flew away, then attack the last small group, so bringing out the final few from a clearing in a remote jungle area caused a bit of tension.

One of us new guys, Richard Whaley, a good, solid warrant officer, was flying right seat with me. Warrant Officer Whaley had the controls as we made the approach to a clearing surrounded by tall trees. Grass grew about knee-high in the LZ so that we could not see the ground as we made the landing. Just as we were about to touch down, I thought I saw the tip of a tree stump in the grass. I would have had to abruptly take the controls from Whaley to land farther ahead, so rather than risk upsetting him and possibly looking a little paranoid, I did nothing.

The troops backed out of the undergrowth, firing their weapons into the trees in case an enemy force was waiting to ambush. They backed all the way to the helicopter and jumped in. The throttle went to idle. This was no place for that!

I turned to Whaley. "Why did you roll the throttle off?"

"I didn't roll the throttle off. You rolled the throttle off."

"I didn't roll the throttle off," I said. "Oh, shit!"

I tried to roll the throttle back on full and could not move it.

That fucking stump! It got the throttle linkage!

No doubt the stump I thought I had seen was real and had gone right through the belly of the aircraft and caught the linkage connecting the engine to the throttle in the cockpit. The crew chief and I got out and crawled under the helicopter. The stump had gone right up through the opening in the bottom of the helicopter called the "hell hole," pinning the linkage so that it could not be moved. We were stuck.

I took a machete and hacked away at the stump until I was able to chop it off near its base, freeing the linkage. I took the controls and we got out of there as fast as we could.

I quickly went to 3500 feet altitude so that, if the engine quit, we would have a lot of glide room. Mechanically the prudent thing to have done would have been to stay on the ground and have maintenance people come get the helicopter. But, given where we were in that jungle clearing, I elected to fly out of there and take my chances with engine problems. We returned to the forward base without incident.

My inexperience and indecision could have cost us our lives had there been an ambush waiting for us. Never again did I hesitate to take the controls if I thought it should be done—which was any time there was the slightest doubt in my mind. Whaley hadn't seen the stump, and I wasn't sure that I had. I made sure from that day forward.

WE WERE WORKING north and east of Bong Son near the coast of the South China Sea where the infantry had just concluded an operation of several weeks. Someone higher up had pronounced the Viet Cong (VC) battalion they were up against as finished. A new operation was to begin west of Pleiku. We were to pick up the troops and fly them to the new area of operations. To get an early start, the decision was made to leave the helicopters out in the rice paddies overnight with the troops.

Sixteen of our company's Hueys were among 48 parked nose-to-tail, with a large, open rice paddy on our left and a tree line on the right. Right away I noticed the troops were not between the helicopters and the trees, where any attack would come from.

Obviously there was no concern of an attack on us. *I was concerned, but I wasn't the leader of anything.* We had parked in a garden area. Nothing was growing, but the earth was plowed into furrows. As I walked in the garden, I found a rake and a hoe carved from wood, no metal on them at all.

My God, these people are 300 years behind us. What are we doing?

I had my .38 pistol and my two knives. I always carried the knives. I thought that if I should somehow lose my firearm, I would always have at least the pocketknife if I kept it in my pocket. I wore the Bowie knife and the pistol around my waist.

As darkness fell, we set up folding cots, with the helicopters between the cots and the tree line. Needing to stay close, I placed my cot only a few feet away from my helicopter. We ate C-rations and talked for a while, then went to sleep.

I awoke in mid-air. I hit the ground scrambling and was five or ten feet away before I had my first conscious thought.

What the fuck! We're under attack! I've got to get away from this damn helicopter!

I did not want to be near a helicopter if one was hit by a rocket and exploded. The loud staccato of machine gun and rifle fire was ringing in my ears. Flares were going off overhead, lighting up the area. I moved in a rapid, low crawl across the garden furrows in the direction of our troops until I felt I was far enough from the helicopters. Cursing the decision not to issue rifles to pilots, I stopped and reached for my pistol. The holster was empty!

Goddammit! I'm in my first firefight and I've lost my weapon. Son-of-a-bitch!

A pistol isn't much in a firefight, but it's something. I didn't know whether I should be scared because I didn't have a firearm or embarrassed because I had lost it.

Facing the tree line, I wriggled, face down, in a furrow as low as I could. If the VC charged the position, they would probably come across the ground where I lay. I pulled out my Bowie knife, lifted my eyes so I could see if anyone was approaching, and hoped like hell no one was. If anyone did come, I figured I would gut the first one with my knife and then see what happened next. I lay there while the firing continued, steeled and ready.

In a few minutes the firing stopped; the attack was over. A small force had apparently come in, shot up the helicopters, and scrambled away in the darkness. Nearly half the helicopters were damaged. We didn't leave helicopters in rice paddies overnight again.

George Rose went home shortly thereafter, but not before I gave him 20 dollars for his World War II sub-machine gun. In the 1940s it was called a "grease gun." It was a small, all-metal, automatic rifle that was extremely effective at short range. I carried the grease gun for months until we were finally issued the Army-standard M-16 rifle.

I had found my .38 pistol where it had fallen from its holster when I was scrambling away from the helicopter. The pistol never provided much defensive comfort. Its main use was for protection while flying. Most of us slid our waist belts around when we were sitting in the cockpit so that our pistols rested squarely between our legs. Some places needed protecting more than others.

Chapter 5

The House

THE ARMY GP tent leaks. Used ones, old ones, brand-new ones—they all leak. Except for the company commander and a few of the more senior officers, everyone in B Company of the 227th lived in a GP tent. We five new guys and the company aircraft maintenance officer, Captain Howe, lived together in one miserable, leaky tent.

One day Chuck got an engineer friend to lay a slab of cement at the front door of our tent. It was the exact width of the tent and extended about 10 feet from the entrance.

"Chuck, what are you doing?" I asked. "What's that cement for?"

"I'm building a porch," he said. "Actually, *we* are building a porch. Come on."

Leave it to Chuck. A porch for our tent! Using two-by-fours for framing, we—mostly Bob and Chuck—built an open-air, farmhouse-style porch right at the front of our tent. In the village we were able to buy a few sheets of regular, corrugated metal, the kind seen on farm buildings, to make the roof. It slanted downward from the tent entrance to the front of the porch. We built a 30-inch–high wall on both sides and the front of the porch. Except for the two-by-four framing, it was open-air from the tops of the walls to the roof.

We put a doorway front and center, built tables and washstands, and hung mirrors to shave by. The item that added real class to the structure was the card table. Bob and Chuck built an eight-sided table and covered the top tightly with a woolen GI blanket. More than a few dollars changed hands there during the next several months.

We were able to buy beer and soft drinks at the Post Exchange store, or "PX." We had a small, camping-type, cooling container, which fit nicely on the porch, but we had no ice. The Army had no facility in An Khe for ice, nor was there any in the village. The closest place to buy ice was in Pleiku, a good 45-minute flight west of An Khe. Every other day or so, as the ice melted, a "training" flight to Pleiku became necessary.

The ice facilities in Pleiku were extraordinary. Because there was nothing in Pleiku to make ice or keep it frozen, Vietnamese entrepreneurs

Pine boards, taken from boxes containing howitzer rounds, were used to build the half wall of our porch. An Khe 1966.

hauled it in daily by truck from Qui Nhon, right past An Khe. The ice was buried in a pit in the ground five or six feet deep and covered with dried rice and blankets to keep it from melting.

The ice itself was something to behold. It was shaped into hollow rectangular blocks about four feet long, eight inches wide, and six inches high, and it had an odd, grainy texture. We dared not put the ice in a glass, but it did chill the cans in the cooler.

In the daily heat, once the ice came out of the ground, it melted rapidly. We wrapped it in GI blankets, threw it in the back of our Huey, and flew as fast as we could back to An Khe before it melted.

With cold soft drinks and beer, a woolen-covered card table, flimsy little lawn chairs bought in the village, washstands, a cement floor, and a tin roof that did not leak, our porch was a classy and popular place. We gathered there at night to talk, read, play cards, and write letters. After rising in the mornings, we went to the porch, poured cold water from five-gallon cans into tinny, lightweight pans also bought in the village, and enjoyed fine, open-air, cold-water shaves while looking into small red- or purple-trimmed mirrors, also bought in the village. It was an incongruous sight, that dirty, dilapidated, faded, sagging GP tent, with a sturdy, tin-roofed, wooden porch at its front.

As much as we loved our porch, we five FNGs disliked our dirty, dilapidated, faded, and sagging, old Army GP tent. It was dirty inside when dry and miserably wet when raining. During the rainy season, that was almost daily. We knew it would be months, maybe even the end of our tours, before the Engineers worked far enough down the priority list to build us a house. So we decided to build one ourselves.

Thank God for Chuck Evans and Bob Lawson. Left to me, the house would never have been built. Chuck and Bob were natural carpenters and builders—and they wanted a house. We all did.

We needed three things—material, space, and permission.

The old guys, especially the captains and majors in the tent beside us, were derisive. They were always good-naturedly giving us hell, especially about our house talk.

"You all can't build any damn house! There are no two-by-fours, no boards, no nails. Hell, you can't even fly! What makes you think you can build a house?"

There was building material in the supply yards in An Khe and Qui Nhon, but it was slated for engineering projects, and thus, tightly controlled and strictly prioritized. But the material existed, so we knew it could be had. We would just have to be a little creative in our procurement methods.

We needed a place to build the house. Because it rained almost every day, it wasn't feasible to tear down our tent and build on the same spot. We would have no place to get out of the rain during the weeks we were building. Even working every spare hour, we figured the construction would take at least six weeks.

We needed permission from the company commander to build. We saw no reason he should not grant permission, but we were not at all sure that he would. Most of us did not think highly of him. He barely acknowledged the existence of us new guys. The officers laughed at how during the night, in his little, one-man house, he would yell to be heard on the field telephone about what a hero he had been that day. All he ever really did was ride back in the gaggle while one of our captains or majors led the flight and made all the important decisions.

So it was with some trepidation that Chuck, being senior among us, went to the company commander to ask for space for our house and permission to build it. The conversation went something like this:

"Sir, we in the FNG tent want to build ourselves a house. Is it okay with you, sir, if we do that?"

"Why, hell, Lieutenant, you don't have any material to build a house with. Forget it!"

"But, sir, if we can get the material, and if we do it on our own time, would it be okay?"

"Look, I don't care what you do, but there is no material to be had, so forget it."

"Well, sir, thanks for your permission," said Chuck, adding, "Sir, can we have that space past the officers latrine over on the other side of the company area?"

"No, dammit. No, you can't."

"Sir, we can build a house, but we need space. We can't tear our tent down to build it."

"Well, Evans, that's what you'll have to do, because exactly where your tent is, is the only space you can have. That's all there is to it. Hell, you all can't build any damn house."

"Okay, sir. Thank you, sir."

We had permission to build—but no material or space. We would figure out the material later. Space was the real problem.

Talking on the porch that night, we gave the company commander hell for not giving us a spot to build on. With the constant rain, he knew we couldn't take the tent down and live in the open.

I had an idea. "Hey, the hell with him. We'll just build the house up around the tent! When we get the house built, we'll take the tent down and pull it out the door. That'll work. That'll torque his mind!"

Bob and Chuck could build anything. They would be the architects, and the rest of us would be nail-drivers. We had two carpenters and five strong backs. We had permission and space. But there was nothing we could do without building supplies, and they simply were not available. The Army engineer units controlled every board and nail in country. They had massive building plans and were putting up all sorts of facilities as fast as they could. They were using every bit of structural supplies that came in and were begging for more.

Yet, if one was inventive and persistent, surprising things could be done. If you had a friend in the Engineers, it might turn out that at the end of a construction job, too much cement got mixed. Rather than it go to waste, it might get placed at a point of your choosing. If you didn't have a friend who could help, contraband would usually do the trick. Cross the palm of the engineer or supply-yard man with a favored item and all sorts of strange and wonderful objects might appear. Whiskey, a flight jacket, a captured enemy rifle, a Montagnard bowgun or a helicopter ride to Qui Nhon or Pleiku could provide very satisfying results.

We needed material to build a foundation for the house. We had seen several six-by-eight-inch wooden beams, about thirty feet long, lying at the end of the Golf Course. We had no idea where they came from, and we didn't ask. We took a company three-quarter ton truck, hooked the beams on to it, and pulled them up to our tent. The beams were solid and heavy, and while not perfect for the job, they would do as a foundation.

We needed two-by-fours. We figured we would have to go to the big supply yard in Qui Nhon and beg, steal or trade for those. However, before we had a chance to get over there, fortune intervened.

One day a two-and-a-half ton truck loaded with brand-new two-by-fours drove slowly by. As Bob, with covetous eyes, took in the sight of that precious material, he was amazed to recognize the driver as a classmate and friend from college.

Bob yelled and flagged him down. "Hey, Bud! Is that you?"

"Robert! What are you doing here?"

"I live here!" Bob exclaimed. "I'm flying helicopters for the Cav. What are you doing?"

"I'm in the Engineers over in Qui Nhon," he told Bob. "I just brought this load of two-by-fours over here, and I can't find where they are supposed to go."

Bob couldn't believe what he was hearing. "Well, hell, I'll take them. I need 'em bad. That okay with you?"

"Yeah, hell, I don't care. But somebody will have to sign for them."

"That's no problem," Bob assured him. "Pull that truck in here."

Bob guided the driver into our company area and up by our tent.

They unloaded the entire truckload of two-by-fours beside the tent. That night when the rest of us came in from flying, we had quite a time celebrating our good fortune. We gathered on the porch with soft drinks and beer, slapping Bob on the back and congratulating him for accomplishing the impossible.

Smiling widely, I said, "Robert, you're a genius, son, an absolute genius!"

In his usual, self-deprecating way, Bob grinned. "Hey, I didn't do anything. I just knew someone. And I couldn't let those two-by-fours just go by."

Chuck laughed and said, "Well, by God, you did good. You did damn good!"

As the levity quieted, I brought up a problem I had been thinking about. "You know, everybody and his brother are going to see this stack of lumber. There is no way we'll be able to keep all this."

"You're right about that," Bob agreed. "But guess what. We don't need them all. We just need enough to build our house."

That gave me an idea. "Hell, somebody will be after these two-by-fours in no time at all. Let's hide what we need under the tent floor, and when the Engineers come to take the stack away—which they will—we'll piss and moan and beg and then finally give them up."

Chuck looked at me and grinned. "Great idea, Ray. Let's do it."

We waited until dark. Then, laughing and chuckling, we shoved the two-by-fours we needed under the wooden floor of our tent. Sure enough, the next morning an engineer officer came to claim the stack of lumber. We feigned ignorance, pleaded for a few of the boards to be left with us, and watched as the entire stack was loaded and hauled away—all except those hidden under our tent.

We lost some good trading material when the lumber was taken away, but we had the two-by-fours we needed to use as studs and joists. But what about siding? And nails? And a roof? The roof would wait. The siding and nails were easy.

Artillery shells, specifically 105-millimeter howitzer rounds, came packed two rounds in a box—a wooden box. The box was made of one-inch pine boards six inches wide and two-and-a-half feet long. The boxes were held together with—*nails*. The artillery used so many

105 shells that the boxes became a nuisance. They burned them in huge piles to get rid of them.

We hauled a lot of ammo boxes to our company area. We broke the boxes apart, straightened the nails, and there we were with semi-straight nails and pine boards for siding. Now we had all the material we needed except roofing.

Bob secured the precious two-by-fours that began to surround our tent, as can be seen over my shoulder. An Khe 1966.

We had built a porch onto our tent; we now set about building a house onto our porch. With Chuck and Bob leading the way, we went to work. We strung those heavy beams around the tent and put them in place as a foundation. Then we began to put up the two-by-four studs and framework for the front, back, and sides of the house. We placed the studs vertically and separated them by the length of the ammo boxes. That allowed us to nail the boards right up the studs with no measuring or sawing required.

The construction went slowly, taking about six weeks, as expected. It all looked pretty comical, the framework slowly over-taking the tent as the days passed. We cut the windows and finished the framework and siding in just three days.

We had a house with sides, doors, windows, and a porch. Protruding upward from the inside, through the top where a roof should have been, was a huge tent.

We needed roofing material. We had two-by-fours for rafters for the roof, but nothing to cover them. The Air Force used a synthetic fabric to cover makeshift dirt runways. Bob and I saw a full roll of this fabric lying by the Air Force airstrip on the western side of the Golf Course one day. The roll was about six feet wide. There was no telling how much fabric was contained in it. Bob and I looked at each other. Huge, heavily loaded airplanes landed on this fabric at high speed and it did not rip or tear. It would damn sure be strong enough to make a roof. We took a three-quarter ton truck, drove to the airstrip, and made a "midnight requisition" of the big roll of runway material.

To build our roof, we would have to collapse the tent. The entire roofing job would have to be done in a day if we were to avoid getting rained on. We prefabricated the rafters so that once we were ready, all we would have to do is set the rafters up, nail them in place, and attach the roofing. We had rafters, scrap one-inch boards to nail them together, and enough roofing material to cover the Pentagon.

We took a lot of ribbing as our architecture slowly went up—the porch, the roofless house, and the tent protruding out the top. Now we were beginning to detect envy in our detractors.

One day we finished flying early and decided to put the roof on after lunch. With growing excitement, we went to work. First we dropped the center pole of the tent, allowing the tent's top to collapse. Then we put the rafters in place and connected them with one-inch pine scraps two or three feet apart. Then came strips of our runway roofing material. We had a roof! Our house had a roof, four walls, ten windows, two doors, a porch, and a large, leaky tent inside. We finished collapsing the tent and pulled it out the front door and across the porch. We could take our time on the inside, building rooms for the six of us.

There were a lot of grins that day. This would be lavish living.

The next morning we received a bombshell of news. Our company commander took one look at our completed house and decided that he would put 10 men in it—in *our* house, conceived and built solely by the six of us. We complained mightily, but to no avail.

We huddled to talk it over. No additional pilots had yet been assigned to live with us, nor had we received any direct orders to take in anyone else. We figured if we finished the inside of the house with six rooms before the company commander issued formal orders to assign more people to us, he might leave it alone rather than force us to tear it all out.

We stayed up all night finishing the inside. There was a hallway down the middle connecting the front and back doors, and three rooms on either side of the hallway. We used ammo boxes to build the interior walls to about five feet. We ran bamboo matting, bought in the village, from the tops of the walls up to the rafters. The matting allowed free air circulation throughout the house while providing privacy for the rooms. Each room had a doorway to the hall and a window on the outside wall. The windows were covered with mosquito netting salvaged from our disenfranchised tent.

Ammo boxes comprised the walls to about five feet high. Bamboo matting was nailed up to the rafters, allowing air circulation and privacy. An Khe 1966.

It was daylight when we finished. We slept a couple of hours, ate breakfast, and waited to see what would happen. When the company commander saw what we had done, he gave up on the idea of adding anyone else. The six of us had our house!

The first night under our new roof, condensation formed on the inside of the fabric and provided us with our very own, indoor rain. That was not in the plans. We beat it down to the village the next day and bought more sheets of corrugated metal to put on our roof. Once we covered the fabric roofing with the corrugated metal, the condensation stopped.

As long as I was there, she never leaked a drop. What heaven it was to be dry and comfortable during those monsoon rains. While the tent-dwellers were pushing pools of water off their tent tops trying to stay dry, we were on the porch playing cards or reading, or in our private rooms sleeping soundly.

My lone contribution to the design of the house was simple, but important. When I was in jungle school in Panama, I saw how windows were covered only with screens, aiding circulation, and long roof overhangs were built to keep rain from blowing in the windows. We did the same for our house. Because of the space limitation we had for our building, one side of the house was only about three feet from a tent. Our overhanging roof dumped a torrent of rain on top of that tent.

Unfortunately for us, the tent was filled with captains and majors. They had no sense of humor about water running onto their tent. We had to trim the roof on that side. The lopsided roof line added character, we thought, although we missed watching water pour onto the majors' tent during rainstorms.

Because most of the material came from 105-millimeter howitzer ammunition boxes and ships' dunnage, Bob christened our beautiful, new house "105 Dunnage Strip." The concrete step at the entryway to the porch had an engraving which was even more eloquent. It read "FNG."

For me it was simply "The House." And a grand one she was.

The House. An Khe 1966.

Chapter 6

Chu Pong Landing

I LOOKED AROUND one day, and the old guys were gone. Suddenly Chuck, Bob and I were the old guys, trying to keep the new guys alive. Three months after my arrival, I was planning and leading combat assaults and teaching combat flying.

In late June we began supporting an operation southwest of Pleiku, in the area of the Chu Pong Massif and the Ia Drang Valley where the 1st Cav had fought so bitterly in November 1965. It was too far from An Khe to fly back and forth daily, so we moved to a temporary camp at Pleiku called the "Turkey Farm."

The Turkey Farm was a flat, rather barren area just outside of Pleiku with plenty of room to park the helicopters and pitch our tents. We

"Old guys" CW3 Norm Taylor, WO1 Parry Etheridge, and WO1 George Rose, pictured, taught me how to survive in the insane conditions in which we flew. An Khe 1966.

were working south of there, refueling at a forward base called the "Oasis." Highway 14 ran south out of Pleiku toward the village of Plei Me and the Ia Drang Valley. The western edge of Chu Pong Mountain lay no more than a half-mile from the Cambodian border.

Sanctuary for the NVA and the VC lay on the other side of the Cambodian border: We were not allowed to cross it. It reminded me of the boundary between Texas and Mexico in old cowboy movies: The bad guys would come into Vietnam, ambush, then hightail it back into Cambodia. Our guys would give chase but had to stop at the border. Our congressmen were playing at war. We weren't.

The weather was often treacherous, with cloud ceilings extending to the ground and visibility down to 100 meters—sometimes almost zero. To keep from getting lost we would fly right down the road, just feet above the surface. That meant helicopters were flying along the same road at the same altitude, visibility so bad we couldn't see another aircraft until we were close enough to see each other smile. Like driving a car, we stayed on the right side of the road to avoid head-on collisions in mid air.

South of Pleiku on the eastern side of the highway was a small, cone-shaped hill with high grass and few trees. In their inimitable way, the GIs named it "Titty Mountain." There were aircraft of all shapes and sizes splattered over that little mountain, their wreckage a grim reminder to stay alert. Nobody wanted to end his career on the side of Titty Mountain.

For immediate support we kept six Hueys and some Huey gunships at LZ Cat, a forward base camp and staging area just a 30-minute flight from the Turkey Farm. LZ Cat was a fixed-wing, dirt air strip cut out of the woods east to west about three kilometers east of Chu Pong Mountain. The 2nd Brigade, 1st Air Cav forward headquarters was at LZ Cat, as was the command post for the 2nd Battalion, 5th Cavalry (2/5), one of the 2nd Brigade's infantry battalions. There was also an artillery battery of 105mm howitzers. A rifle company from one of the infantry battalions provided security.

ONE MORNING IN early August 1966 we were flying log missions out of LZ Cat, delivering ammunition, and food and water to various units. Our troops were scattered all over Chu Pong Mountain. We knew the enemy were heavily encamped in their safe haven just across the border west of Chu Pong. I got a spooky feeling, flying in that tight zone between Chu Pong Mountain and Cambodia. The extreme ruggedness of the mountain terrain—trees 120 feet high and thick jungle canopy—and large numbers of enemy

LZ Cat looking west toward Chu Pong Mountain and Cambodia. August 1966.

troops camped just across the border would make rescue of a downed helicopter highly improbable. It was no place for an engine failure.

I got a call to check out a mission on the back side of Chu Pong. There was a rifle company up on a ridge on the Cambodian side of the mountain that needed supplies and also wanted to get some people out. They had hacked a landing zone out of the jungle and asked for one of us to fly over to see if he could get in. The instructions concluded with "Don't worry about it if you can't get in. It may be too tough."

That struck me as odd. Never before had I heard that from an infantry unit. They always said, "We need you," carved out a place for us to land, and we went. Period.

"This is going to be interesting, Mac," I said. "Let's go check it out."

Bill "Mac" McManus was one of my warrant officers, a solid performer from McDonough, Georgia. I always liked having Mac with me.

We flew west toward Cambodia until we reached the western side of the mountain, then headed south.

I spotted the high ridge where the troops were supposed to be and called for smoke. "Black Diamond 6, this is Gunslinger 3-6, over."

"Black Diamond 6 Alpha, over."

"Gunslinger 3-6," I said. "I'm about a half-mile north. You wanna put some smoke out?"

"6 Alpha, roger."

"This is 3-6. We're gonna take a look and see if we can get down in there. I got red smoke, over."

"6 Alpha, roger red smoke."

As the smoke rose marking their location, I got a sinking feeling in my stomach.

"Holy shit, Mac. Would you look at that? Damn."

"I don't know, sir," Mac said. "I don't know about that one."

We continued flying south toward the company, entering the open end of a U-shaped, jungle-covered mountain ridge. From the highest point of the ridge the terrain sloped down a few hundred feet, then flattened into a narrow ledge. From that point the elevation dropped nearly a thousand feet in a sheer cliff. Our landing zone was on the ledge.

I made a low pass over the troops to get a better look. The ridge behind the landing area rose so high that if, at the last moment, I determined we couldn't make the landing, we would not be able to pull up and fly away—in any direction. Once we got past a certain point in the descent, I would be committed to land the aircraft. I would stick the helicopter on the side of that mountain or we would bounce off it and roll down that cliff.

Adding to our difficulties was the swirling wind inside that deep U-shaped ridge. A sharp gust or downdraft as we approached touchdown could throw us into the side of the mountain.

I circled and made another low pass. Once our skids were on the ground, there would barely be room for the blades—but there would be enough.

"There's no way we can go around, Mac," I said, "not once we get committed. No way."

Mac didn't say anything. He didn't like it either.

"The wind isn't too high right now, though," I said. "I think we can do this."

I got on the radio. "Black Diamond 6, this is Gunslinger 3-6. I think we can get in there all right, but I'm not sure we'll be back."

"6 Alpha, roger."

We circled again to set up for the approach. I focused on a tiny spot of red dirt on the edge of the cliff. The last few feet of the approach would be critical. With too much speed we would hit the trees. Too little speed or not enough power, the aircraft would lose lift and crash into the cliff, tumbling down that mountain like a runaway wagon in an old western movie.

I reduced power and started the descent. We continued at a steep angle, slowing as we descended. I could feel the machine groan and begin to work hard as airspeed dissipated. Little by little I pulled in power to compensate for the loss of airspeed. I would rather stop a tree with the rotor blades than tumble down that cliff, so I kept a little extra speed.

Jesus, I hope I don't run out of power.

Troops were backed against the trees, watching us.

The angle looks good...she feels strong enough...take her right on in there...hold whatcha got...fly it right on down to the ground.

I planned to put the blades within inches of the tree line and set the skids down. I gave no more than a cursory glance to the edge of the cliff, keeping my eyes focused on the edge of the trees.

We were 50 feet from the cliff and closing fast. Maintaining lift depended more and more on pure power from the engine. I was tense, but I had to stay smooth. Any erratic move by me could cause us to lose lift and miss the landing.

She's okay...she's okaaay...she's okaaay...we're gonna make it!

We crossed the cliff's edge, I pulled the nose up slightly, brought in more power, and set her down. We landed cockeyed: The back end of the left skid was in a hole, the front of it on a mound of dirt, the right skid on a tree stump. The blades cleared the trees by just inches all around, and the entire tail boom hung off the edge of the mountain. Our perch was so precarious I did not dare take the pitch out of the blades.

After the troops unloaded the food and water, mailbags, and ammunition, they loaded some gear, and three troopers got on.

"Sir, how are we going to get out of here?" Mac asked.

There was no room to turn around, and we didn't have enough power to hover straight up.

"No way to go but backward, Mac," I said. "We'll just back it up off the cliff, do a right pedal turn, and let her fall.

"Chief, you tell those boys to hang on back there," I said over my shoulder. "I don't want anybody falling out."

"Yes, sir, I'll tell 'em."

I pulled in power, lifted off, and began to fly backward. As we broke away from the cliff, I kept the aircraft moving back until the blades were well clear of the mountainside. When we began to fall from lack of speed and power, I did a right pedal turn, using the natural torque of the aircraft, pushed the nose downward to keep flying and to gain airspeed. We ripped down the side of the mountain.

Hueys in nose-to-tail formation. 1966.

Once we got to 80 knots airspeed, we rounded out the descent and turned north to fly out of the horseshoe.

Everything had gone as I had planned. Still, after falling that two or three hundred feet into the valley, I breathed a sigh of relief once we rounded out and began climbing.

We returned to the ridge a little later, but the winds had picked up significantly. We radioed our regrets and flew back to LZ Cat.

Later that afternoon we were sitting in line nose-to-tail, the helicopters running, blades spinning at full force. Sitting in the Huey behind me, Bob watched a young trooper walk directly into my tail rotor. The tip of the blade zipped by his chin, somehow missed the end of his nose, and caught the front edge of his steel helmet, knocking him backward. It shattered the end of the tail rotor, ending our flying for the day. He was unhurt.

Unbelievable.

Chapter 7

Only One Way Out

IT WAS SUNDAY, August 14, 1966. I was flying with one of the new guys, 1LT Harry I. "Butch" Decker. From Kingsport, Tennessee, Butch was a good man and would become a great friend. Although he had been in country only three or four weeks, it was easy to see that he was going to be a top aviator.

We were flying log missions that day on and around the Chu Pong Massif. I was leading the mission with two ships and helping Butch learn the ropes. We went out to deliver food and ammunition to a rifle platoon operating alone in the rainforest. We found them in a deep depression ringed with small hills and tall trees. We got in there to them, dropped off some C-rations and ammunition, took on some five-gallon water cans they had, and got ready to leave. As I looked around at the terrain to decide how to take off and in what direction, I realized I had made a bad mistake.

We were in a hole, surrounded by hills and trees. I was in a D model Huey that wasn't as strong as some of the others, and I was still heavily loaded. The clearest path was behind me, but that was downwind. Taking off downwind, I might not clear those trees—not a risk worth taking. The only direction that would give me enough room to clear the hills and trees was straight ahead. Straight ahead was also into the wind, which I needed for takeoff.

The problem was the tree directly in front of me and another to the right of it, both dead and limbless, like two telephone poles. If I tried to squeeze between them, the rotor blades wouldn't clear. The angle from which we would approach would give us about 45 feet, and the blades were 48 feet in diameter. If I could maneuver 20 feet to the right for a more straight-on approach, I might have just enough room for the blades. Unfortunately, 20 feet to the right sat a dead tree stump. Hovering over that 15-foot stump to take off would consume so much power that we wouldn't have enough left to clear the hill and trees.

The only way out was between those two pole-like trees, and we would have to approach from an angle. If I caught the tip of a rotor blade on one of those trees, we would crash and burn. I turned the helicopter 180 degrees to confirm. No way. I looked left, then right. No way. I turned back to study the two trees ahead.

With Butch Decker. An Khe 1966.

If I fly right up to them and bank the blades, I can slide right through there. I can do that.

"Butch, you ready?"

"Yeah, I'm ready."

"Hang on, guys," I said. "We're going between those trees."

I lifted off and flew straight for them. We were about 20 feet off the ground when I banked the helicopter to the left, putting my blades at an angle, and squeezed through the tight space. I leveled the aircraft, and we continued to climb. As we drew nearer to the green mass of trees, I knew we wouldn't clear them. We had lost engine and rotor speed in the ascent, and our RPM was down to 5700—way too low. While holding just enough throttle to keep the blades above the treetops, I flew the helicopter into the trees. Leaves and branches pushed through the doors and windows.

Come on, sweetheart! Come on, sweetheart! Fly, goddammit, fly!

Up to 5800...5900...she began to feel smoother...6000—we cleared the trees. Engine and rotor speed returned to 6600 where it belonged, and she began to feel good and strong again. So did I.

ON THE WAY back to LZ Cat, I got a call to pick up a KIA, a soldier killed in action. We found the troops in a small, tight clearing ringed by jungle growth and trees 80 or 90 feet tall. The KIA was a German shepherd scout dog. I was relieved it wasn't a soldier, but was touched by how this dog had given his life. The scout dogs did great work, saving the lives of an untold number of soldiers. They were special to their handlers in a way that we could not fully comprehend.

The troops treated the dog's body with the same care as they would a soldier's. Two men carried the dog, carefully wrapped in a poncho, and laid him gently on the floor of the helicopter.

We were ready to go. The clearing was so small, there was almost no room for forward movement in the takeoff.

"Chief," I said, "I'm gonna back up and stick the tail rotor back in the woods as far as I can to have a little more room for takeoff. Don't let me hit anything."

"Yes, sir."

I lifted up and began easing the helicopter backward.

"Come on back, sir…come on back…don't go left, sir! Don't go left!"

I stopped the Huey, dead still. His tone told me we were very close to something that could destroy the tail rotor and put us on the ground.

"You're okay, sir. You're okay," he said. "Just bring it straight back about another foot. Okay, sir, that's it."

I set the helicopter on the ground, then lifted off and over the trees. We headed north to the Oasis to deliver the KIA and pick up more ammunition.

We were sitting on the ground at the Oasis, the engine running and blades turning, when a trooper pulled up, driving under our blades. The long radio whip antenna mounted on the back of his jeep was thrust into the blades. The blades whacked the antenna off, but not before the antenna put a dent about the size of my thumb in the leading edge of each blade. That meant the blades would have to be changed. The dent did not create any bad vibrations or bumps when we flew, so we decided to fly the ship the rest of the day.

In the end, the blade dent didn't mean much. In another 24 hours those blades would be reduced from forty-eight feet to about four. The unusual takeoff between the two trees was only a warm-up. The real fun was about to begin.

Chapter 8

Don't Do It, Sir

South Texas was losing a steady number of young Mexican-American men to the Vietnam War. The Basilica of Our Lady of San Juan del Valle in San Juan, Texas, began issuing Virgen de San Juan medals to the mothers of young soldiers destined for combat. A woman who lived 200 miles away entered the church. She collected her medal from the priest, then stepped into the sanctuary. Before her stretched a long center aisle leading to the altar. She knelt, then traversed the length of the aisle — on her knees — clutching her Virgen de San Juan and praying for the safe return of her son....

PFC Joseph E. Rodriquez of Beeville, Texas, carefully inched his way up Hill 534 on Chu Pong Mountain. Sent ahead of B Company to scout, Rodriquez saw fresh dirt. When he saw the outline of bunkers through the foliage, he dropped to his belly behind a tree. Watching from behind, CPT William Taylor called for him to continue. Rodriquez ran left. A bullet to the shoulder took him down. Still drawing fire, he lay there, motionless, praying to the religious medal he wore that he would not be hit again. His best friend, James Sawitski, called out to him. "I know you're alive, Joe! I know you're alive! I'm going to count to 10. When I say 10 we are going to lay down fire for you! You get up and run like hell!" At 10, gunfire erupted, and Joe Rodriquez ran for his life. Safely back with B Company, he reached for his Virgen de San Juan, given him by his mother. It was gone.

WE HAD SPENT the afternoon flying log missions in the Ia Drang area, working for the 2/5. Except for the takeoff between the trees and the antenna strike, it had been a relatively uneventful day. After we returned from the Oasis, Butch had gone to fly on another mission while I took Karl Marrott, one of the new warrant officers, to fly with me. Marrott had been in country only a couple of weeks. I found him arrogant, but he did have above-average ability. The question in my mind was whether his arrogance would kill him before or after he became proficient in combat flying.

Just before 6 in the evening, the 2/5 supply officer, a captain, told me he had one more mission for us. Both helicopters would carry ammunition to B Company on Hill 534 on Chu Pong Mountain. B Company was under the operational control of 1/5, commanded by LTC Robert H. Siegrist. I was ready to finish this last routine mission and get back to the Turkey Farm before dark.

The captain gave me the radio frequency, call sign, and map coordinates for B Company. He said there were no clearings in their area so the ammo would have to be dropped down through the trees.

He turned to walk away. As if an afterthought, he turned and said, "Oh, yes. They're in contact up there."

Well, thank you very much.

I liked that captain, but his informing me as an aside that the LZ was hot was perplexing. Flying in and out of tight and dangerous jungle clearings is one thing. Doing it while people are shooting at you from close range raises the intensity level considerably.

I spoke to the crew chief as we set about loading the ammunition. "Chief, let's just stack those ammo boxes in single, tall columns by the doors. That way when we are ready, you can just push the columns, and all the boxes will topple out at once. Throwing all those boxes out one at a time would take way too long. I don't want to be hanging around up there any longer than necessary if they are going to be shooting at us."

We had used this technique many times before, and it had always worked well.

"Okay, sir," he said. "That's fine with me."

This crew chief was one of the old crew, and the next day was his last scheduled day in country. He was probably 10 years older than I and well-experienced. These older, experienced crew chiefs were far more knowledgeable about the aircraft than we young officers were. I did not know this man well personally, but I had a strong and good opinion of him.

About that time the executive officer of 2/5 walked up. He was a major, and tall, nearly six feet and a half. He wore a dark expression. "Lieutenant, I want you to put this ammo in a sling load."

Carrying the ammo suspended under the helicopter in a big net or sling was not something I intended to do.

"Sir, that's not the best way to do that," I said. "We're going to stack the boxes in tall columns by the doors. Then when we get over the troops, we'll just push the columns, and all the boxes will topple out at once. We'll have them all out in no time."

The major furrowed his brow, scowled at me and said, "Lieutenant, did you hear me? I want sling loads! Throwing those boxes out will tear them all to hell. Now, I want sling loads. I want you to take nylon ropes and hang the loads under the helicopters. That way you can let them down through the trees all the way to the ground and the ammo won't get all broken up!"

I thought that was a ridiculous idea. Hovering a hundred feet or so in the air while troops rappelled to the ground from those ropes was one thing, but carrying a large load of ammunition was quite different. The trees on the mountains were 100 to 120 feet tall, and the nylon ropes were Army-issue ropes 120 feet in length that would stretch out as much as one-third of their length. The problem I saw was if we let down a sling holding a huge load of boxes, the jungle canopy might trap it and hold it in the canopy. Worse, that load of ammunition was the weight of several men, not just one. I could imagine a broken rope flying up and getting entangled in the tail rotor or main rotor system and bringing us down.

Furthermore, although it made no difference in what I would or would not do, I didn't like his attitude. Regardless, I was well-versed in the areas of discipline and obedience to orders, and I had no intention of arguing with this senior officer. I found myself on the weak end of an escalating verbal confrontation with this demanding and highly agitated battalion executive officer. He was trying to force me to do something which, if I were right and he were wrong, could kill us all. I had learned not to put myself in a position where, if a mishap occurred, my crew and I would be killed.

I was the aviation expert here. Perhaps we could tie that ammunition under the helicopter with a 120-foot rope and fly off with it, maybe the rope would not break, and maybe the huge package of ammunition boxes would slip easily down through the triple canopy jungle to the ground—maybe. But it didn't sit right with me. We had nylon web slings made specifically to carry loads under the helicopters. The longest was 20 feet. I assumed there was a reason for that. I was no engineer, but I knew the dynamics of carrying weight 120 feet under the helicopter were quite different from those attendant at 20 feet. I figured the Army would have given me a 120-foot sling if it had intended me to use one.

As hard as the major was coming down on me, this wasn't the toughest man I had ever seen. I was the son of Richard W. Clark, possibly the toughest good man in the western hemisphere. Furthermore, while I was a rookie flyer and young officer, I was also an experienced, professional soldier.

As I stood facing the major, the crew chief positioned himself immediately behind me and hissed in my left ear, *"Don't do it, sir! Don't do it! Don't do it, sir! Don't do it!"*

I laugh every time I think of that great crew chief. He didn't know me well either. As far as he could see, I was a young and inexperienced first lieutenant, his aircraft commander, and I was being eaten alive by this infantry major. If there was any doubt about what I should do, the good chief removed it.

I spoke to the major in an even tone. "Sir, I can't tie that ammo on with nylon ropes. That won't work. Why, they stretch a third of their length—"

"Goddammit, Lieutenant!" He stopped me in mid-sentence. "I said I want a sling load with those ropes. Now you get it done!"

"Don't do it, sir! Don't do it! Don't do it, sir! Don't do it!"

"Sir, please, that will not work," I said, trying to convince him my way was more sound. "I have done this plenty of times before. The boxes will be okay. Those ropes are too dangerous."

"Dammit, Lieutenant, you hover a hundred feet in the air and rappel people with them. Why can't you do this?"

"Don't do it, sir! Don't do it! Don't do it, sir! Don't do it!"

"Sir, it just won't work," I said. "It's not designed to work that way, and I'm not going to try it here."

Enraged, he began to shout. "Goddammit, Lieutenant, you fucking aviators are all alike! You won't do a goddamn thing when you're needed!"

He had pushed me too far. For the first time ever, I raised my voice to a senior officer. "Goddammit, sir, this is not Fort Benning, this is Vietnam! You can't do that kind of shit over here! Now we've got six more helicopters sitting right over there, and every one of them has two drivers. If you can get one of them to come do this, then you fucking have at it, sir, because I am not going to do it!"

His comment was uncalled-for, totally untrue, and insulting to my profession and to me personally. He was trying to force me to use the ropes, and, though I was outranked, I held the high cards. I was not about to be bullied into doing something stupid and dangerous when there was a safer, easier alternative.

"Lieutenant, I am going to have your ass!" the major roared. "What's your name?"

"Sir, it's right there on my name tag! My name is Ray Kenneth Clark! I'm a first lieutenant, Infantry! I belong to B Company, 227th. And I am not going to take a 120-foot sling!"

"Well, goddamn!" said the major. "I've never seen such bullshit in all my life! How big of a sling will you take?"

"Take the 20-foot sling if you have to, sir! That's all, sir! That's all!"

"Sir, a sling is not the way to do this," I told the major, "but if you just have to have a sling, I'll take 20 feet."

"Well, all right then, use 20 feet," he said, "but I'm going with you!"

"Well, sir, maybe you will, and maybe you won't. Once we get loaded, we'll have to see if we can carry you."

The major walked away. The crew chief retrieved a 20-foot sling for each helicopter, and the crewmen stacked the ammunition boxes in the slings. The next step was to attach them to the hooks under the helicopters. Each of us would pick up our loads and hover to test the weight. If engine and rotor speed were lost at hover, the load would have to be reduced.

We started the engines. The major got in the back of my helicopter. I hovered over the sling loaded with ammunition boxes and lowered the aircraft so the end of the sling could be attached. Standing on top of the load, the trooper attached the sling to the hook, then jumped off the mass of boxes. I pulled in power and slowly brought the aircraft to a hover, the sling load of ammunition dangling beneath. The weight just exceeded the maximum allowable, although I knew I could handle it. The small drop in engine speed was all I needed. The major was dead weight overloading my helicopter. I wasn't taking his sorry ass anywhere.

I lowered the sling to the ground, flicked a switch to disconnect the sling load, moved the helicopter sideways a few feet, and set it down. I half-turned in my seat, raised my fist with thumb extended, and motioned the major out of the helicopter.

I picked up to a hover again, connected the sling load, and we were off, headed west for Hill 534.

AS WE APPROACHED the drop area, I spotted a large clearing at the top of the hill, a place to land where the supply officer had said there was none. There seemed to be a lot about this operation I didn't know: Air Force F-4 Phantom jets were making diving bomb runs on the clearing.

I called the infantry company commander we were trying to supply up there on Hill 534. No answer. I called again. Still no answer. A third call yielded the same result.

"Damn!" I said to myself. "His radio must be out."

I could get close to him with the map coordinates, but that would not be enough to find him under that solid jungle canopy. I needed him to mark his location with smoke.

I called the battalion commander, Lieutenant Colonel Siegrist, to see if he could reach the company. No reply there either.

Damn. Maybe it's my radio. Goddamn. I've gotta get smoke.

Maybe the FM channel was the problem. Only helicopter pilots had both UHF and FM radios. On a UHF channel I called the pilot of the command-and-control helicopter. I preferred to speak to the commander on his FM radio, but that was not an option.

"Saber Tooth 4-4," I said, "this is Green 3-6, over."

"This is Saber Tooth 4-4, over."

"This is Green 3-6. Listen, I can't raise the company on the ground and I can't get the 6 [commander's call sign] in the back of your helicopter either. I need some smoke or some instructions on where to put this load. Also, what's the deal on all these jets? Ask that 6 back there where I should put this stuff and come back to me, will you?"

"Roger, 3-6."

We continued toward Hill 534, two D model Huey helicopters with 20-foot sling loads of ammunition. The F-4 Phantoms were wreaking havoc with their 500-pound bombs, diving in at speeds substantially greater than our 60 knots.

"Green 3-6, this is Saber Tooth 4-4, over."

I was very glad to hear back from him, as we were rapidly closing on the mountain.

"This is Green 3-6, over."

"This is 4-4. You see that big clearing down there? Put it right in that clearing. That jet moving in there right now is the last pass so you are clear to go in. Over."

"Roger, 4-4. We'll put it in the clearing."

I called my trailing helicopter. "Green 4, this is Green 3-6, over."

He answered with two quick clicks on his mike.

"This is Green 3-6. We're going in that clearing down there. We'll probably be drawing fire, so let's not hang around in there. We'll zip in there, drop it, and keep moving."

Two quick clicks signaled he understood.

We were approaching from the south. From a quarter-mile away I viewed an F-4 Phantom screaming in on its last pass. Huge columns of black smoke rolled up out of the tree line. I was pretty sure we would draw fire. Because the NVA battalion was in dug-in positions, automatic weapons fire seemed likely. I wanted to get in there as quickly as possible behind that jet while the NVA still had their heads down. I planned to zip in just above the treetops, move into the edge of the clearing, cut the load loose on the fly, scoot quickly back over the trees, and get out of there.

I could smell the smoke as we came in over the brilliant green canopy, rotor blades popping their familiar sound. As we moved into the open area a hundred feet off the ground, I braced myself for enemy fire from near-point-blank range.

No noise yet. No muzzle flashes. Hey! There's no fire! We're not getting any fire!

I pulled the nose up and flared the helicopter to a quick stop, cut the load loose, and darted back over the treetops. We headed down the mountain right on top of the trees.

What a relief! No fire at all! No fire at all!

We headed back to LZ Cat, a little excited and feeling good about getting the ammo in there.

We landed at the LZ where we had lifted off just 15 minutes before. The supply officer and several others ran to meet us. They were so happy we had gotten the ammo to their friends, who I learned were in dire straits: They were a single company of 140 men, almost out of ammunition, up against five or six companies dug in at the top of Hill 534.

Before I could get out of the helicopter they were asking for my name and unit so they could put us all in for awards. I thought that an overreaction. The run in behind the F-4s had been a little scary, but nothing happened after that. I wasn't expecting any accolades, but the infantry supply people were not to be denied. They were still talking excitedly when the major I'd had the altercation with strode up.

"Lieutenant!" he barked. "Where did you put that stuff?"

"I put it right in that clearing, sir, right where your CO asked for it."

"Well, goddammit, they don't have it!"

"What do you mean they don't have it?" I said. "I put it right in there!"

"You put it in the wrong fucking place, goddammit! They don't have it! Where the hell did you put it?"

"Sir, I told you, I put it right in the goddamn clearing! That is exactly where the battalion commander said put it, and that's where I put it! Now, if you have a problem with that, sir, talk to the battalion commander. I put it exactly where he said!"

"Well, what it means is the fucking Vietnamese have it!"

With that he turned and stalked away.

If our guys didn't own the clearing, I supposed the NVA did have the ammo. I couldn't believe we had supplied the NVA and not our own troops. More than a little on my mind was the fact I had landed smack in the middle of an NVA battalion position.

Marrott spoke up. "Sir, maybe that's why they didn't shoot at us."

"No, I don't think so," I said. "They probably didn't shoot because they were still down in their bunkers hiding from those 500-pound bombs. We just had good timing."

I was sick that our mission had failed so miserably. If I could have reached that company commander by radio, I would have gotten his position marked by smoke and that mistake would not have happened.

IT WAS NEARLY 6 p.m., and darkness was closing in. Low clouds covered LZ Cat except for a small opening directly above us. How strange, I thought to myself. Solid cloud cover everywhere—everywhere except for a small hole directly above us.

The infantry battalion supply officer came back. "Clark, we've gotta get those people resupplied up there."

"What's the deal, sir?" I asked. "How did they get in so much trouble up there?"

"They were walking up that big finger [a large ridge sloping down off the top of the mountain with lower ground on both sides] and they ran right into an NVA battalion dug in around the top of the mountain," he told me. "We haven't been able to get to them to reinforce them or resupply them because there is no place to land up there."

"Well, there is a big clearing up there on top of the hill," I told him, "but apparently the NVA own it. Your guys must be down the hill from the clearing."

"I guess so," replied the captain. "Anyway, they are in contact up there and can't get loose. They are out of food and water and almost out of ammo. We have to get supplies up there tonight. The ammo you took up there was the last we had here at Cat. Can you go to the Oasis and get two loads of ammunition and bring it back here? The CO wants to resupply the company tonight as soon as possible."

I now had a real problem—the cloud cover. We could see stars up through the small opening above us, but how long would the hole stay open? I knew I could get out of LZ Cat and up to the Oasis. There was a portable Ground-Control Approach (GCA) radar system set up there. While loading ammo there earlier in the day the GCA operator asked if he could practice by giving us a radar approach into the Oasis. I had his radio frequency to do that. The problem would be getting back to LZ Cat. The entire valley floor was covered with clouds. How would I find the opening? Would it still be there?

There was a small, portable non-directional beacon (NDB) at LZ Cat, and we had the radio equipment in the helicopter to use it. In theory, you could simply tune in the NDB radio frequency and home in on it. The portable NDBs were notoriously unreliable. It would bring us back to LZ Cat—if it worked.

"Well, we can get out of here and we can get to the Oasis," I told the captain, "but I'm not sure we can get back in here. If this hole stays open, we'll find it. But if it closes over while we're gone, we'll just have to go back to the Oasis and wait."

"Do the best you can," he said. "I'll call the Oasis and tell them you are coming."

In addition to my two helicopters, we had six more Hueys and two B model Huey gunships at LZ Cat for an early combat assault the next morning.

As we discussed the situation, one of the gunship pilots, a lieutenant from Texas I had never met, offered a suggestion. "Tell you what. It ought to take you all about an hour or so to get up there, get loaded, and come back. About 40 minutes after you're gone, I'll turn on my radio. If the NDB doesn't work, and it probably won't, you call me. I'll turn my beacon [a rotating red light on top of the Huey] on and fly up out of this hole. You'll be able to see the beacon and you can home in on us."

I held him by the forearm and shook his hand. "Damn good idea! That'll work. Thanks a lot. Now just don't let that hole close in."

The lieutenant laughed. "Don't worry. We'll keep the bastard open."

I liked this lieutenant. I got his call sign and radio frequency and went about stacking the odds in my favor as much as I could. There were people around who could fly instruments better than I. I talked to the pilots in our group. CPT Everett "Ev" Greenwood was a good, solid aviator fully instrument-qualified in fixed wing aircraft—a levelheaded, good man. I asked him to fly the mission with me. I got the two most experienced pilots to fly the other ship.

"Captain Greenwood, I appreciate you doing this for me," I said.

"Hey, no problem, Clark. We'll get it done."

"Good. Just one thing, though, sir. You're a captain and I'm a first lieutenant, but I'm the aircraft commander. It's my mission. I'm in charge all the way. What I say goes, no conversations. Okay, sir?"

"Hey, no problem," Greenwood said. "I'll just be Peter Pilot. You run the show."

"Great," I smiled, happy he agreed. "I just don't want to get up there and get in trouble and then start having a conversation about who's in charge."

"No sweat, Ray," he said. "Let's get going."

We fired up both helicopters and moved to the center of the dirt airstrip, under the opening in the cloud cover.

"You want to do an instrument takeoff [ITO] or try to go up through the hole?" Greenwood asked.

"Stay in the clear if you can," I said.

We lifted off, climbing nearly straight up, trying to stay in the hole. It was so small we began to lose visibility.

"You want to go up through the clouds or try to stay in the hole?" asked Greenwood.

I liked being able to see. "Stay in the hole if you can."

He banked left in a tight spiral upward. We were back in the hole and climbing. Suddenly we were out of the hole and on top, flying in a beautiful, clear, black sky filled with stars. The beauty of it took my breath away. The soft, dark white of the cloud cover lay below us as we turned north toward the Oasis and began a steady climb.

"Nice going, sir," I said.

"Well, it wasn't too thick, was it?" Greenwood said. "About 300 feet, I guess. Man, this is pretty, isn't it?"

"It sure is," I said. "Those stars are beautiful. Let's go to about 3000 feet.

"Chief," I said over my shoulder, "is Green 4 with us?"

"Yes, sir, he's back there."

After 20 minutes of smooth flight, we were at the Oasis. Even though the weather was clear there, I called the GCA operator to get a radar approach as he had requested. With no threat of enemy attack at the Oasis, we came in with the landing light on. We hovered over to the supply area where troops were waiting for us. We shut the engines down and waited for them to load the helicopters.

As we were running the engines up to leave, I had an idea. "Hey, Captain Greenwood, let's get that radar operator to give us a radar vector back to LZ Cat."

"Sure, good idea," he said. "Let's do."

B Co. platoon leader CPT Dennis Engen and CPT Everett Greenwood. LZ Hammond 1967.

I called the GCA operator with the map coordinates for LZ Cat and asked for a radar vector.

"No problem, Green 3-6," he said. "It will take me a couple of minutes to work it out. Can you wait?"

"Green 3-6. Sure, we'll wait right here, over."

This was such a good idea. I was happy about this radar vector business. He would put us precisely over LZ Cat. I had made the trip from the Oasis to LZ Cat many times and knew it was 186 degrees, ever so slightly west of due south. The GCA operator would tell me how far to go and exactly when I would get there. The huge Chu Pong Massif and the Cambodian border lay southwest. I was after all the insurance I could get to fly straight back to LZ Cat.

In about five minutes the radar operator called. "Green 3-6, this is Oasis. Take radar vector 217. That's 217. Over."

"This is Green 3-6. 217? Are you sure? 217? Over."

"This is Oasis. Roger, 217 degrees. You are cleared for takeoff."

"This is Green 3-6. Thank you very much. We appreciate it. We won't be needing you further. Out."

I was disappointed, perplexed, and deeply relieved that I knew the route to LZ Cat was precisely 186 degrees.

"Sir, can you believe that? The stupid son-of-a-bitch just gave us a radar vector into the side of Chu Pong Mountain! It's been 186 degrees every time I've been down there. I'll bet you it still is."

Greenwood laughed. "I'm with you. Stupid bastard."

We lifted off into the starry night, climbed to 3000 feet and set our direction at 186 degrees. Soon we were back over the cloud cover. It was about a 20-minute flight, so we began to descend after 15.

"Let's try the NDB," I said. "I don't have any idea if it will work, but let's try."

I dialed in the radio frequency for the non-directional beacon and looked for the needle to pick up the radio signal. It fluttered all over the place. There was no indication at all.

"I wonder who makes this Mattel son-of-a-bitch," I grumbled. "Scratch that. Let's see if we can get the boy from D Company. Trooper 25, this is Green 3-6, over."

"This is Trooper 25, over."

Hot dog!

He was right there, just as he said he would be.

"This is Green 3-6. We're two or three miles north. Can you still get out of there? Over."

"Trooper 25. The hole looks tight, but it's still there. We'll be right up."

"Green 3-6, roger."

In a moment, to the left and a mile or so ahead, a red rotating beacon came into view.

"There he is, sir," I said. "Now, how nice is that?"

"I like it, Clark, I like it," Greenwood said. "Let's get over there."

"Trooper 25, this is Green 3-6. We gotcha. I'm turning our beacon on now. Do you see us? Over."

"25, roger."

"3-6, okay. Head on in. We'll be right behind you."

"25, roger."

"This is 3-6. Hey, 25. You do good work."

"25, we aim to please."

After giving our friend time to get down through the hole and out of the way, we followed, spiraling down through that opening in the clouds, leaving the starry sky behind. We hovered over to the supply area, landed, and shut the engine down.

I spoke to the crew chief. "Chief, you all rig this ammo for sling loads, and I'll see when they want us to go up there and do the resupply."

"Okay, sir."

Fifteen minutes after we landed in LZ Cat, the hole in the clouds was covered over. We were entirely socked in by weather.

Chapter 9

Hill 534: B Company, 2/5

B COMPANY WAS in real trouble. They were up against a force that was entrenched in well-fortified positions and outnumbered them perhaps five to one. They were nearly out of ammunition and they had no food or water. They had suffered serious casualties. The enemy owned the only clearing in the area so it had been impossible to reinforce our people with new troops. Our guys had them by the nose and couldn't get loose.

I went to see the operations officer of 2/5 twice that night to find out when he wanted us to go back to Hill 534 to deliver the ammo and supplies. Both times I entered the command post I found the 2/5 battalion commander immersed in intense, grave conversation with the young captain and company commander of B Company.

I had never heard such an exchange over military radio. I felt as I did when I walked into a church sanctuary, that I should be reverent and still. As he spoke to CPT William Taylor up on the mountain, the lieutenant colonel's voice was quiet and intimate. I could hear only one side of the conversation, but the intensity of the hushed, low tone of the colonel's voice made clear the gravity of the situation.

I never met Bill Taylor. I wish I had. I heard several officers and enlisted men speak of him that day and the next. He was tremendously respected, held in the highest regard. This was one hell of a good man, and he and his boys needed saving.

After waiting several minutes at the command post, I told the operations officer we were loaded and ready to go. I was intent on making myself clear. "There is just one thing, sir," I said. "We are entirely socked in here with cloud cover. I don't know how long it will last. I can get out of here up through the clouds, but I won't be able to get back in until the clouds go away. So you had better be damn sure the top of the mountain is not socked in when you send us up there, because if it is, I won't be able to get in to them and I won't be able to get back in here either. I'll have to go to Pleiku where I can get an instrument landing. And of course the ammo will have to go with me. So don't send me until you are sure I can get to them."

"Okay, okay, I understand," the major said. "We're going to send an Air Force helicopter up there after a while with a winch and chair that will go down through the trees to bring out some of the wounded. You go back down to your helicopter and wait there. We'll call you when we're ready for you."

It was 9:30 or 10 at night. I went back to the helicopter, briefed everyone and told them to get some sleep. It started to rain. The crew chief and door gunner were sprawled out on the cabin floor, so there was no room inside the helicopter. I crawled under it and lay down. That's when I learned the Huey is not an efficient rooftop. Because of the curvature of the sides and bottom, rainwater runs down both sides of the helicopter, clings to the bottom until it meets at the center of its body, then falls. That night it fell on me.

I crawled into the only spot in the helicopter that I could call mine—the left seat—and soon began to doze. Trying to sleep in that straight-backed seat was agitating and uncomfortable. The aches and cramps of sleeping upright and the anticipation of a call to fly the mission kept me in and out of a fitful sleep. It was close to 3 a.m. when fatigue finally won out and I slept.

Shortly after 6 a.m. Captain Taylor began to issue instructions in preparation for the coming day's battle plan. Each of the platoons were gathered in groups making last-minute preparations. Thwump! Thwump! It was the sound of enemy mortar rounds being fired. The company was under attack. Captain Taylor called for artillery fire, then shouted to his men to prepare for the enemy ground attack which was sure to follow. Moments later Captain Taylor and his command group took a direct hit. Captain Taylor, 1SGT Kenneth Hawsey, and the radio operator were killed instantly. The company's chief medic, SP4 Teddy G. Barger, was critically wounded, as were several others. A human wave assault came at the company. Responding to Captain Taylor's instructions, the troops were ready. The enemy ran into a wall of fire, forcing them to the ground. For the next four hours B Company traded shots with the enemy at an average range of 25 meters. The company's second radio operator, Tiger Shark 6 Alpha, though seriously wounded, remained on the air.[1]

I AWOKE A little after daylight. I wondered why they had not called us. It was Monday, August 15, a rain-soaked, beautiful morning with sunshine and a clear sky. I ate a pecan nut roll out of a can from a C-ration box, and went to the command post to find out what was going on.

I saw the operations officer first. "Sir, you didn't call us. What's the deal?"

"I was just coming to get you," he said. "They had a rough night up there last night. That Air Force helicopter got some of the wounded out. They are still out of food and water and almost out of ammunition. And they still are in contact. I want you to go up there now and take that resupply in there to them."

"Okay, sir. We'll get going right now."

I figured the resupply shouldn't be too difficult, although we would not be able to see the troops on the ground because of the thickness of the jungle canopy. We would fly up the side of the mountain to where I estimated them to be. I would call the company and ask for smoke to mark their exact location. We would hover over the smoke, make one final check by radio, and drop the two loads of C-rations, ammunition and water.

I went back to the helicopter and briefed the two crews. "Okay, here's the deal. It's pretty simple. We'll go up the mountain and call for smoke. I'll drop mine."

Nodding at the two pilots flying my second helicopter, call sign Green 4, I continued. "You come in and drop yours and we'll be outta there. We'll come back here and see what's next. Any questions? These guys are in a lot of trouble up there. They have

[1] AAR, 1st CAV Division at Hill 534, 1st Cav Div (Ambl), Report No. H-534, p. 27.

apparently taken a lot of casualties and they are still in contact. They are completely out of food and water and almost out of ammo. We've gotta get this stuff in there to them. Let's go."

It was about 7:30 a.m. We cranked up our two Hueys, picked up the sling loads and took off for Hill 534 on Chu Pong Mountain.

We flew over flat, fairly open rainforest with trees 90 to 100 feet high. The treetops nearly grew together in the area around LZ Cat but you could sometimes get a glimpse of the ground. As we started up the mountain, the jungle canopy became so thick we could not see down through the trees at all—it was a solid sheet of green.

Once we were airborne the first thing I noticed was that a huge cloud covered most of the mountain. LZ Cat and the valley floor were clear, but this cloud hung over the mountain, almost to its base.

As we approached Hill 534, I called B Company for smoke. "Tiger Shark 6, this is Green 3-6, over."

"This is Tiger Shark 6 Alpha, over."

"6 Alpha, this is Green 3-6. We're inbound with some goodies for you. We're about a minute out. You wanna put some smoke out for us? Over."

"This is 6 Alpha. Roger, 3-6. Poppin' smoke."

We were at the base of Hill 534 now and near the bottom of the cloud.

I spoke on intercom to Warrant Officer Marrott who was flying right seat. "Boy, I hope they are not under that cloud. If they are, we will never find them.

"Anybody see smoke?" I asked, addressing the crew.

We looked in all directions. No smoke.

Worried, I called the company again. "Tiger Shark 6 Alpha, this is Green 3-6. Put some more smoke out. I don't see anything, over."

"This is 6 Alpha. We don't have any more smoke. That was the last one. It's red smoke. It's red smoke, over."

"This is Green 3-6. Roger. There is cloud cover hanging down over the mountain. You may be under it. We'll keep looking."

As we circled looking for the red smoke, I was thinking out loud on the intercom. "Damn. They must be under that cloud cover. We should have seen that smoke by now. They have to be under that cloud cover. No telling how long that cloud will lie there. It could burn off in an hour or it could stay three days or a week. We have to get in to those guys. Somehow we have to get in to them. Their last smoke grenade. No ammo. No food. No water. Damn. Somehow we have to get in there."

I decided to fly down along the ragged edges of the cloud where the bottommost part met the treetops. Maybe they were just under the edge of the cloud. If so, I might be able to see the red smoke.

The sling load limited our maneuverability and slowed us down. Also, as I got right down on the treetops to look under the edge of the cloud, I couldn't get as close to the trees as I wanted. Those supplies should have been inside the helicopter. Dumb-ass major.

I called the troops again. "Tiger Shark 6 Alpha, this is Green 3-6, over."

"This is 6 Alpha, over."

"This is Green 3-6. I'm going to try to look up under the edge of this cloud a little bit. If you hear us or see us, yell. Over."

"This is 6 Alpha. Roger."

I flew down as close to the treetops as I could and moved in to where the edge of the cloud mingled with the tops of the trees. Surprisingly, as I peered under the cloud, I could see 30 or 40 meters up the hill. While the cloud formed a solid cover over the mountain, here was a space of hazy visibility between the treetops and the bottom of the cloud.

I bet I can fly up this damn hill!

"Green 4, this is 3-6. I'm gonna see if I can fly up under this cloud. You stay out there and circle till we get this figured out. Don't you come in here till I tell you to. Over."

"Green 4. Roger."

As I moved slowly under the cloud, whiteness and haze enveloped us. The treetops were my only visual reference, but they seemed to be enough. Excited at the prospect of being able to fly under the cloud, I began to think about what I could and could not do. This was beyond dangerous. I needed a plan.

Shoot, I can see these treetops! I can fly in here!

I was moving so slowly that I didn't have to see very far. The cloud cover wasn't thick and I could fly up through it quickly if I had to. I would fly up the hill until I found the red smoke or until I couldn't see anymore. The finger I was flying up fell away to lower ground both to my left and right. I would fly up the hill using the treetops below me as a visual reference. When I could no longer see I would go on instruments, climb 500 FPM and turn left until I broke out on top of the cloud cover. Climbing would break me out on top of the cloud, and turning left would put me over lower ground in case I got vertigo and ended up descending when I thought I was climbing.

I can do this. All I gotta do is keep that sling load out of the trees and keep moving up the hill. Need to keep at least 30 knots airspeed because of that damn sling load. If I get in trouble, climb and turn left. I can do this.

We began inching up the mountain at about 30 knots airspeed. I couldn't see well enough to go faster, and I felt like I shouldn't go slower. We were carrying maximum weight, and the sling load severely limited our maneuverability. I was in an unfamiliar and perilous predicament. Simply flying the aircraft demanded most of my attention. I deliberately kept my eyes looking out and ahead and away from the instrument panel.

When the horizon is not visible, a pilot must depend on his aircraft instruments to fly straight and level. He must guard against going back and forth, from looking down at the instruments to looking outside for a visual reference—a fast way to end up with vertigo. You can suddenly find yourself in the bewildering state of not knowing whether you are right side up or upside down.

I was in wonder at our visual surrounding: hazy, green treetop canopy under us, the panorama of white that enveloped us, and the simple fact that we were in there. I didn't know what to expect as we crept up the hill, whether the limited visibility would last, if we would draw fire, or if we would even find B Company. With the cloud lying over the trees, I figured the smoke would not have dissipated.

We had to find them. Being an infantryman myself, I had a pretty good idea of what was going on down there. Maybe *I* had time to wait for better weather conditions—the troops did not.

"Green 3-6! Green 3-6! We hear you! We hear you!"

There was no smoke to reveal the location of the excited voice on the radio.

"You've gone by us now! You've gone by us!"

Damn!

"Okay, 6 Alpha, okay. We'll try it again. I'll go around and start up the hill again. We'll be right back. Over."

I pulled in power, switched my gaze from the treetops in front of me to my instrument panel and began to climb. We were enveloped by a dense, murky whiteness. We couldn't see a thing. After climbing for a few seconds, I began a left turn to get over lower ground. Suddenly we broke out on top of the cloud into sunshine, blue sky, and clear visibility. I was exactly where I had intended to be—off the crown of the ridge and over lower ground.

We were fired up after hearing the strain and excitement in 6 Alpha's voice, and breaking on top of the cloud pumped us up even more. I wanted to find those people and deliver that ammunition in the worst way.

I flew back to the valley floor and the bottom of the cloud. The green sameness of the treetop canopy made it difficult to spot where we had started before. I guessed where our starting point was, moved a few meters left, and began our second trip up the hill.

"6 Alpha, this is Green 3-6. We're coming in again. Over."

"Roger, 3-6. We're watching."

"You all watch for this smoke, now," I told the crew.

They did not need the instruction.

Holy Shit!

I could see nothing. The impenetrable whiteness of the cloud descended all the way down into the trees. Startled and frightened by the abrupt loss of sight, I felt a cold tightness in my stomach. Just as quickly, we were through it, and I could see again. After that, 20 or 30 meters of hazy sight felt pretty comfortable. Losing all visual sight for that few seconds was unnerving, but we could handle it if it didn't get any worse.

We continued up the mountain. After a certain amount of time passed with nothing from the radio, I knew I had missed them again. I pulled in power, climbed, turned left and broke out on top again.

"6 Alpha, this is Green 3-6. We'll try it again. We'll be right back. Over."

"This is 6 Alpha. Roger."

We went back in.

"6 Alpha, this is 3-6. We're coming in again. Over."

"This is 6 Alpha. Roger."

I thought if I made enough passes up the hill and kept starting from a position farther left each time, eventually I would find them, but I was never sure how far left I had moved or if I, in fact, had moved at all.

We were under the cloud and climbing slowly up the mountain again. We hit the whiteout spot again, and I lost all visibility. I held the controls steady, and, as before, we passed through it in two or three seconds. I took a breath, and we continued.

Jesus Christ! There's the fucking clearing!

There was only one clearing on that part of the mountain, and the NVA owned it. We were behind the NVA's defensive line at treetop level, moving slowly over open ground. I pulled in power and got up into the cloud as quickly as I could. I turned left. We broke out on top again and started to descend back down the mountain.

"Chief, did we take any fire there?" I asked. "Did you hear anything?"

"No, sir, I don't think so. I didn't see anything."

I had flown too far up the mountain; that was for sure.

Damn, I cannot fly over those fucking NVA positions again! One machine gun burst in the right place and we're through!

"6 Alpha, this is 3-6. We're coming around again. Over."

"This is 6 Alpha! Roger! You were real close that time! You were real close! Over!"

Normally those guys were dead calm and cool on the radio, but when the bullets were flying and the situation was hot, you could hear it in their voices. I heard both desperation and anticipation in this radio operator's voice. I didn't know if they were under fire at the moment, but they needed us and badly wanted us to find them. That was more obvious each time 6 Alpha keyed his mike.

We flew back to the bottom of the mountain, ducked under the cloud, and started up the hill again. The whiteout area was becoming passé. We would hit it, go blind for a few seconds, hold everything steady, and quickly pass through it.

"6 Alpha, this is 3-6. Here we come, over."

"6 Alpha, Roger!"

We hit the whiteout. I held steady. We passed through it.

Holy shit!

In front of me was a big treetop that loomed 15 or 20 feet above the others. Twenty feet to the right of it was another, extending above the canopy exactly like the one in front of me. I had that damn sling load, so any quick maneuvering was difficult to impossible. My blades would not fit between the trees, and there was no time to climb.

I broke right and, keeping my rotor blades above the trees, flew between them, passing the fuselage of the aircraft and the sling load through the narrow space.

"3-6! We hear you! We hear you!"

This time as 6 Alpha spoke, I could hear other charged voices in the background saying "I hear them! I hear them!"

Seeing no smoke, I continued up the hill, climbed into the cloud, turned left and broke out on top. We had missed them again, but I was greatly relieved to have gotten between those two trees.

We moved to the bottom of the hill to start again.

"Sir, the 20-minute warning light is on," Marrott said.

"Shit!" I glanced at the red light on the instrument panel, not knowing how accurate those 20-minute warning lights were.

Do I have exactly 20 minutes left? 25 minutes? 15? Fuck, I got no idea!

I would get us out of there as soon as I could, but finding those Americans on the ground was what I was thinking about.

We moved up the mountain, passing through the whiteout. We heard more shouting on the radio. We missed them again.

Damn!

I pulled in power, climbed into the cloud and turned left. We broke out on top again. Something didn't feel right.

I was out of the cloud and in the clear. I had made my left turn and was headed away from the mountain.

Something isn't right! Something isn't right!

I checked the instruments.

Airspeed...that's okay. I'm climbing at 700 feet per minute.

I checked the climb indicator again, which indicated we were descending 700 feet per minute.

No, goddammit, no! I'm climbing *700 feet per minute!*

I read the indicator again: descending 700 feet per minute. Instruments don't lie.

Confused, frightened, and not knowing which way was up or down, I believed the climb indicator. I brought in power and pulled the nose up, leveling the aircraft.

In control again, I felt better, but I was shaken—really shaken. I obviously had had a touch of vertigo. I knew I was pushing it, going on instruments and off instruments, looking inside the aircraft and then out, going in the cloud and then out of it, over and over.

The left turn, which was a part of every recovery as we climbed up through the cloud to break out, turned us away from the mountain, so the 700-feet-per-minute descent had us flying down nearly parallel to the mountainside. If we had not made that left turn, we would have flown into the side of the mountain. It was turning left every time we climbed up through the cloud that saved us.

I started the descent back down the mountain again.

"6 Alpha, this is Green 3-6, over."

"This is 6 Alpha. You went right by us that time! You went right by us! Over!"

"This is 3-6. Yeah, yeah, I know, I know. Now, we almost crashed that time, but we didn't."

I was talking too fast. I needed to calm down. "We're coming back in there and we are going to find you."

"This is 6 Alpha. Roger."

"This is 3-6. Look, I'm on my 20-minute fuel warning light. We'll make another pass or two and then I'm gonna have to go and get fuel. But don't worry. If we do, I'll be back. We'll stay right here, by God, till we find you."

"6 Alpha. Roger."

"Green 4, this is 3-6. Why don't you go get some fuel, then come on back. Soon as we find these guys I'll lead you in so you can drop your load."

"Green 4. Roger."

We made another pass. And then another. We flew over the NVA clearing twice more. Another time we came out of the cloud descending again instead of climbing.

On the ground, SSG Ed Walsh, newly promoted from squad leader to B Company's 3d Platoon sergeant, was down to his last magazine of ammunition. He had no food and little water left in his canteen. Each time he heard us fly by he thought, "Just drop the damn stuff!"

I was really worried about fuel now. We had been on the 20-minute warning light close to 20 minutes.

I don't know how many times I said "I'll make one more pass." It must have been a dozen or more, as we kept going back up the mountain "just one more time." But this time *had* to be the last.

"6 Alpha, this is 3-6. This is definitely the last pass. If I don't find you this time I will refuel and then I'll be right back. Over."

"This is 6 Alpha! Roger! You went almost right over us that time! Over!"

We went under the cloud and started up the hill for one last pass. This time, after we broke through the whiteout, we heard: "3-6! 3-6! We see you! We see you! We see you!"

I looked out my left window. There in the haze, about 30 meters away, lay a pall of red smoke—and we were passing it by. With the limited visibility, closeness of the cloud to the trees, the low airspeed, and the clumsiness of the sling load, I couldn't make the turn to get to them.

"6 Alpha, this is 3-6. I've got your smoke. I've got your smoke. I can't get stopped so I'll have to go around again. I know where you are. I'll be right there. I'll be right there."

"This is 6 Alpha! Roger! You were almost on top of us! Over!"

"3-6. Roger. We'll be right back. We'll get you this time."

I began the climb through the cloud and turned left one more time.

We'll get 'em this time. Jesus, I hope this fuel holds.

We went back under the cloud and passed through the whiteout. There on my left again lay the red smoke, hanging in the haze.

Christ! I'm almost by them again!

I pulled in power and made a sharp left turn I didn't like. The aircraft shuddered and came around. We moved into the red haze with the nose of the helicopter pointing downhill.

6 Alpha shouted over the radio.

"Kick it loose! Kick it loose! No, wait! Move forward! Move forward! Kick it loose! Kick it loose!"

"Roger, 6 Alpha. Comin' to you."

I pressed the electrical

BRAVO COMPANY
2ND BN , 5TH CAV
"THE NIGHT HORSEMEN"
You have just supported The Highlands finest fighting Soldiers. We are listed in your SOI For references call "CHARLIE" at CHUPHONG, BONG. SON or IA DRANG.

Calling card. B Company, 2d Bn. 5th Cav. 1966.

switch with my thumb to release the sling load. It did not release. I hit the button again. Nothing.

"Goddammit! Let go, you Mattel son-of-a-bitch! Marrott! Kick the release! Kick the release!"

Marrott kicked the manual release and the load of ammunition went crashing down through the trees.

"It's clear, sir," said the crew chief.

"Okay," I said. "We're outta here."

I pulled in power, climbed into the cloud, and broke into the clear. "Let's go get some fuel."

On the ground Staff Sergeant Walsh heard a crashing noise and looked up. Above where he lay, but out of reach, hung the sling load of ammunition and supplies. The troops had to stay low because of small arms fire. It didn't take long for Walsh to solve the problem. They used C-4 explosive to blow down the trees that held the load.

The men of B Company, on their bellies, looked up to see C-ration boxes in the trees, ammunition belts hanging from limbs—and something else, dropping through the bushes, falling from the trees. Oranges. It was *raining* oranges.

I STAYED AT the controls. If we ran out of fuel, I wanted to do the autorotation. We made it to the refueling point at LZ Cat—a landing I was glad to make. As soon as we refueled we headed back to the mountain to take Green 4 in to deliver his load. On the way it became apparent that the cloud was lifting.

As we approached the mountain, I was surprised to see Green 4 climbing out with no sling load. "Green 4, this is Green 3-6. Did you get in there already? Over."

"This is Green 4. Roger. Sure did. They have both loads. Over."

"Okay. Good work. Let's go back to Cat."

I spoke to my crew on intercom. "Can you believe that damn cloud is lifting now?"

I had put my crew, myself, and my helicopter at major risk—some would say foolish risk—flying up that mountain under the cloud the way we did. But if we had not done it, and B Company had been overrun....

I never gave the decision a second thought.

WE LANDED AT the 2/5 battalion supply area and shut the aircraft down. It was late morning. As I got out of the helicopter the infantry battalion executive officer walked up. After my previous encounter with the major, I was ready for anything.

"Lieutenant Clark, I want you to do a rappelling mission," the major said. "The company commander was killed up there early this morning. The first sergeant was killed, and all their medics are either dead or wounded."

ॐ

When I went to the mountain the morning of August 15, I didn't know that Captain Taylor had been killed. During those many passes we made up the hill I wondered why I never got him on the radio. My only direct contact with B Company was with the radio operator, Tiger Shark 6 Alpha—SP4 Caney Greene.

PFC Joe Rodriquez survived the battle on 534 and the remainder of his tour. He was medically evacuated on Monday, the 15th, but not before his Virgen de San Juan medal was discovered by a soldier and returned to him. Rodriquez would lose the medal twice more during combat operations, and twice more it would be returned. His mother, Concepcion Rodriquez, wears it proudly today.

As for SP4 Caney Greene, I thought his conduct in his interaction with me was superb. Though I did not know of the Monday morning attack or that Greene was himself seriously injured, I knew those men on the ground badly needed us to get that ammunition to them. It was understandable that 6 Alpha and those around him were excited and even desperate as we made pass after pass without getting to them.

Major Wesley G. Jones, the 1/5 operations officer, recalled talking to Greene from Lieutenant Colonel Siegrist's command-and-control helicopter.

Here was a man who, when we first called him, was about out of his mind. I asked him, 'Where is the company commander?' 'He is dead!' 'Do you have the weapons platoon leader coming to your position?' 'Sir, nobody there can move. They just got the word.' Very shortly this radio operator calmed down, and he really ran the company with his radio. He was the center link. He got reports. He calmly passed on what was going on, and we passed our instructions to him. He did a tremendous job.[2]

Knowing his situation in as much detail as I do now, I must say 6 Alpha comported himself in a supreme manner. We have had many true heroes in our country's history. Tiger Shark 6 Alpha ranks with the best. SP4 Caney Greene, heroic radio operator, son of North Carolina, died in combat later that day, that 15th of August.

---

[2] AAR, 1st CAV Division at Hill 534, 1st Cav Div (Ambl), Report No. H-534, p. 28.

Chapter 10

You Take the Left

"I **WANT YOU** to take a new company commander and three medics up there and rappel them in to B Company," said the major.

"Okay, sir," I said. "No problem. We'll have to get the ropes and rig the helicopter for rappel."

I turned to my crew chief. "Chief, do we have the equipment here?"

"Yes, sir, we do," he said.

"How long will it take us to get ready?" I asked.

"About a half hour, sir. That should do it."

I addressed the major. "That okay, sir?"

"Yeah, that's fine," he said. "Let me know when you're ready. By the way, your gunships are on another mission and won't be available to support you. We'll send a pair of ARA with you."

"Okay, sir. I'll go talk to the ARA people, and I'll let you know when we're ready."

It was unusual for an ARA ship to fly close support for us on any kind of mission. It was the role of the gunship to protect the lift ships as they landed and took off, making passes low to the ground, spraying the area with rockets and machine gun fire. The job of the ARA was to fire rockets at a target from a few hundred feet in the air. The ARA ship was armed with only rockets, fixed weapons that fired straight ahead. The gunship protected itself with machine guns on swivel mounts in the cargo doors. The ARA had no machine guns to protect themselves when making a pass at low level.

The leader of the platoon assigned the mission was CPT Sam Vanderbilt. Vanderbilt and his pilots from the 1st Platoon, B Battery,

2/20th Aerial Rocket Artillery, flew B model Hueys, large pods of rockets hanging on both sides. Captain Vanderbilt had argued with his superiors a number of times against his helicopters flying close air support, as they were to do for me on this day. This was the first time he was overruled.

Three medics and B Company's new company commander, a Captain Snyder, were set to go on the rappelling mission. The mission involved my helicopter, the two ARA ships, and the command-and-control helicopter carrying Lieutenant Colonel Siegrist, who would watch from overhead and coordinate any contingencies.

Huey gunship. D Company, 227th Avn Bn, 1st Air Cav. 1966.

The crew chief secured four 120-foot nylon ropes to rings in the helicopter floor. Two ropes would go out the right cargo door and two would go out the left. Each man would strap a small rope harness on his body and attach a snap link at the waist. The 120-foot rope, anchored to the floor of the cargo compartment, would pass through the man's snap link and be tossed out the door to dangle to the ground. With the helicopter hovering in a stationary position, the four soldiers, two on each side, would jump backward out of the wide cargo doors and slide quickly down the ropes to the ground.

I thought it should be a fairly simple operation. The bad guys were at the top of the hill. I would approach from the bottom of the hill where I had spent a good part of the morning under the cloud. I would hover up the side of the mountain and halt just short of B Company's position. That would put me well short of the enemy positions. The dense trees, undergrowth, and jungle canopy should mask us from enemy fire. My plan was to fly slowly up the hill at treetop level, then hover until the captain and medics rappelled to the ground. Tension released from the ropes would indicate the men were on the ground, signaling the crew chief and gunner to cut the ropes and let them fall from the helicopter.

The ARA pilots had been circling overhead during the resupply mission that morning. Their call sign was Armed Falcon. LT Charlie

Huecker, in the ARA lead ship, and I agreed to use his UHF frequency for communication between helicopters, and communication with the ground units would be on the 1/5's FM.

The rigging secured, I gathered my crew and our four passengers for a briefing by the side of the helicopter. "Okay, here's what we're going to do. We'll fly right up the side of the mountain and stop at B Company's position. We'll come to a hover and then we'll wait. I want to make sure we're not drawing any fire before you all get out, so don't get out too early. You don't get out until you get two signals. The crew chief or gunner will grab you with his hand and tell you to go. Also, Mr. Marrott in the right seat will turn and throw his left arm straight out and point at you. When you get both signals, you go. Understand? Both signals. You get both signals or you don't go.

"Marrott, you got it?" I asked.

He nodded.

I turned back to Captain Snyder and the three medics. "He will throw his arm and point at you to go. Don't get out of this helicopter until you have both signals. Any questions anybody? Okay, let's go."

It was about 11:30 a.m. on August 15 when our four passengers got in and sat down on the floor of the helicopter, the seats having been removed. Each man hooked his snap link to his rope.

"Chief, are we clear?" I asked.

"Clear, sir."

"Okay, Mr. Marrott. Fire it up."

Marrott started the engine, and we lifted off. I had the controls as we approached the now familiar Hill 534. We flew slowly up the mountain, staying close to the treetops. There was green canopy below and lovely blue sky above. Although there was no terrain feature to accurately locate the troops, I hoped to recognize their location.

I called the infantry company to ask for smoke. "Tiger Shark 6, this is Green 3-6. Over."

No answer.

"Tiger Shark 6, this is Green 3-6. Over."

"Green 3-6. This is Black Horse 6."

Black Horse 6 was Lieutenant Colonel Siegrist in the command-and-control helicopter overhead.

"They hear you, but you are not hearing them. I'll relay for you, over."

"Green 3-6. Roger," I said. "Tiger Shark, this is Green 3-6. You wanna put some smoke out for us? Over."

"Green 3-6, this is Black Horse 6. He's puttin' out smoke for you. Over."

"Green 3-6. Roger."

I didn't know for sure if we were in the right spot, so I asked the ARA ships for help. "Falcon 47, this is Green 3-6, over."

"This is Falcon 47, over."

"This is 3-6. Hey, help us keep a look out for this smoke, will you?"

"Falcon 47. Roger, we'll look."

I heard the Armed Falcon leader tell his second helicopter, "You take the left, and I'll take the right."

"Roger," came the reply.

We hovered and waited for the smoke to work its way up through the trees and into view. About 10 meters in front of us I spotted green smoke filtering through the canopy, furling gently upward.

I grinned in satisfaction.

"Tiger Shark 6, this is Green 3-6. I have green smoke, over."

"Green 3-6, this is Black Horse 6. That's affirmative. The smoke is green. Over."

"Green 3-6, roger."

"Green 3-6, this is Black Horse 6. Move about 30 meters to the east. Over."

"Green 3-6, roger."

Thirty meters to the east? Damn! Which way is east?

I always knew which way I was headed, and this was simple. I had been right here all morning. Even so, at that moment I did not know which direction was east, west, or anything else.

The needle on the aircraft directional indicator showed east to be behind me to my right. I turned, saw a depression in the treetops about 30 meters away, and moved over to it. I turned my nose back into the wind, lowered the aircraft as close to the trees as possible, and came to a steady hover. Looking ahead, I spotted a clearing through an opening in the treetops. The NVA owned the only clearing on Hill 534. I was a little surprised that we were close enough to see it. Still, I trusted the ground troops would not have me hover in a spot where I was vulnerable to enemy fire.

I keyed the mike. "Black Horse 6, this is Green 3-6. Is this where you want us?"

Thunk!

A bullet struck the aircraft. I had the odd thought that it was like a rock hitting the right front fender of a car.

My first hit ever, I flinched, the slight movement of my hand on the cyclic causing the helicopter to jerk. Embarrassed and angry at myself for this lack of personal control, I steadied the aircraft and began talking to myself.

You sorry bastard! Hold this son-of-a-bitch still! You've just taken a round or two! Now hold this son-of-a-bitch still! You've got to get those guys in there!

My gunner began firing his machine gun steadily.

Damn! He's shooting straight down!

The crew chief spoke calmly over the intercom. "Sir, we're taking hits."

No shit. What was your first clue?

"Roger. I can see that."

I held at a steady hover and waited to see if we had taken someone's lucky shot or if we were in someone's sights. If it was only a stray round or two, there was no need to run. If we took more hits, I would leave.

Warning lights burst forth in full color on the instrument panel as we took more hits, the center of the panel lighting up like a Christmas tree.

AC generator.

No sweat.

DC generator.

I can live without that.

Engine oil pressure.

Uh-oh. This engine is going to quit. I might have three or four minutes. If it will just get calm right now, I might have time to get them in there.

A new warning light. Transmission oil pressure.

Oh, shit. It's over.

This would result in transmission failure: The blades would stop turning. I didn't know how long the transmission would last, but I figured longer than the engine.

I keyed the mike. "I'm taking hits. I'm getting out of here."

I broke left and started down the mountain, right on top of the trees. I had to get on the ground—fast. Every gauge on the instrument panel read zero except airspeed. We were doing 85 knots. I wanted to fly faster, but I was afraid to, given the oil pressure situation.

My mind was racing. I knew that either the engine would fail or the transmission would freeze up. Fly at altitude or low level?

If we went off the mountain at altitude and the engine quit, we could hopefully find a clearing and autorotate.

But if we were at altitude and the transmission froze, we would plummet in.

If we were low level and the transmission froze, we would at least be close to the ground. Maybe it would not kill us all when we hit the trees.

If the engine quit at low level, we would have to autorotate into tall trees, essentially a controlled crash.

Go low level. Eliminate the one that kills you for sure.

Marrott reached up to flip the hydraulics switch off. "Hydraulics comin' off!"

"Okay," I said automatically. Then it hit me. "Hey, wait!" I raised my hand to stop him. "There's nothing wrong with the damn hydraulics! Hell, it's the only thing we've got that works! Leave it alone!"

Marrott was following the emergency procedure for a failed hydraulic system. I could see why he might think it was out— everything else was.

I heard a loud boom.

Oh, shit. They're shooting at me with something big now.

It sounded like a big gun. I had no other explanations.

We would later learn the second ARA helicopter exploded and crashed. 1LT John Boyce, WO1 Mike Dundas and PFC Byron Ludwig were killed. No one saw them go down. No one heard from them. No one knew the cause of the crash. We had only the sound and Falcon 47's instruction. "You take the left, and I'll take the right."

I knew of three places in the area I could land. The closest belonged to the NVA. There was a small forward outpost a thousand meters or so away, but I did not know exactly where it was. The third was LZ Cat. It was too far to suit me, but it was straight ahead in my direction of flight, and I knew where it was. It was long, wide, and flat—perfect for an emergency. It seemed my only choice.

I flew toward LZ Cat, but I wanted to confirm I was exactly on course. "Falcon 47, this is 3-6. I'm headed for LZ Cat. Am I headed right?"

"This is 47. You're okay. You're headed right at it."

"3-6, roger. Thanks."

"Chief," I said, "tell those guys in the back to stay on the floor and hold on. We might not make it all the way back."

"Yes, sir," he replied.

Everything was going fine—85 knots airspeed, treetop level.

LZ Cat came in to view.

Ah, it looks like we're going to make it. As soon as I clear those trees I'm going to set this baby down.

Another 200 meters.

Phtttt!

It sounded like a burst of steam escaping from a car radiator. The sound was followed by abrupt silence and loss of momentum. The engine had quit. I entered autorotation, taking the pitch out of the rotor blades and allowing them to spin freely. That would give us one attempt at a landing.

Trouble was, there was no place to land.

I keyed the mike. "The engine just quit. We're going in the trees."

In flight school we were told in the classroom how to execute this maneuver. I didn't know anyone who had actually done it.

I headed where the treetops were lower, about 90 feet. I pulled the nose of the helicopter up high, stopping all forward movement. For an instant we hung there, suspended, nose high, tail pointed down at approximately a 30-degree angle. As we began to fall, tail down, I pulled full pitch into the blades to momentarily fly, cushioning our fall into the trees. I pulled the pitch control up under my left arm as far as it would go, kept my feet on the pedals, my right hand on the cyclic, and held on. The spinning rotor blades hit the treetops.

Clip! Clip! Clip! Clip! Whap! Whap! Whap Whap Whap Whap—
WHAM!

Sunshine and greenery all came together in a smooth, vertical blur as we slammed violently down through the trees. My grease gun flew off the back right corner of my seat and smashed into the instrument panel. The tip of the tail hit the ground first, the tail boom breaking away from the cabin area. The transmission that held the rotor blades was pushed up and back as the cabin area crashed to the ground. The diameter of the blades were slashed from 48 to 10 feet. We landed on the skids with a hard jolt.

I flipped the battery switch off, unfastened my seat belt, and got out. Marrott and I checked on our passengers and crew. The crew chief was lying on the floor, but he didn't appear to be hurt. I grabbed him and helped him out. The passengers were sitting on the floor, each still attached to his 120-foot nylon rope by his snap link. They were tugging and pulling at their ropes instead of simply releasing the rope from the snap link.

"Marrott!" I called. "Help those people out over there. Just let the rope out of the snap link."

I freed two of them and helped them out on my side of the aircraft, and Mr. Marrott got the other two out on his side. The gunner got out by himself.

"All right, get away from the aircraft!" I yelled. "This thing might explode and burn!"

As we ran from the helicopter, I counted heads.

Wait! There's only seven!

I ran back. On the left side of the aircraft where I had helped him get out, my stalwart crew chief lay by a tree. His back was sprained and he was having trouble moving. Instead of

1st LT. RAY CLARK

Interviewed by NBC correspondent Howard Tuckner after the crash. I was worried my family would be frightened if they saw the story on television. As it turned out, only my grandmother and a family friend caught it. Seems my grandmother was more delighted than anything else. LZ Cat. August 1966.

strapping himself tightly in his seat as we had started down through the trees, he had been half standing, leaning out the cargo door, watching his tail rotor go into the trees. He knew it wouldn't help to watch; he knew he couldn't prevent the crash or stop the damage. But watching the tail rotor when it was close to foreign objects was what crew chiefs did. He wasn't trying to save himself. He was doing his job. I picture him even now leaning out the left side of that helicopter, watching the tail rotor as it began to dip down into the treetops. I see him behind me with his face to my ear in LZ Cat. "Don't do it, sir! Don't do it! Don't do it, sir! Don't do it!" And I think of him. It was his last scheduled day in Vietnam.

Marrott came running back to the helicopter. We helped move the crew chief to where the others were.

"Captain Snyder," I said, "make a perimeter with everybody here. I'll go get help."

He nodded okay, and I ran toward the LZ.

We'd gone in only 50 meters from LZ Cat, but I had to run nearly a half-mile to get to anyone. When I got to the command post, headquarters personnel had already been alerted to the crash. I took two small vehicles and some troopers back to our helicopter. Of the eight people on board, seven walked away. Until a Chinook from maintenance could lift it out, a squad was sent down to guard the heli-copter. The last three digits of the Huey's tail number were 848, a number I would not forget.

Our helicopter after getting shot up on Hill 534. LZ Cat. Aug. 15, 1966.

Chapter 11

Pompous

THERE WAS A constant turnover of personnel in Vietnam. When I came in, we had a number of strong, competent captains and majors. Unfortunately, our new leadership was not as strong as the old guys.

Several days after we returned to An Khe from LZ Cat, Chu Pong Mountain, and the Turkey Farm, a newly assigned major walked into my room with a notepad. We didn't know much about him at that point, but he seemed likeable and, more importantly, a competent officer.

"Good morning, sir," I said.

"Hi, Ray. Listen, the company commander has asked me to write up the recommendation for your award for that business where you were shot down on Chu Pong. You want to tell me about it?"

I was honored when our company commander, Major Eaton, shook my hand following the events on Hill 534, telling me he intended to put me in for a Silver Star.

"Sir, there's nothing to tell, really, unless you have some questions," I said. "I have already written the story of everything that happened, just as Major Eaton asked me to. It's all in there."

"I've read that," he said, "but let's get real. All that never happened and you know it. I want the real story."

I was stunned. "Sir, are you serious? Do you mean that?"

"Look, Ray, nobody could have done what you say you did. It just isn't possible."

Incensed, I got to my feet. Had he not been a field-grade officer I would have pummeled him to the floor.

My hands clenched at my sides, I fought to control my emotions. "Sir, are you calling me a liar?"

"I'm not calling you anything," he said. "It just isn't possible to do what you said you did."

"Not possible? Not possible! Hell, sir, do you think I was the only person in the aircraft? Go over there and ask Mr. Marrott. He was there. There are a crew chief and gunner down there in the enlisted tents. They were damn sure there! Why don't you go ask them?"

"I don't have to ask them," he said. "No one could have flown up that mountain the way you say you did. It just isn't possible."

"Sir, you really haven't been here long, have you?"

"That has nothing to do with it," he said. "You could not have done those things."

"Sir, you don't get to call me a liar," I said. "I am going to ask Major Eaton to take you off writing this. And right now, sir, I think you had better get out of my room."

He turned and left.

I went to see the company commander and told him what had happened. He covered for the major and said he would get someone else to write up the award. The junior warrant officer in the company was assigned to write it. He was a good kid but not especially talented in that area as far as I could tell.

The company commander had told me face to face that he was putting me in for the Silver Star. A few months later I was awarded the Distinguished Flying Cross for the action on Chu Pong.

I RECALL IN particular a new incoming officer I will call "Major Pompous."

Pompous wasn't a bad guy—he was just...well...pompous. He outranked most everyone in the company. Problem was, he thought that meant something. The helicopter did not care about rank, and Vietnam paid no attention to flying experience. It simply did not matter how long anyone had been an aviator or how many hours of flight time he had. Flying those overloaded Hueys in the conditions we faced required special skill and experience, and there was only one way to acquire them—fly Hueys in Vietnam. Pompous didn't quite understand that.

There were so many helicopters so close together—taking off, landing, and flying in tight formation—that vigilance to safety was paramount. You could spot a D model Huey lift pilot by watching his helicopter: Every move was slow and deliberate, his turns concise and sure. He was adept at parking close to the next helicopter, the two sets of rotor blades almost touching. The three-foot hover he was taught in school was fine—at school. In Vietnam the aircraft was often overloaded, so he hovered 18 inches off the ground—and he *knew* it was 18 inches.

The D model required skill and touch. If a pilot did not have them, he had to get them. All this had to be taught to the new guys. Pompous did not take kindly to that. He was a major, and he was "already experienced."

Soon after Pompous arrived, he flew with me. I was a first lieutenant, but as the aircraft commander, I was in charge of my helicopter and everyone in it—including the good Major Pompous.

We were on the ground with three other Hueys around a fuel pump, the four helicopters facing each other with only a few feet separating us. After refueling, the procedure was to come to a low hover, back slowly away from the fuel pump, turn in the direction of takeoff, and safely fly away.

After we refueled, rather than slowly backing away, Pompous jerked the aircraft straight up 20 feet, putting us right on top of the other three helicopters.

I went ballistic. "Goddammit, sir! What the fuck are you doing!"

He looked at me, incredulous. "What do you mean? What are you bitching about?"

"Goddammit, sir, you don't jerk this aircraft around like that. Look where you are. You're sitting up here at a 20-foot hover right over the top of these other helicopters. If one of them takes off like you did, he's gonna fly right into your ass. You're slow, you're smooth, and you don't go to a 20-foot hover over other helicopters. Ever!"

"Bullshit, Lieutenant! There's nothing wrong with what I did. We're not in anybody's way."

"Sir, you are gonna fucking kill yourself, but you are not gonna do it with me. You fly the way I tell you to when you're with me, sir, or you won't fly at all. Now get us out of here."

"You don't know shit, Lieutenant," Pompous said.

"I guess you're right, sir," I said. "I guess that's why I'm the aircraft commander and you're Peter Pilot."

Pompous didn't get it. Fortunately, I didn't fly with him often.

OUR NEW EXECUTIVE officer was another incoming major. We called him "Sister Sam."

When a man is a leader in combat, he had better be out there taking some of the risks his boys are taking and sharing some of the load. His troops need to know that he understands what they are up against, and he needs to demonstrate some degree of competency in what they do every day. The best leaders will get their noses into the wind at crucial moments and will risk everything when necessary, just as their boys are doing.

Sister Sam was a nice man and was concerned for our welfare, but that was about as far as it went.

Sam seldom flew with us. I was surprised one day to learn that he was scheduled to fly right seat with me. Sam was like everyone else who had not flown much in Vietnam—he could handle the aircraft when it was empty and light, but he got a little nervous when it was loaded.

We were on a combat assault west of Pleiku, halfway back in a gaggle of 20 Hueys. Sam was flying. Two miles out from the landing zone we began a long, shallow descent. About a mile out, Sam started to get rough on the controls—and he got rougher as we got closer to the LZ. He began to move the cyclic around like he was stirring soup.

"Sir," I said, "easy on the cyclic."

No response. As we closed in on the landing zone, he began jerking the cyclic back and forth.

I was more insistent in tone. "Sir, easy on the cyclic."

Still no response. By now we were almost on top of the trees. I put my hand on the cyclic but could not steady it. As we began our final approach, the door gunner and crew chief began to fire their machine guns, and the gunships cut loose with their machine guns and rockets. The major was now maniacally shoving the cyclic back and forth.

I clamped both hands on the cyclic. "Sir! Quit jerking the cyclic! Goddammit, sir, let go of the cyclic!"

He never heard a word. He had a death grip on that cyclic. He did not let go.

The landing was plenty rough. We bumped the ground hard, the troops jumped out, and we were in flight again.

After taking off, I could tell he had regained his senses. I could think of nothing to say that would make a difference for him.

Chapter 12

Crazy Charlie Fairchild

PROBABLY THE TOUGHEST and meanest among my peers—certainly the orneriest—was CPT Charles Henry Fairchild from Woodville, Mississippi. He was and is a Mississippi redneck of the first order. He is the greatest character I've ever known, and one of my best friends.

Of medium height with a crew cut shaping his red hair, his body alternated almost yearly from slim to rotund. With a ready smile, he was full of wisecracks. He never forgot his roots, and in many ways, never moved far from them. He was funny, cantankerous, and absolutely dependable. If I were down behind enemy lines and I could choose one person to come after me, it would be Charlie Fairchild. I have friends who would die trying to save me. Charlie would get there.

Charlie and I first met as officer candidates at Fort Benning. Academics was serious business in OCS. If you didn't meet a minimum standard, you were kicked out. I worked as hard as I could to make good grades. Not Charlie. He didn't believe in working harder than necessary on anything academic. The minimum passing grade was 70. On Charlie's first test, he made a 72. He kept the pencil he took that test with and used it on every test he took in OCS. As far as I know he never made above 74 or below 70 all through the six-month course. He called the instrument his 70 pencil.

I knew the man well. Had he wanted it to be a 95 pencil, it would have been.

Charlie was a cook in the Coast Guard before he was in the Army. His culinary skills were exceeded only by his ability to eat.

When Charlie, Wesley Coltrane and I were in flight school in Mineral Wells, Texas, there was a popular eatery called Hoppe's. Fried chicken was served on Thursdays and fish on Fridays, all you could eat. We ate there almost every Thursday and Friday evening. Being in our early 20s and on limited budgets, we ate gargantuan amounts at Hoppe's. By the time we moved on to Fort Rucker for advanced training, Hoppe's was out of business.

After our second year in Vietnam, Charlie, Wesley and I were assigned to Fort Benning. Wesley was newly married to his first wife, a young lady not of Charlie's choosing or mine. Thanksgiving was coming up and Wesley invited Ann and me and Charlie and his wife, Peggy, for dinner. He proudly announced this would be a lavish spread, the centerpiece a magnificent holiday ham.

Our budgets were tight; a whole ham was a large expenditure for any of us. We were pleased to be invited to this nice dinner celebration. Then Wesley began to brag about this huge and wonderful ham he had bought for our dinner. To hear him tell it, this was the largest, finest ham ever. He told us how his wife could "flat pinch a penny" and that she already had plans for the many meals she would provide with this ham. Why, it would make this wonderful holiday meal, and the leftovers would feed him and the new Mrs. Coltrane for weeks.

Wesley continued to carry on about that huge ham as the holiday approached. He went on and on—which, considering his audience, he should not have done. During the three days prior to the holiday, Charlie and I ate almost nothing. Then on Thanksgiving Day we went in and ate the entire ham. There was nothing left but bone.

Although she said nothing, Wesley's new wife was mortified. Charlie and I could see her swelling with anger as we steadily devoured the ham.

Wesley, not being from such genteel circumstances as she, couldn't contain himself. "You sons-a-bitches! You sons-a-bitches! You ate the whole goddamn thing! You ate the whole goddamn thing!"

Charlie and I, holding our bulging stomachs, roared with laughter. Wesley's wife gave him pure hell for days, which he let us know about, cursing us for weeks.

After flight school, Charlie was assigned to a medical evacuation unit in Pleiku, not far from An Khe where Wesley and I were assigned with the 1st Cav. I stopped in Pleiku one day to look Charlie up. While we were living in tents and sleeping on folding cots, Charlie and his group lived in buildings with corrugated metal roofs. They slept on real GI beds with real mattresses.

"You son-of-a-bitch!" I said. "Look at you, living over here in luxury. Tin roofs? Damn!"

"I can't help it if you boys in the Cav ain't got enough sense to get in out of the rain," Charlie said. "I bet you don't eat good, either."

"Well, you're right about that," I said. "Hey, Charlie, you got any extra mattresses? You think we could slide one or two of those things on my helicopter before I leave here?"

"Why, hell yes. It ain't nothin' but a damn mattress. How many you want?"

"Two will do," I said.

"All right. Let's go load 'em up before some do-good major comes around."

I gave one mattress to Bob and put the other on my cot. Life was getting better.

THE ROLE OF medevac helicopters in Vietnam cannot be overstated. The capability to send a helicopter to retrieve the wounded saved countless lives. In daylight, the threat of ambush meant driving the roads only when necessary and with great caution. Traveling the road at night was unthinkable.

Few pilots, medevac or otherwise, were like Charlie: fearless, determined—"hellbent" would be a better description—and borderline crazy. He was as smart as anyone, but I'm convinced he never operated with a full load of gray matter.

One day, in a hot LZ west of Pleiku, troops were loading wounded soldiers into Charlie's aircraft as he hovered. Charlie had flown into enemy fire so intense and heavily concentrated that a general watching from a nearby helicopter ordered him out.

"Dustoff, you get out of that LZ! You get out of there right now!"

With no intention of leaving the wounded, Charlie replied over the radio: "Don't worry about the mule, just load the wagon!"

One night when Charlie was the on-call medevac pilot, a call came in from a unit of the 4th Infantry Division. They were 10 or 12 miles south of Pleiku, near Highway 14. They had a sergeant who was badly wounded. Could the unit send a medevac helicopter right away?

Charlie took off in his helicopter. As he began to climb he ran into heavy fog, losing all visual reference. Fortunately there was an Air Force base at Pleiku with aircraft navigation facilities. Charlie got a radar vector back to his landing area. He parked, went inside, and called the 4th Division unit with the bad news.

Observing firsthand the sergeant's grave condition, the soldier on the radio was unmoved.

"Well, Dustoff," he told Charlie, "he's gonna die if you don't get him out."

I have friends who would die trying to save me. Charlie would get there. Pleiku 1966.

Trying to fly in fog that heavy was crazy. Just two nights before, a Chinook had gone down in similar conditions, killing all on board.

"Hold tight," Charlie said. "I'll try again."

He went back out, this time flying right on top of the ground, trying to stay under the fog. That was near-suicide. He got about a hundred yards before the fog swallowed him again. He climbed and called again for a radar vector to guide him back.

Charlie called the unit again. "There ain't no way we can get out there right now. I tried hovering along the ground and still couldn't make it. We'll have to wait until the fog lifts."

The voice on the radio was adamant. "This man is gut-shot. If you don't get him out of here right away, he's going to die!"

"I have an idea," Charlie said. "I'll try it again."

He went out, started up, and hovered a foot or two above the surface, right down the narrow two-lane road. Soon the fog was all the way to the ground. Charlie had no choice but to climb and call for a radar vector back to the airfield.

He called the unit to deliver this final, sad news. "There is no way we can make it. I just hovered down the highway and got into fog. It's all the way to the ground. I'm sorry. We'll get there as soon as we can."

"'As soon as you can' won't work," the soldier exclaimed, his voice rising. "This man is going to die if you don't get him out of here right away. He doesn't have much time."

Charlie looked at his map. "Do you have any armored personnel carriers or tanks you could bring him in with?"

"Yes, we have APCs and tanks," the soldier affirmed.

"Well, bring him in in one of those APCs or tanks," Charlie said.

"Are you crazy?"

Even with tanks, it was ill-advised to drive that road at night.

Steadfast, Charlie continued. "There's an intersection on the main highway just east of your location, right?"

"That's affirmative, there is," the soldier said.

"Well, can you get him that far?"

"Roger," said the soldier. "We can do that."

"Good," Charlie said. "You have your man out there at that intersection at 0130 sharp, and I'll be there to pick him up. Do you understand?"

"Roger. Understand. We'll be there at 0130."

His medic and crew in tow, Charlie drove a truck 10 miles down the highway to the intersection. No one was there. Armed with only their personal weapons, Charlie and his crew waited 20 long minutes before an APC, escorted by a tank, rumbled up. The sergeant was loaded into the back of the truck. They returned to Pleiku without incident, delivering the wounded man to the hospital.

Charlie had driven a maniacal 40 miles an hour in dense fog, his head hanging out the window.

Chapter 13

A Precision Maneuver

THE VC HAD been sneaking in and firing mortar rounds onto the base camp during the night. This had been happening on a regular basis. Finally someone decided to do something about it.

An infantry platoon would be on alert through the night, a ready reaction force to be airlifted to the site of the attack within minutes of the first VC round. Troops, pilots and their crews would sleep in tents beside parked helicopters, poised for action. Going in first would be the pathfinders, an elite group of young rascals whose job was to set up landing lights, marking the way for the main assault group.

We were assigned to be the lift force. We moved six Hueys to Hotel 12 and parked them in formation, ready for takeoff. Four Hueys would transport the assault group and two would carry the pathfinders. Because the main assault group would touch down just 45 seconds behind the two lead helicopters, the pathfinders would have no time to waste getting the landing lights set up. It would be a precision maneuver.

A good captain who didn't fly so well was leading the mission that night, his call sign Gunslinger Yellow One. I was Yellow Two. All I had to do was follow the leader. He had the tough job—he had to find the landing zone.

It was Wednesday, November 9, 1966. The VC attacked that very night, around 4 a.m. We dashed to the helicopters and took off. The night was totally black with a heavy overcast that blocked any moonlight. It would be impossible for us to see without some kind of light. Even with the 105mm howitzer battery we had off to the east lobbing illumination rounds, the landing zone would be hard to find in the absolute black of that night.

I didn't like it from the start. The LZ was only 2000 meters north. We could have simply jumped up to 300 feet and flown straight north to the LZ. Instead, our leader went immediately to the bottom of the cloud cover at 1700 feet, taking us north and east in a classic rectangular flight pattern. In doing so, we flew across the howitzers' gun-target line.

When a howitzer fires an illumination round, a bright parachute flare is deployed. While the flare floats to the ground, illuminating the area, the large brass canister it rides into the air continues to tumble through space along the "gun-target line," or the imaginary line from gun to target.

I prayed that one of those canisters would not collide with our helicopter and take us to the ground with it.

Skimming the bottom of the clouds, we flew past the landing area, then turned left 90 degrees, heading westward. After a short distance we made another 90-degree left turn, flying south, again crossing the gun-target line.

The young warrant officer flying right seat with me had been performing poorly and not catching on in the unit, so I had him flying every mission with me. I told Warrant Officer "Smith" to widen the gap between us and the lead helicopter to a distance of about two football fields. I did not trust our leader.

We were still at 1700 feet above sea level. Ground elevation was 275 feet above sea level. We could see nothing except two tiny, dim lights on the lead helicopter. All I knew for sure was that our altimeter read 1700 feet, and when it read 275 feet, we would be on the ground. So I wanted a little room.

Suddenly the leader started down, descending rapidly. Smith stayed straight and level, not reacting to Yellow One's sudden decline.

D model Hueys cruised at 80 knots. A normal descent was 500 feet per minute (FPM) in daylight. At night we liked 200 FPM. We had plenty of room and time to descend nicely and still catch up before we got to the LZ.

Smith continued to fly straight and level.

"He's descending. You'd better start down now," I said gently.

Smith dumped the nose down and suddenly we were at 110 knots, diving at 2000 feet per minute.

"Whoa, whoa, whoa," I said. "Slow this thing up—80 knots, 200 feet per minute. Easy here. Easy."

Nothing changed.

"Here, I got it," I said.

"You got it," he replied.

I brought the helicopter back to 80 knots and 200 FPM descent. We had gained on Yellow One.

"You got it," I said.

"I got it."

Here we went again, 110 knots, 2000 FPM.

"Slow it up, now, slow it up," I said.

He did not.

"I got it," I said.

I cleaned it up again, back to 80 knots and 200 FPM descent. We had gained a little more on the leader.

"Okay, you got it," I said quietly. "Now just take it easy. Just reduce power a little bit. Keep 80 knots, let her start down. She'll go."

He leveled off at 80 knots, but no descent. Ahead I could see Yellow One's lights turning left and descending rapidly.

"He's moving down pretty fast," I said. "You'd better go ahead and get down on it. Just ease into it."

Again 110 knots, 2000 FPM descent.

I wanted to instill confidence, not rattle him further, so I kept my voice low. "I got it. Here, let me see this thing a minute. The way he's flying up there, couldn't nobody follow him."

I made the left turn, following our leader, then turned left again to fly north on a one-mile final approach in to the LZ. With our series of rapid descents we had closed the gap to about four rotor-blade widths. The illumination from the artillery was so far away that I could see nothing but Yellow One's lights and the dim lights of our instrument panel. We were now following at a two-blade distance and descending far too rapidly to suit me. I was watching the needle on the altimeter unwind. I thought about pulling in power, gaining altitude, and breaking off the approach. But if I did that, it would screw up the whole operation. Heck, we had the pathfinders.

The altimeter went below 500 feet, putting me further on edge.

If that son-of-a-bitch gets to 300, I'm going around. We can't get lower than that without landing or crashing.

I gave the controls back to Smith. "You got it. Just stay cool. Keep 80 knots and keep that descent easy and slow. Give yourself plenty of time."

He was doing nicely now, holding the necessary airspeed and rate of descent to keep us right behind Yellow One. I was watching his lights, making sure he was always below us.

Well, as long as he doesn't go up in a big ball of flame, I won't either.

One of our gunships pulled alongside Smith's window and cut loose with rockets and machine-gun fire.

Shoooo! Shoooo! Shoooo!

The rockets flared orange and red as they sped by us in the darkness toward the LZ. The brilliance of the colors flashed by us, becoming quickly smaller against the blackness of the night. It was a startling and strangely beautiful sight, standing in stark contrast to the danger of the moment.

It rattled Smith. He dumped the nose and in a flash took us to 1500 FPM descent and 105 knots.

"Come on, now," I said. "Pull the nose up. Slow it down—80 knots, 200 feet descent. Let's just stay up here behind him. Easy does it."

He slowed the aircraft and got us back into a gentle descent.

While dealing with Smith I remained focused on our dwindling altitude and the aircraft leading us. We were very close to the ground and still descending, our altimeter reading down to 300 feet. I could see absolutely nothing, but turning on the landing light was a dangerous thing to do in enemy territory and would have been no use in the fog. If Yellow One hit a big tree or a small hill now, I might not have time to prevent the same fate. The only safe thing to do was break off the approach and gain some altitude.

I took the controls. "I got it."

"You got it," Smith said.

I pulled in power to climb and turned left to break off the approach. I keyed the mike. "This is Yellow Two. I'm going around."

As we broke left at about 70 knots, I felt the aircraft bottom and begin to round out its descent. I saw leaves on my windshield. As black as the night was, I could see they were green.

Goddamn! I'm gonna hit that fuckin' tree!

I had waited too long. I jerked the cyclic back into my stomach to try to flare up over the tree, but we were already into it. Smith, who was supposed to be ready to take the controls in an emergency, threw up his arms and screamed so loudly I could hear him over the engine noise.

Why, you sorry bastard!

All the instrument panel lights went out. I had the sensation of being suspended in mid-air. We had no airspeed. The tree had stopped us dead.

Oh, shit! It's not gonna fly.

The jet engine was whining loudly, and I could hear the RPM go way down. I was hoping we could still fly. The engine noise got louder as the engine RPM revved back up.

Okay, it's gonna fly! It's gonna fly!

Then the engine noise and RPM went down again.

Oh shit! It's not gonna fly! It's not gonna fly!

I rolled the throttle on tight to make sure it was all the way on. I heard the engine rev back up.

It's gonna fly! It's gonna fly!

I realized I was just hoping. I was sitting in the air with no visibility, no power, and little control. Fear hit me in the stomach, a silent shriek of stark terror. I concluded the helicopter was not going to fly and that I must take it to the ground. The fear left as quickly as it came. "Take the helicopter to the ground" is different from "I'm going to crash."

Half of one of the two main rotor blades had broken off, but we were still right side up, just hanging in the air with the engine racing and whining. I kept the power where it was and looked out my window to the ground. My view was simply black on a darker black. I could distinguish the air from the ground because the ground was darker, but I had no depth perception. All I could do was let the machine sink into that dark abyss and try to control it as much as I could.

I reduced power and let the helicopter fall. We came straight down, fortunately remaining level. When we got close to where I thought the ground was, I pulled in what power we had. We landed upright on the skids on the side of a hill covered with scrub trees and undergrowth 10 to 12 feet tall. I bottomed the pitch control. The ship rocked to the right once, twice, then rolled over on its right side.

I flicked the battery switch off, quickly got out of my seat harness and crawled between the two pilot seats into the rear cabin area. I wanted to be sure we weren't on fire, something I worried about in a crash. With the helicopter lying on its right side, the left cargo door faced the sky. I stuck my head out and looked back toward the engine compartment. No flames.

I turned to get the troops out. The crew chief's seat was up in the air. He had run from the helicopter without trying to help anyone. I was not happy about that, but at least he was safe. I worried about my door gunner on the underside of the aircraft, afraid he might have been trapped or crushed.

The cabin area was an entanglement of arms, legs, rifles, and torsos of the six pathfinders. Appearing to be dazed, they were completely unresponsive to my attempts to get them out of the helicopter. I wrestled and cursed and shouted, to no avail. Smith sat neatly in his pilot's seat, still strapped in by his seatbelt and shoulder harness. He was looking straight ahead, making no effort to free himself.

I stuck my head out the cargo door and saw a flame licking up out of the engine tailpipe. I ducked back inside and yelled, "This son-of-a-bitch is on fire! You'd better get the fuck out of here!"

Only Smith didn't move. The rest came out like a shot, my door gunner included.

I unbuckled Smith's harness and seat belt. "Come on, you stupid son-of-a-bitch. Let's go!"

I pulled him into the cargo compartment, shoved him up and out the cargo door and climbed out after him. We ran into the undergrowth. The flame I had seen was apparently from a small pool of fuel in the engine tailpipe, which quickly burned out.

I counted heads. All 10 of us were there—me, Smith, the crew chief, door gunner, and six pathfinders. Except for a minor cut on the back of a pathfinder's hand, there were no injuries.

We knew the VC were close by. We had the two 30-caliber machine guns off the helicopter, eight M-16 rifles, my World War II grease gun and two .38 pistols—good firepower for 10 people. For security I put one man uphill from us and one down the hill while I thought about how to get the hell out of there. I could see the lights of our helicopters circling overhead, so I knew there had been no landing. No helicopters made any move toward us. Yellow One, unable to find the landing zone, had left the area, his crew chief erroneously reporting we had followed him out. The main flight had been too far behind to see us go down. No one knew we were missing.

I needed radio communication. I wasn't about to crawl back into that helicopter and turn the electrical switches on to activate the radios. I could imagine an electrical charge igniting fuel and the helicopter exploding with me in it. Maybe it wouldn't have happened—maybe it couldn't have happened—but I never did like choices where, if things didn't go as planned, I died.

The crew chief retrieved a small Air Force emergency radio from an external rear cargo compartment. There were two modes of transmission—voice and tone. In tone mode a beeping signal was transmitted on the aircraft emergency frequency that all U.S. aircraft radios were tuned to, unless the channel was intentionally turned off. This meant that all of our helicopters should hear my emergency transmission.

I tried the radio. It would not transmit voice. I switched to tone transmission. The radio began transmitting a continuous stream of beeps to all aircraft emergency receivers in range.

Well, they won't know where we are, but at least they will know someone is down and will begin to look for us.

Coincidentally, the emergency audio signal sounded the same as the low-RPM warning signal in a Huey. On hearing the constant *beep beep beep of* our emergency signal, pilots checked their tachometers for possible engine problems. When the beep wouldn't go away, they turned off their emergency receivers.

I had to figure out a way to be found.

The landing lights! I'll use the pathfinders' landing lights!

We put them on top of the helicopter and turned them on. A few minutes later, a Huey approached our position. The ship flared to land, paused, and then flew by. The landing lights had worked perfectly. The pilot thought he was landing in the LZ, only to see our overturned helicopter at the last moment. I couldn't see a place for the helicopter to land. We would have to wait until first light for someone to come for us. We settled in to wait for daylight, staying alert in case of enemy contact.

Shortly after dawn, two Hueys dropped off troops nearby to secure our helicopter until a Chinook from maintenance could lift it out. They flew us back to An Khe. I took the rest of the morning off.

That afternoon I was flying with our new brigade commander, a full colonel, on an administrative mission north of An Khe where I had hit the tree.

"We had a helicopter go down out here somewhere last night," the colonel said.

I was looking for a tree with the top chewed out of it. "Yes, sir, we sure did. It was B Company. Some eight-ball drove right into that tree, right down there on top of that little hill...see it, sir?"

Chapter 14

Sergeant Earnest

"HEY, RAY! LET'S go join the paratroopers!" My older brother, Jerry, could not contain his enthusiasm.

I was at home in Jenks after my first semester at Oklahoma State in Stillwater. I was 17.

"The paratroopers?" I asked. "What's that?"

"What's that? Man, they jump out of airplanes!" he said. "They run five miles before breakfast every day! And one of them can whip any three guys on the street!"

"Boy, that sounds great. Let's go check it out!"

I enlisted the next day with a guarantee of jump school and assignment to either the 82nd or 101st Airborne Division. Jerry and I went to talk to the Army recruiter in Tulsa, but Jerry backed out, citing his acceptance into the Naval Air Cadet program. I was so excited I didn't care. Finishing college could come later—I wanted to be a paratrooper.

And so I was. I was assigned to the 82nd Airborne Division at Fort Bragg, North Carolina—B Company, 1st Airborne Battle Group, 325th Infantry. I am proud of my three years' service with the 82nd. I jumped as often as I could, ran miles before sunrise, and whipped no one on the streets of Fayetteville, North Carolina.

I had come into the company as a private, fresh from eight weeks of basic training, followed by eight weeks of advanced infantry training. I went through the 82nd Airborne Jump School in January 1959, and was assigned to the weapons platoon. There were three outstanding noncommissioned officers (NCOs) in my platoon: the platoon sergeant, MSG Charles J. Hurley; SSG "Shubie" Blount, whom I worked for directly; and SSG Willie Lee Earnest. It wasn't easy, but soldiering and learning under those three NCOs provided me with a military foundation that few enjoyed. They were American classics. Of the three, it was Sergeant Earnest whom I found the most intriguing.

Sergeant Earnest, a black man about five-feet-nine inches tall, was from Sunflower, Mississippi. He was handsome, I thought, with a powerful build. I would say he left his last ounce of fat in his baby crib. He was immaculate, a model of how soldiers in the nation's most outstanding division should look. Every time I saw him he looked freshly scrubbed from head to toe, dressed in his stiffly starched 82nd Airborne war fatigues.

What impressed me most were his high standards, his starched, crisp, ever-pristine, spotless appearance. Everything about him was clear, sharp, incisive. When he spoke to you, he looked you dead in the eye. And you listened. He could really burn you up verbally—and he never hesitated to do so when you had it coming—yet he never bullied. If you could soldier for Sergeant Earnest, you could soldier for anyone.

I was 18, trying hard to learn and advance. The same was true of my friend Harold "Pappy" Butler. One day Pappy and I were called to task by Sergeant Earnest. For what, I don't remember, but I do remember Sergeant Earnest. He met us at the entrance to the platoon bay, a large barracks room where our platoon slept. He directed us to the far end of the bay for privacy. Pappy and I exchanged glances and braced ourselves for what was to come.

He sat us down on a bunk and stood over us. In a low, even voice he began. "Gentlemen, I am surprised at you. Two fine, young soldiers like yourselves, involved in something like that. I am amazed. You're better than that. Both of you. I don't ever expect to hear of anything like that, from either of you, ever again. Agreed?"

Oh, yes, it was agreeable. And that was it. It was my turn to be amazed. I did my best never to disappoint him again.

As I advanced in rank, finally becoming a sergeant myself, I came to know Sergeant Earnest well. It was clear how much he loved his children and family. He loved the Army. He loved his troops. He loved to soldier. It pleased him immensely to see young troops learn, advance, attain rank, and do well.

After those three years in the 82nd, a lot happened for me. When my enlistment was up in May of 1961, I briefly left the Army to return to college. Instead I married, returned to the Army, was assigned to the 101st Airborne Division, and became a father. I attended OCS in 1963 and became a Regular Army second lieutenant. I served a year in the 501st Airborne Infantry Battalion, 101st Airborne, the same unit I was in when I was an enlisted man. In 1965 I went to flight school. In April 1966 I went to Vietnam.

Late in 1966 Mac and I were flying resupply missions to isolated infantry units. One December afternoon we landed on a wooded knoll overlooking a valley. It was a 1st Air Cav weapons platoon position, and there were several troops standing about. As water and ammunition were unloaded, I stayed at the controls, ready to take off in case we began to receive fire. As I looked ahead, I saw Sergeant Earnest talking to two soldiers. I had no idea he was in the 1st Air Cav. I was overjoyed.

I couldn't leave the controls, so I sent a trooper over to him with instructions to come to the helicopter. I was sitting in the left seat, 30 feet away, engine running, rotor blades turning, a flight helmet covering my head and most of my face. I don't know how he knew, but when he looked my way I saw the light of recognition on his face. He turned and fairly ran to my side of the chopper, leaned in the window, threw his arms around me and hugged me like a child. He was crying and laughing at the same time, and so was I. We talked excitedly for two or three minutes. He kept telling me how proud of me he was—one of his boys, an infantry captain and aviator! I asked him to ride with me for a while, promising to bring him back soon, but he couldn't leave.

We clenched hands tightly, agreeing to try again when I came back. He was watching as we lifted off through the trees.

Three weeks later I went back to his unit. This time I would insist he go for a ride with me. I landed on an open hillside where his company was deployed. The wash from the rotor blades flattened the tall grass around us as troops came to unload the ammunition, C-rations and water.

I motioned a sergeant over, and he leaned into my window to hear over the roar of the engine. "Hey! Where is Sergeant Earnest? Is he around?"

"Sergeant Earnest? Sir, Sergeant Earnest was killed a week ago."

"What?" I asked. "Are you sure?"

"Yes, sir. No doubt about it, sir."

"Damn…damn! Thank you."

I sat there, numb, as the troops unloaded the supplies.

Thank you? Thank you?! That was a stupid thing to say.

The troops backed away from the helicopter. It was time to go.

"Hey, Mac. You fly."

Chapter 15

God Bless Us, Every One

CHRISTMAS IN WARTIME is still Christmas. The Army did its best to serve traditional holiday meals to troops everywhere. The 1st Air Cav hadn't been served many hot meals the last couple of years, but kitchen and culinary amenities were improving. In 1966 a delicious Christmas dinner would be served hot to troops on Christmas Day.

The food would be prepared in a kitchen located in a safe area and packed in large, insulated containers to keep it hot. One container would be filled with mashed potatoes, one with gravy, one with dressing, one with turkey, and so on.

On Christmas morning Operations asked for a crew to fly dinner to five outposts surrounding An Khe. The outposts were platoon-size, 30 or 40 men at each site. Two containers of hot mashed potatoes, two containers of turkey, and so on—right down to the pumpkin pie—would go to each site. I readily agreed to fly dinner out to the troops.

We fired up one of our Hueys and eased over to the infantry battalion area to pick up the food and get instructions and locations for the deliveries. As the containers were loaded, someone was trying to give me instructions as to which containers went where.

"No, no. You don't understand," I said. "I fly—you disburse. Put a man on here to ride with us who knows where everything goes."

A soldier charged with disbursing the containers of food got on board, and off we went. As we settled in to each location, the expectant looks on the men's faces told me they knew what we had.

The flights that morning were most pleasant.

It took about an hour to make all the deliveries. We dropped the young trooper back at the infantry battalion area, returned to the Golf Course, and went down to have dinner ourselves.

About the time I was reaching for my pumpkin pie, a warrant officer from Operations came charging into the dining area. "Sir, you'd better get back over there. Those people are madder than hell. They want you back over there right now."

A Christmas present to ourselves: a refrigerator, powered by a portable generator. What a blessing. An Khe 1966.

I had just spent an hour flying a hot Christmas dinner to five outposts, and they were mad at me? I soon learned why. The first outpost got all the turkey, the second outpost all the potatoes, the third all the gravy, and so on. I couldn't help but laugh. We got right back out there, picked up all the containers, properly sorted them and delivered them again. This time we waited at each location until we got a thumbs-up.

DECEMBER 2, 1966, I was promoted to captain. When I was commissioned a second lieutenant in March of 1964, I had never heard of An Khe. Now at 26, I was flying Hueys, leading combat assaults—and taking it to the edge almost every day.

I had said a prayer almost every night of my life from about the age of 10. Recently I had stopped those nightly prayers. I made no conscious decision to do so. They just sort of went away. I had lost all intimacy with God.

As Christmas drew near, we were back at the base camp at An Khe. One night Billy Graham held an outdoor candlelight service. He stood on a small, white stage elevated about three feet. There must have been a hundred or so of us in attendance. We sat on the ground in a loose semicircle, each of us holding a small, burning candle.

I had always admired Reverend Graham. His delivery that night was even more powerful than what I had seen and heard from him on television in years past. I found myself less interested in what he was saying and more focused on the fact that he was there with us, being Billy Graham. It was his presence that touched me.

When the service was over, I went forward with several others to say hello. I stood at the left side of the stage, looking up as I waited. Finally, he came my way.

His blue eyes were piercing as he gazed down at me, gripped my hand tightly and said in that distinctive, resonant voice, "God bless you, Captain."

I'll never forget that.

WHEN I GOT a call the next day from the leader of a patrol I was picking up between An Khe and Mang Yang Pass, Billy Graham was not on my mind.

"Yellow Three! We've got a dink running across the paddy down here. What should we do with him?"

It's a short journey from civilized thought to "kill him," and I believe we all instinctively know the route. Make him a thing, a "dink," justify the killing, and you are there.

My response was instantaneous. "Kill the little bastard."

In a combat environment, you had better be in that place of "kill or capture him," or one day you will die while deciding if you should go there. I found it a frighteningly easy place to reach.

ONE DAY THAT December we were called to evacuate a rifle company that was reportedly in bad shape. The troops had been in a major fight and had taken a lot of casualties. We were warned we would be under fire as we went in for the landing.

It was a tense 20-minute flight to their location. We went in steeled and ready, but the fight was finished before we got there. The landing zone was on the side of a hill that sloped steeply down to our right. At the foot of the hill was a creek and thick rainforest. We flew down into the clearing, nose high, and landed. I was perched precariously on the hillside, the left skid on a tree stump.

Troops from the battered rifle company walked from the creek bed and up the hill to get on board. I looked over my shoulder through the cargo door to see Robert Williamson, my OCS roommate, climbing in. I had neither seen nor heard from him since we had left OCS more than two-and-a-half years earlier. He was dirty and sweaty and looked tired and haggard as he crawled in and sat on the floor.

I reached for him and fought to hold the tears.

Chapter 16

LZ Hammond

A NEW FIRE support base called LZ Hammond had been established near the coast of the South China Sea. Located north of Qui Nhon and near the Air Force base at Phu Cat, LZ Hammond was mostly a collection of tents and a place to land and refuel helicopters. In early January we began working out of LZ Hammond nearly every day, flying there from An Khe in the mornings and then flying back to An Khe to spend each night. The trip was 25 to 30 minutes each way and a simple trip—when weather conditions were clear.

While LZ Hammond was near sea level, An Khe sat inland on a plateau about 300 feet higher. Where the highway from the coast to An Khe met the plateau, it wound almost straight up. This was An Khe Pass. We could take the direct route from Hammond to An Khe in clear weather, flying high enough to clear the plateau.

When weather forced us to fly low-level, we had to get creative. It was difficult and sometimes impossible to get up that sheer wall of earth to the top of the plateau, but if we could find a way through the clouds to the top, we could fly to An Khe under the clouds, or even at altitude if the plateau was clear.

In late afternoons a huge mass of clouds would often form atop the plateau and, like a waterfall, roll vertically off the high ground all the way down to the coastal plain below, blocking our route to An Khe. When that happened we would fly low-level to An Khe Pass and look for an area along the road with visibility. Flying five or ten feet above the road where it was cut into the side of the plateau—the mountainside only feet away from us on either side— we could sometimes sneak up to the top and scoot on home. If the pass was closed-in, we would fly northward along the edge of the plateau, looking for a break in the clouds. That usually worked if you knew where to look. Failing that, we flew back to Hammond to spend the night.

WE WERE A flight of six leaving LZ Hammond to return to An Khe for the night. I was weary after a long day of combat assaults and was looking forward to getting back. We were led by the same major who did not believe my account of the flight on Hill 534. Although he had been in country several months, he still was not a regular flight leader.

As we flew toward the high ground, I watched as unusually heavy clouds rolled down off the plateau and covered the pass. The clouds, closing nearly to the ground, rolled on toward us. It was too close to dark to challenge the pass. In conditions like this, we would typically return to Hammond.

I was surprised to see our flight leader slip on top of the first cloud he came to.

"What the hell's he doing?" I said to Mac. "Surely he's not gonna go on top."

"It looks like it, sir."

"Nah, no way. He ain't that dumb."

It would be dark in five minutes, and our major had just flown on top of light cloud cover. I hoped he would realize his mistake while there was still some light.

With only a 1:50000-scale topographical map and the aircraft's direction finder to guide us, we flew visually. Because of the all-encompassing darkness, night navigation was especially difficult. We had instruments but no navigational aids to guide us. The radio beacons set up for us rarely worked. There were no lights anywhere except in the major cities and, thankfully, An Khe. We relied on those lights in An Khe.

As long as we were over clouds, we would never see them.

Low fuel could eventually compel you into a blind descent through the clouds. That was unthinkable in the mountainous terrain we flew over. I fully expected Yellow One to dip back down below the clouds while there was still a bit of light.

Day or night, we never—*ever*—flew above solid cloud cover.

I waited for our flight leader to correct himself. Ahead the clouds billowed higher.

I watched in disbelief as he flew *above* them.

As our formation of helicopters followed, my disbelief transformed into anger. Ghostly whiteness beneath us, blackness above us, the deeper black of a mountain ridge in front of us, we flew on. As the clouds billowed higher, so did we, all the way to 6000 feet. Unbelievable. Any confidence I'd had in Yellow One was gone. I no longer trusted him to do anything right.

I checked the direction indicator. "Jesus, Mac, he's flying too far south. If we keep this direction we won't see An Khe even if it's crystal clear. The stupid son-of-a-bitch."

I had made this trip more times than I could count. I knew the exact direction that would get us over An Khe. I could just imagine our leader sailing past An Khe, his flight dutifully in tow.

I had to say something. Voicing my concern over the radio would hopefully wake him up to the seriousness of our situation.

"Yellow One, this is Yellow Three. I think maybe we are flying a little too far south. Over."

"This is Yellow One. Roger."

He maintained his heading with no further reply. I was livid.

"Well, this is fuckin' stupid. What the hell is he thinking?"

"I don't know, sir," said Mac, "but this ain't good."

"Mac, all we can hope for is this damn cloud cover to break. If it doesn't, we are in deep shit."

I was surprised to hear other pilots in our flight, all too aware of the danger we were in, get on the radio and ask the flight leader where we were and what was going on. If the cloud cover was solid all the way past An Khe, what would we do? Where would we go? Would we have enough fuel? I had never seen this happen. And Yellow One had no answers.

We continued flying in a direction too far south. We carried enough fuel to stay up about an hour and a half. Running out of fuel was a distinct possibility if we did not find An Khe.

The deep blackness of the mountain ridge in front of us would be the mountains between An Khe and Pleiku. There was an Air Force base at Pleiku that had radar and navigation aids that could get us down. If we missed An Khe I would recommend to Yellow One that he take us there. If necessary I would lead us there myself. I had no authority to challenge him, nor did I want to, but I was not about to allow the flight to get lost over mountains at night or run out of fuel.

I would give the major every opportunity to solve this dilemma himself. If only we could fly off this cloud cover.

"Sir, there's An Khe! There's An Khe!"

The door gunner spotted the lights off to our right.

We had flown off the cloud cover. Incredibly, Yellow One continued on his heading.

I had had enough.

"Yellow One, this is Yellow Three. There's An Khe off to your right. We're breaking off and going in."

We turned right, breaking out of the formation, and headed for the lights. Yellow Four and the rest of the flight followed. I did not care if Yellow One did not follow. With the cloud cover gone and the lights in full view, surely he could get himself on the ground.

"An Khe Tower, this is Gunslinger Yellow Three. I'm about three miles south for landing. There is a flight of six out here. Over."

"Roger, Gunslinger. Winds are light. Landing is to the south. Enter left downwind. Report entering. Over."

"Yellow Three. Roger."

We entered downwind in the flight pattern at the Golf Course, turned left on base, then left again on final approach to the south end of the Golf Course. I hovered over the parking pad, then set her down. I rolled the throttle off and let the engine idle a minute. I shut off the switches and listened to the engine and blades whine down.

I removed my helmet and protective vest, then opened the door. I took a deep breath and let out a long, slow sigh. Then, another. I sat there several minutes, then got out. I shifted my pistol to my right hip, zipped my helmet into its bag, and took my rifle from where it hung on my seat.

The crew chief was tying one end of the rotor blades to the tail boom.

"Good job, chief. See you tomorrow."

"Okay, sir."

I took my helmet and rifle and walked into the house. I expected the major to say something to me about the flight. He never did.

Chapter 17

Quarterbacks and Pitchers

WE MOVED TO Hammond about a week after the scary flight on top of the clouds, effectively ending all those evening flights to An Khe. That meant living in tents again. They were octagonal, two-man tents with a fair amount of room, and they did not leak as badly as the GP tents. The camp was only a few hundred meters from one side to the other, and was flat and barren. We were pretty much in the center of the camp with our helicopters, while the infantry protected the perimeter.

At Hammond I was often awakened at night by rifle fire. When it woke me, I would listen intently for a moment to the intensity and volume.

Oh. The little bastards are just probing the perimeter.

Then I would roll over and go back to sleep.

ONE OF OUR door gunners, a 19-year-old private, was going to Tokyo on R&R. Pompous gave the young man a hundred dollars with instructions to buy a new Seiko watch. The kid spent the money on geisha girls and saké and returned with no watch. We couldn't wait to see what Pompous would do when he found out. I was lucky enough to be there.

"Sir, I wasn't able to buy the watch, so I spent the money. I didn't think you would mind, since I couldn't get the watch. I'll pay you back on payday, sir."

Pompous was hot. "What do you mean you weren't able to buy a watch?"

Then the private explained.

Apparently satisfied with the story, Pompous bellowed, "Well, you be damn sure you pay me back on payday!"

"Yes, sir, I will, sir," the private assured Pompous.

The boy's explanation? Tokyo was out of Seikos.

ALONG THE MAIN highway, about halfway between Hammond and Bong Son, was a small forward base called LZ Uplift. The 2nd Brigade had established a forward headquarters there. One morning I was making some routine, administrative flights carrying troops from LZ Uplift northward. We had just left Uplift and were at about a thousand feet. Mountains were to our left and ahead of us. To our right, open rice paddies stretched to the South China Sea and its beautiful beaches.

Suddenly over the radio: "Any helicopter! Any helicopter! Please come to the beach! Please come to the beach! We have troopers lost in the surf! We have troopers lost in the surf! Any helicopter! Any helicopter! Please come to the beach!"

We were maybe a mile-and-a-half away. I turned right and took our Huey from its customary 80 knots airspeed to a near-maximum 115.

"Unit on the beach. This is Gunslinger 3-6. I'll be there in two minutes. What's your situation? Over."

"We got five troopers lost in the surf! We got five troopers lost in the surf! We need you to find them! We need you to find them! Over!"

"This is 3-6. Roger. We'll be right there. I'm about a minute-and-a-half out."

This pickup would not be easy. I would have to circle a few hundred feet up to locate the soldiers in the water and then hover right on top of the water's surface to pull them out. Depth perception over water is distorted, making it easy to fly right into it. Hovering over the water would be safer and easier with an empty ship. I hated to take the time, but I had to get rid of the six troops I was carrying. And I wouldn't be able to pick up five if I already had six on board. I could drop the six at the beach, which would mean coming to a full stop, or I could drop them at a company camp on the way. There I could keep my airspeed as I descended, bump the ground, kick them out, and be gone and back to speed in no time. We could fly low level the rest of the way. That should save precious seconds.

"Chief, tell those guys back there what is going on. Tell them we are going to come in fast at this camp up here and for them to un-ass this thing in a hurry. All we are going to do is bump the ground and be gone."

I began a shallow, high-speed descent as we moved toward the camp and the beach. I came in fast and hot and bumped the ground. The troops jumped out and I kept moving, regaining speed as quickly as I could.

As we approached the beach I flared up about 300 feet for a wide view of the water. It looked fairly calm.

"Everybody, look. There are five people out here somewhere."

I circled, and we looked. Nothing. I went higher, circled wider. Nothing, nothing but water.

"Dammit! This can't happen. We've gotta see 'em, guys, we've gotta see 'em!"

We circled wider and wider. We went higher and higher, and then lower. We went south, then north, and farther out to sea.

Eventually I gave up and went back and landed on the beach. There, side by side on the sand, lay three beautiful young men, naked, cold, and dead. None of them looked to be more than 20. They were such fine-looking boys—quarterbacks and pitchers and shortstops.

The other two were not found.

We left the beach, picked up the troops we had bounced out, and continued our work.

Chapter 18

The Corridor

SOMETIME LATE IN 1966 I developed a sense of impending disaster. I was flying one afternoon when I began to feel an awareness, almost a presence. It was as if I were flying in a corridor that became narrower and narrower. At the apex of the corridor lay disaster. I was sure it was death.

I did not get this sense of impending danger every day. When it came it was unexpected. When I sensed the corridor, I did not always become more cautious in my flying right away. But at some point, as I moved closer to the apex, I would sense I should go no further along the corridor. For the rest of that day I would back off, become more conservative in my thinking, the choices I made. I no longer stayed the extra minute, or went in where I couldn't see, or did something with my helicopter because I thought I could. I no longer accepted the invitations to go to the edge and dance with disaster. I did not stop flying or ground myself—I simply quit pushing as I normally did.

Was this experience irrational? I didn't think so. I felt it so solidly, so vividly, that I never questioned its reality or its validity.

This "corridor" business intrigued me. My father, bull of a man that he was, was extremely sensitive and intuitive. Growing up, my brother or I could be away for hours and it seemed my father knew within minutes when we would arrive back home. In my eyes I never measured up to my dad. I was happy anytime I thought I saw some of my father in me.

I was also drawn to the supernatural aspect of this intuitive knowing, or whatever it was. I was aware that the corridor experience came not long after I had lost touch with God. I wondered if this might be a way for God to communicate with me, perhaps even to take care of me. But I couldn't reconcile that. Good men were dying every day. Some were so young that going into the military was their first time away from home. They were vibrant young men, many with wives and small children and babies who would grow up fatherless.

I took comfort in the thought that the corridor gave me some degree of protection, but the gulf between us was such that I gave God no credit for it. And it did nothing to alleviate the anger and sadness of the destruction of young and precious lives, as I was reminded one evening at LZ Hammond. We had lost a young warrant officer that day. I stood looking at the mess tent, thinking about his not being there.

When they are killed, they don't come to dinner.

I felt older for the first time in my 26 years.

THE NEXT DAY we were flying in and out of the mountains just west of Bong Son and as far south as LZ Uplift. Strong winds swirled around the mountaintops, making the pinnacle landings doubly tough. The weather deteriorated throughout the day so that by early afternoon many of the mountaintops were no longer visible. A hard, driving rain set in. We started back toward Hammond, finished for the day because of the weather.

On the way I was asked by Operations to stop at LZ Uplift for a special mission. I went to the 2nd Brigade Operations tent to see what they had.

The operations officer pointed to a map as he spoke. "Captain Clark, we've got a patrol on top of this mountain right here."

The mountain was a short flight away, about three miles north and slightly east of Uplift, across the plain of rice paddies with which we had become so familiar the past few days. The mountain rose abruptly from the plain, forming the northern boundary of the vast paddy area.

This would be an easy mission, assuming weather had not covered the top of the mountain by the time we got there. Another pinnacle landing meant nothing to us.

He pointed to the map again, showing me the locations of two rifle companies. "There are five men in the patrol. Three of them go to B Company and the other two here to A Company. I want you to go over there and pick them up and take them to their units."

"Sir, we'll have to hurry. The weather is getting bad over that way. They are going to get socked in up there if they are not already."

"Well, get on over there and get them off that mountain."

"Okay, sir," I said. "We'll get on it."

We flew to the mountain as fast as we could, but before we arrived, clouds had rolled in and covered the mountaintop completely. There was no way to get to the patrol. I called Brigade operations and was told that the men would walk down the mountain, that we were to pick them up when they reached the rice paddies.

It would take an hour or so for them to get down, so we went back to Uplift and waited. When they had reached the foot of the mountain, I was given the map coordinates of their new location.

The flying conditions could not have been much worse. During the wait, clouds had lowered to less than 50 feet above the ground, and the rain was torrential. We had to fly three miles and back across this foggy sameness of rice paddy in the driving rain, 25 or 30 feet above the ground, unable to see 50 meters ahead.

With visibility so limited, we could easily fly within 150 feet of the patrol and never see them. As usual I had only my 1:50000-scale map and the helicopter's direction finder. The direction finder would allow us to find their general area. The map was useless.

Although I could see very little, I knew where the mountain was, so I was sure I could find them. I was anxious as we set off northward across the plain of rice paddies. With such poor visibility the possibility of a mid-air collision was all too real. I could only hope that no other helicopter crossed our path.

As soon as we reached the base of the mountain, we saw the patrol. I was relieved that we had flown directly to them. I did not want to fly one minute more than I had to in those conditions.

We picked them up, and the intensity of the rain increased. As we started back, 30 feet off the ground in the turbulent rain, I began to sense the narrowing walls of the corridor. I was already near the apex, where the sides were coming close together.

Growing increasingly tense and uneasy, I considered our situation. We were moving extremely well in this dangerous weather. B Company's location was nearly astride our route back to LZ Uplift. Company A was about a half-mile west of B Company. It should be easy to fly that extra half-mile and deliver those two men to their unit.

Should be.

But I was in the corridor and very near the apex. I dropped all five at B Company.

Chapter 19

Just Let Me Walk Away

IT WAS MONDAY, January 16, 1967. The day was all blue sky and sunshine. I was flying command-and-control for Lieutenant Colonel Siegrist, commander of the 1/5 Cavalry, whom I knew from Hill 534. We were north of Bong Son and west of the An Lao Valley. As we flew over the sheer, treeless grass-covered mountain peaks, I noted with concern the abruptness of the steep mountainsides.

You know, if we have an engine failure up here in these peaks and try to land on the side of one of these mountains, we will never stop rolling downhill. I think I would like to get out of here.

About three that afternoon we were released from our mission and headed south to return to Hammond when we got a radio call. We were directed to help with a routine troop lift of B Company, 2/5 Cav, the same company we had worked so hard to resupply on Hill 534 in August. They were in the nearby Soi Cau Valley, southwest of Bong Son.

As we continued south, I was glad to leave those steep peaks west of the An Lao. A few minutes later I joined other helicopters from our unit as they flew down into the Soi Cau, an area of rice paddies framed by forest-covered mountains. We landed, two ships at a time, on the valley's western side. I had the controls as we nestled down into the small clearing.

Six troopers got on board, and the crew chief and door gunner signaled we were ready for takeoff.

"Clear left!"

"Clear right!"

We lifted out of the trees and over the vast, wide expanse of open rice paddy that was the valley floor. The panorama was spectacular: Flat paddies the color of jade stretched before me, rising into the deeper green of the tree-covered mountains, then brilliant blue sky.

Sheeeennnnggggg!

It came from the rear of the helicopter.

What in the hell is that! Son-of-a-bitch! The fuckin' engine's flying apart!

"You'd better get this thing on the ground, sir," the crew chief said calmly.

"We're going, son, we're going."

We were only 100 feet in the air, having just taken off—the worst time to have an engine failure. There is little time to react and no margin for error. Sometimes there was nothing you could do but just "pancake" in and hope you survived.

I bottomed the pitch control and went into autorotation, putting us in a quick descent. I let the helicopter fall, then pulled the nose up into a flare to slow both our rate of descent and forward ground speed. Fifteen feet off the ground I stopped forward movement, leveled the aircraft and pulled in pitch. We settled softly into the water and mud of a rice paddy.

I shut the switches off and got out.

Damn!

We had flown over those peaks near the An Lao most of the day, leaving them behind just 15 minutes earlier. I didn't know what held that engine together through those mountains, but I was plenty thankful for it.

Later when the maintenance officer came to retrieve the helicopter, he tried to start it. He always did that. It didn't make sense to me. Did he think it wasn't really broken? Did he think he was going to fly it out after I had just made an emergency landing?

A big, twin-rotor Chinook helicopter flew in and carried my Huey back to An Khe to be repaired.

ABOUT FOUR IN the afternoon on Friday, another beautiful, clear day, we were picking up B 2/5 troops again, near where we had picked them up four days before. This was a routine flight, six slicks and two gunships carrying troops to LZ Hammond. Flying right seat with me was a first lieutenant, a solid performer who had been with us about four months.

We had just refueled with the usual 1200 pounds of JP-4. We also had two five-gallon cans full of water and three cases of C-rations. Once six troops in full combat gear got on board, we would be about as heavy as we dared get.

We loaded the six troops and lifted off, the lieutenant at the controls. We closed into formation, one-rotor-blade distance between aircraft, turned south and began climbing out of the valley along the eastern side. I was relaxed, looking at the mountain to my left, my hand in the hanging strap above the door.

Bammm!

The noise was loud and sharp. The nose jerked hard to the right and the aircraft began plunging downward.

The engine had failed.

Four hundred feet above the ground with no power, we were falling from the sky.

Beep! Beep! Beep! Beep!

The low-RPM warning was screaming in my ears, and the red warning light was flashing with a will of its own. I was on the controls in a flash to get the pitch out of the blades and enter autorotation. Even so, the split second it took to get my left hand from the overhead strap to the pitch control cost us valuable altitude and rotor speed. We were heavily loaded, over trees, at very low altitude, and headed downwind. My pilot, who had the controls when the engine failed, had frozen. He neither moved nor said a word when the engine quit or during what was to follow.

Our situation was critical. We had only seconds left in the air. I had to get airspeed to 60 knots to maintain optimum rotor speed, turn 180 degrees to land into the wind, find a clearing in the trees big enough for my helicopter, and land in that precise spot—all without engine power.

I would get one attempt at landing.

I glanced at the instrument panel to check the airspeed. The sun cast a glare on the gauge—I couldn't read the numbers.

Dammit!

I looked ahead to check the helicopter's attitude against the horizon for an estimate of airspeed.

The nose is too high.

I pushed the nose down and keyed the mike.

"MaydayMaydayMaydayThisisYellow3Ihaveanenginefailure I'm goingdown!"

Dammit! I'm on intercom!

With my left hand on the pitch control, I held the cyclic between my knees, freeing my right hand to reach for the radio switch on the console. I turned the switch from intercom to UHF, took the cyclic back with my right hand, keyed the mike and made the emergency call again.

"MaydayMaydayMaydayThisisYellow3Ihaveanenginefailure I'm goingdown!"

We were falling so fast.

Just let me walk away from this one. Just let me walk away.

I looked out my window for a place to land and spotted a small rice paddy, surrounded by trees, directly beneath us. It was big enough for one helicopter.

Boy, I'm glad that's there because that's where I'm going, straight down.

I would have to come in high enough to clear the trees, yet land softly. There could be no forward movement when we touched down or I'd risk the front tips of the skids catching in the mud and flipping us over. If our nose was not into the wind when we reached the clearing, I'd hit the trees on the far side. I didn't know if I was high enough to complete it, but I *had* to make that 180-degree turn into the wind — that was crucial.

As I leaned the aircraft into the left turn, the nose started up. Nose up, the feeling is wonderful because the rate of descent slows — but the rotor speed declines — rotor speed needed for the landing. Suddenly I could see the stage field at Fort Rucker where I had done this in training. I sucked in my stomach, pushed the nose down, and let her fall.

I felt like a meteor.

Just let me walk away from this one. Just let me walk away. I don't care what happens to the chopper. Just let me walk away.

We were already 75 feet from the ground and only halfway through the turn. There wasn't time to complete it.

I'll take injury. Just let me walk away. I don't want to be injured, but I'll take it if I can just walk away. Just let me walk away.

At 90 degrees of turn I pulled the nose up into the flare. With a rush of gratitude I thought of Harold Jones, my civilian flight instructor at Fort Wolters, Texas, who first showed me this maneuver. For a moment I could see the trees and that clearing in Texas where I had flared through the last half of a 180-degree turn and landed safely in a small, confined area the first time.

When we came out of the turn we were right at the treetops — *we would clear the trees.* It was the first indication I had that we might make it.

As we crossed over the treetops and descended into the clearing, the trees on the far side of the paddy became a threat. About 15 feet off the ground, keeping the nose up, I popped the pitch and stopped forward momentum. Then I pushed the nose down and pulled in all remaining pitch. We hit the ground, rocked back and forth two or three times, and came to a stop. The blades managed one final, lazy spin, then stopped turning.

The troops were out the doors in nothing flat. I shut off the switches and got out. There were no bad guys around, and our helicopters were circling overhead. We were safe for the moment.

The paddy turned out to be hard ground, not soft mud. I hoped the landing had not spread the skids. A hard landing generally implies poor flying skill, and spreading the skids is an embarrassment second only to running out of fuel.

I walked around to the front of the aircraft and looked under it. "Goddamn, I spread the skids," I said wistfully. "If only I had been a little smoother."

THE NEXT DAY a major from battalion headquarters came into the operations tent at Hammond to see me.

"Captain Clark, you got a minute?"

"Yes, sir."

"Listen, you're being charged with a major accident on that forced landing yesterday."

"What? Are you serious? But, sir, how can you call that an accident?"

"There's a dent in the bottom of the tail boom. It has to be replaced. The reg says that if any major component is replaced, it is a major accident and goes on the pilot's permanent record."

The major was quoting peacetime regulations.

I replied forcefully, "Sir, have you heard? This is Vietnam. People are being killed here. Why, some are even calling it war."

"Look, I did not write the regulations."

I couldn't believe what I was hearing. What an idiot. Hell, if I had lost it and killed everyone, I probably would have been decorated.

"Sir, let me get this straight. I just had an engine failure with a full load of fuel, a full load of troops on board, downwind at 400 feet—*maybe* only 300. I did a 180 into a confined area, saved the aircraft and 10 people—and I get a major accident?"

"That's about it," the major replied.

"Sir, I don't think so. I don't think that's 'it' at all."

Ludicrous as it was, if Battalion forwarded the paperwork, this could slip through the cracks and actually be posted on my record. The company commander might have been able to take care of this, but I would not trust him to do so.

I went to see the division safety officer, a lieutenant colonel. This being my fourth surprise landing, we had come to know each other, and I had already spoken with him about this latest adventure.

As I related my conversation with the major, the lieutenant colonel's expression grew dark. I didn't know what he was thinking, but he appeared to be mad as hell at somebody.

When I finished, he smiled and put his hand on my shoulder. "Don't worry about it, Ray. That isn't going to happen."

No one in his right mind would have penalized me for that landing. What we had done out there was possibly the single most difficult maneuver in the helicopter world.

More important to me, my crew and six young soldiers were alive.

Chapter 20

My Very Own Mess

I WAS OFFERED the job of company instructor pilot. I turned it down. A few days later I was appointed mess officer.

Being mess officer was the worst possible extra duty an officer could have. This rotten job usually fell to a lieutenant, sometimes a captain. In early 1966 Bob had the hated job. And it looked as though he would never get rid of it.

Not long after our house in An Khe was completed, I was in my room and overheard voices coming from the tent just a few feet from my window. A lieutenant named James Joyce, roaring drunk, was loudly giving his cohorts a dissertation on the evils and overall poor quality of our mess hall. As he ranted and raved in his drunkenness, he began to talk about what he would do to straighten out the entire problem—if he were the mess officer.

Butch Decker holding his friend "Gook." Everything was under a tent at LZ Hammond. 1967.

"By god if I was the mess officer, I'd straighten that place up!" he ranted. "Why, I'd make those damn cooks toe the line! I'd make sure we had fresh food to eat! I'd have coffee sittin' outside all the time!"

And then he said it. "By god I wish I was the mess officer!"

I called out to Bob in his room across the hall. "Listen to this clown," I said, when Bob came in.

The lieutenant was still at it. "By god I wish I was the mess officer! I would...."

Bob and I laughed as Joyce's tirade went on and on.

"Hey, Bob," I said, "why don't you go to the company commander and tell him that Lieutenant Joyce wants to be mess officer? He's said it over and over. He's even talked about what great ideas he has to improve the mess hall. Might be a way out."

Bob didn't say anything. He just laughed, turned and left.

You had to watch Lawson. He was sneaky quiet.

The next day Lieutenant Joyce was appointed mess officer. He never knew what happened, and we never told him. Bob had gone straight to the commanding officer and quoted Joyce verbatim, citing his admiration for the lieutenant's great ideas and strong desire to serve in a way that would benefit his fellow aviators and crewmen. Bob neglected to mention that the lieutenant was inebriated when he had said these things. But, as he mentioned to me, a person cannot be expected to remember everything.

Now at LZ Hammond, the prank that Bob and I pulled had come full circle. I didn't like it, but I was the new mess officer. I set about doing all I could to create an outstanding mess hall.

A new mess sergeant had just joined the company. A career soldier, he was long overdue for promotion. Promotions usually went to the sergeants in front-line combat. My man seemed to have given up hope on his promotion and his career. I had no idea how competent he was, but he was my mess sergeant. So we talked. I liked him and empathized with his career plight.

"Sergeant, as far as I can see, you should have been promoted a long time ago," I said. "Now, I don't know that I can do anything at all, but if you will bust your butt in making this the best damn mess hall in the Army, I'll do everything I can to get you promoted before you leave here."

I had no authority to promote him and no direct influence to get it done, but I could aim some amount of persuasion toward those who did.

"Sir, I've been waitin' a long time."

"I know you have. You get this mess hall up and running and I'll do my damnedest to get you that stripe."

"Okay, sir. I'll get it going."

"Good. Anything you need, you let me know."

I started talking hard to the company commander about getting the sergeant promoted.

Everything was under a tent at Hammond, which didn't help matters. We got lucky when three new cooks were assigned to us. Two of them could bake—even better, they liked baking. I told them I wanted hot, freshly baked bread served twice a day—three times a day if they could do it. Fresh, hot bread makes everybody happy. The kitchen was not issued enough flour and other ingredients to make fresh bread every day, let alone two or three times a day, but we got lucky there too. Air Force rations were far superior to Army rations, and there was an Air Force base just five miles away at Phu Cat.

We had a supply sergeant who may have been the world's greatest scrounger. Almost every day we loaded him up with enemy rifles or bowguns and other tradable items, and put him in a helicopter to Phu Cat to prey on the Air Force. Those on the periphery of combat seem to be susceptible to being traded out of their gold watches for mundane items related to combat action. He came back with choice cuts of meat, fruit and ingredients for baking. As a result we had more—and better—food than the mess halls that relied simply on what they were issued.

Bob built tables and benches from ammunition boxes for the mess tent. We had great cuts of well-prepared meat, hot bread at nearly every meal, and freshly baked desserts twice a day—our fine mess hall gained a reputation. Senior division officers were showing up regularly to eat. People we had never seen were stopping by at mealtime.

With the supply sergeant's unique ability to trade and scrounge, those great cooks' baking abilities and positive attitudes, and the mess sergeant's supervision, the mess hall became truly outstanding. For several weeks, until we moved to Bong Son, it was the best I ever saw. My contribution was sampling the hot bread and desserts to make sure everything was in order.

A few weeks later an NCO promotion became available in our company. It went to the mess sergeant. I was delighted; he was ecstatic. It had been a long time coming, and he had certainly proven himself deserving. He thought I was a miracle worker because he had been promoted, and so soon. I had lobbied for him with the company commander, but that was the extent of what I could do. Even the company commander had limited authority to promote—the stripes had to come from higher up. I didn't know if his promotion finally caught up with him or if someone higher up really liked the biscuits.

THE MESS TENT was not only where we ate our meals, it was a natural meeting place. There being no other place for private conferences in our company area at Hammond, I asked the chaplain to meet me there. I was aware that my experiences had been tame in comparison to many. Still, I had seen enough to affect me. My small-town, Methodist faith was shaken to its roots. I felt empty. We sat opposite each other at one of Bob's pine-board tables one morning. The sides of the tent were rolled up, and we talked in the morning light. I told him I had stopped praying. I described the emptiness I felt.

"Well, son," he said, "I felt like that once. It went away in time. I'm sure yours will too."

I stared at him.

Is that all you've got to say? Is that all?

"Thank you, sir," I said. "I gotta go fly."

He was as empty as I was.

Chapter 21

Little White Lights

IT SHOULD HAVE been routine. It was a simple mission. We were at LZ Hammond, about to be released to return to An Khe, when my trail helicopter and I were assigned to fly with C Company on a night combat assault.

It was twilight when we moved our two aircraft to the pickup area and parked behind several C Company Hueys. We shut the engines down and got out, awaiting our briefing from the flight leader.

After about 10 minutes a C Company pilot came walking quickly down the line and informed us there would be no briefing from the flight leader. He told us there would be eight Hueys flying single-file. My other Huey and I would take up the rear of the eight-ship gaggle. We would fly five miles due north across a small mountain ridge and drop our troops in the rice paddies where a fight was going on. All lights on the helicopters would be off except for a small white light on each side, near the top of the aircraft. There was also to be strict radio silence. This made no sense to me and appeared unnecessary, but I was not the flight leader.

What the C Company pilot did not say was that, with only those two little white lights on a helicopter, you couldn't tell whether the aircraft was coming or going.

Up front the flight leader was already starting his engine. I wondered who he was.

Mac and I jumped in and started up. "Well, we'll just follow the leader, Mac," I said. "This can't be too hard—long as the son-of-a-bitch doesn't get lost. He's just going up there past Uplift, land in those paddies and come back."

I added, "It would have been nice to have had a real briefing, though."

My chief concern at this point was the darkness. All I had to do was follow the helicopter in front of me, but with no lights on the ground and no moonlight, it was like sitting inside a closet that night. Weird things can happen in the dark.

I had the controls as we lifted off, six Hueys in front of me and one trailing behind. We headed north, quickly climbing to 1700 feet.

"Mac, why in hell do you suppose he's going to 1700 feet? We don't have that far to go."

"You got me, sir. We don't need to go this high."

Again I wondered who our flight leader was.

We were shrouded in darkness. There was no moon, no horizon, no visual reference at all. All I could see were the two little white lights on the helicopter in front of me, occasionally glimpsing the small, ethereal lights on the helicopters in front of it.

I told the crew, "You all keep your eyes open here tonight."

I had an uneasy feeling. We were flying in formation with these guys we didn't know, we were unnecessarily high, we could not see, and we could not talk to each other.

"Mac, there's something about this deal that ain't right. I hope he finds this landing zone all right. I don't really want to keep this up for a long time."

Halfway to the ridge, where we should have begun our descent, I spotted two little white lights to my left front. They did not appear to be with our little gaggle heading north. What was this? *Who* was this? The two white lights floated past us, going south. Then came another two! And there were more....

"What the hell's going on here? My God, Mac, he's turning the whole gaggle around."

There was no reason to turn around unless we had gone too far.

"Wait a minute..." I said. "I *guess* it's our gaggle. Hell, I can't tell. I can't see a goddamn thing except those stupid-ass little white lights."

There were little white lights in front of me and little white lights passing me going the other direction.

"Jesus Christ. The son-of-a-bitch is lost, Mac. He's goddamn lost!"

When I no longer had white lights to follow, I turned left 180 degrees to follow in trail, restoring our single-file formation.

Oh no. Not again. This can't be.

Ahead to the left were little white lights that should not have been there. They appeared to be coming toward me. Was it our flight leader? The radio was silent; I could only guess.

Damn! This is like Twilight Zone.

Two little white lights wafted by my window.

"Jesus Christ, Mac, the dumb son-of-a-bitch is going north again. Fuck this! I'm getting on the radio. What the hell is he doing?"

I keyed the mike.

"Yellow One, this is Green Three. Is that you going north again?"

Silence.

"Yellow One, this is Green Three. You want to tell us what is going on?"

Nothing. He was not going to respond, even though I had broken radio silence. Our leader was lost, his flight was in chaos, and he had no instructions? Nothing to say?

Who *is* this guy?

Ghostly white lights continued gliding past us in the opposite direction. I tried my best to follow the helicopter in front of me, but by then we couldn't tell who was who. We turned back north and passed over the top of a helicopter.

"Sir, we're over the top of Green Two! We're over the top of Green Two!"

"I know, I know, I see him," I told the crew chief. "What a rat fuck! I can't believe this! You all keep looking in all directions. Don't let us run into anybody."

We were no longer part of a single-file line. We were surrounded by little white lights. They were under us, in front of us, behind us. I only hoped there were none above us.

I slowed and worked my way to the pair of lights I thought I was supposed to follow. Suddenly the leader began to descend rapidly.

"Thank God," I said to the crew, "the dumb son-of-a-bitch has found the LZ. At least I suppose he has. You all keep your eyes open. No telling who's out there."

We turned 180 degrees back south once again and made our own rapid descent into the rice paddies.

"Turn on the landing light!" I told the crew. "Turn on the searchlight! Turn on every goddamn light we have! We may get shot but I am not going to crash following this damn fool because I can't see."

We made the landing and returned to Hammond unscathed.

I never saw that flight leader from C Company. I did not know who he was and I no longer cared.

It should have been routine. It was a simple mission. We added darkness, silence, little white lights, and a dumb son-of-a-bitch…and had our very own episode of…the *Twilight Zone*.

Chapter 22
Attitude Adjustment

WITH 10 MONTHS in country, I had become one of our most experienced flight leaders. Months earlier I was tense leading flights, but with experience I had become confident in my ability to plan, navigate, improvise, get to the landing zone right on time, and fly the Huey in the worst of conditions.

I had gone down violently four times in the past seven months. I asked my crew chief what he was thinking on that last engine failure as we were falling so rapidly to the ground.

"Well, sir, when you went into the turn, I knew you had it."

I laughed aloud. It was nice to know there was a point at which my crew chief had confidence we'd make it. I asked him what the other crew chiefs and door gunners were saying about my going down four times.

"Well, sir, about half of them don't want to fly with you because something is always happening. The other half don't want to fly with anyone else because you always bring everyone back."

"That's fair enough," I said, grinning. "That's fair enough."

I DIDN'T KNOW if the company commander was trying to save my neck by keeping me from flying every day or if he just wanted an operations officer with experience as a flight leader. Whatever the reason, my platoon was given to another young captain, Don Walker, and I was made the company's new operations officer. I would hold that position just three days. Captain Walker was shot down in action near Bong Son. Troops pulled him and his young warrant officer from the wreckage, saving them from advancing enemy soldiers.

Walker took a small arms round through the ankle, and his warrant officer suffered a broken leg and a broken jaw.

The company commander and I flew to the hospital in Qui Nhon to check on them. Walker was in some pain but was in good spirits. The warrant officer was sleeping. He was a good-looking, dark-headed kid, age 22, with a wife and two-year-old daughter. His face was so swollen I almost did not recognize him. The doctor, however, assured us that he was okay and would recover completely.

The next morning the young man was dead. We were told he had suffocated during the night. I flew back to Qui Nhon to identify his body. He was such a fine-looking kid. He had been with us only 30 days.

With Walker out, I was back flying with my platoon the next day.

ON VALENTINE'S DAY of 1967 I had two ships flying resupply missions to troops north of Bong Son, where I had seen my first action 10 months earlier. About midmorning, as we headed north over the rice paddies, I was again struck by the lush, green beauty of the mountains to the west, and the beach and the South China Sea to the east.

After dropping off my cargo of ammunition and supplies, we continued to our second location. One of our rifle companies had taken position in a small, wooded area that was bordered by rice paddies on three sides and a narrow river on the north side. About a mile south of the location I called the company and asked for smoke. My number two ship landed in a clearing in the woods and delivered its cargo. Then we headed back to Bong Son to load up again and returned with more supplies.

I called about a half-mile out. "Black Diamond, this is Gunslinger 3-6, over."

"This is Black Diamond 6 Alpha, over."

"This is Gunslinger 3-6. I'm a half-mile out with two more loads for you."

"6 Alpha. Roger. Do you want smoke?"

"3-6. Nah, I've already been there. I know where you are."

"6 Alpha. Roger."

Because my number two had landed in the clearing before, I had him take the clearing again. He keyed his mike twice in recognition of the instruction. I would land in the open rice paddy west of the trees, just feet away from the troops, with the riverbank immediately in front of me.

The approach across open rice paddies made me feel a little vulnerable, so I came in pretty fast, landing with the nose on the edge of the riverbank. I didn't like sitting out in the open, but I knew they would unload us quickly and we'd be in the air again.

Troops began to unload my number two ship. No one made any move to unload us. Those not busy unloading the other helicopter were standing around looking at us. As a rule the crew chief and gunner didn't unload in such a situation, instead remaining on their machine guns, at the ready. I was getting agitated by the delay. The warrant officer with me was new, so I talked to him about what was going on while I got hotter and hotter.

"Damn, I don't like sittin' out here in the open. Those little bastards will lay some fire on you if you sit out in the open like this very long. This is not a good idea. What in the hell are they waiting for?"

Now unloaded, the other helicopter lifted off out of the clearing. I was really angry now. "Look at that! Look at that! They've already unloaded him! I'll tell you what those sorry bastards are doing. The sons-a-bitches are too damn lazy to walk over here and carry this stuff 30 feet. They're waiting until he leaves the clearing, and now they expect us to move over there and land in that clearing so they don't have to walk, while we're sittin' over here with our asses hanging out. Well, fuck them! I'm not about to move over there. We'll sit right here, by God, till hell freezes over! Jesus Christ. This is really stupid."

"Gunslinger 3-6, this is 6 Alpha. You're sitting in a minefield. You wanna move over here?"

Instant attitude adjustment. I may never have spoken with a sweeter tone. "3-6. Well, sure, I'll be right over."

Everything else was forgotten. My intention was simply to get the hell out of there. I pulled in power and lifted off.

The explosion was deafening. The helicopter began to gyrate wildly, bucking and thrashing about as we moved over the river. I was fighting with all I had to get the helicopter under control and keep it right side up as it continued to flail wildly. I had never felt anything like it.

They must have shot the push-pull tubes in two. If I turn this son-of-a-bitch upside down, it'll kill us all. Fuck it! I'm puttin' this thing down.

I didn't know how deep the water was, but it didn't matter. I had to get out of the air before I lost all control. I bottomed the pitch and got us down, right side up, in about three feet of water.

In previous emergency situations, I hadn't remembered to pull the quick release on my door, which would literally blow the door off the helicopter and allow a rapid exit. I had since schooled myself on this, and at last—when I didn't need to—I did it. I was astounded at how that door flew off the helicopter.

I stepped into water waist-deep in a serene countryside. There was no incoming fire. The aircraft was stable on its skids in the water. Apparently we had armed pressure-release mines when we landed, and they exploded as we lifted off. Given the gyrations we went through, I was sure the external control linkage was damaged. I was fortunate to have gotten the helicopter down on its skids.

Now I wanted that company commander. How could they watch us make an approach from a good half-mile away and not warn us of the mines? How could they let us land and then sit there for minutes before warning us? What if my crew chief or door gunner had gotten out and walked in the minefield? I waded toward the rear of the helicopter and headed for the troops. Being an infantry officer myself, I figured we could relate, and I definitely intended to get his attention.

One of the troops yelled at me from the trees. "Sir, you'd better not come across there! There may be mines in there too!"

I stopped. "Aw, the hell with it." I turned around and waded across the river where the other chopper waited on a sandbar.

I was walking to the operations tent when the company commander and executive officer came out.

"What happened to you, Clark?" asked the CO.

I was wet up to my fanny. "Well, sir, I just broke another one."

Chapter 23

Down in the Valley

A FLIGHT LEADER'S sense of timing was critical. He had to find the landing zone with only a 1:50000-scale topographical map and land into the wind—precisely on time. If he were late to a landing zone, he lost the protection of the artillery barrage. If early, he flew into it. A timing error by the lead helicopter magnified itself from ship to ship all the way to the rear of the flight. A less-than-gentle turn by the leader became an impossibly sharp turn for ships back in the gaggle.

Just as turning abruptly caused problems for trailing pilots, slowing abruptly could force them to fly S-turns to remain airborne. A good flight leader would go quickly and smoothly from 80 knots to zero at touchdown, allowing the rest of his flight to do the same. The 227th drilled this technique into its flight leaders. Other units we sometimes flew with might hold a steady 80 knots right up to the LZ and then go into a slow and steep descent to land. We would be in the back of their flight, slowing abruptly from 80 knots to 30, doing S-turns, trying not to run into each other. No pilot wants to fly slowly into an LZ—he wants to get in there and get out as quickly as possible.

The number of helicopters an LZ could accommodate determined how the flight gaggle was formed. If an LZ could hold four helicopters, it was a four-ship landing zone, meaning a group of four would fly in formation together and land together. A flight was formed in groups of two for a two-ship LZ. While four helicopters were a platoon, two were a section.

Accurate LZ reconnaissance was crucial. Flight leaders were best qualified to determine how many helicopters could land in a clearing at the same time, but there often wasn't time or opportunity for them to perform their own LZ reconnaissance. Many infantry commanders considered their own reconnaissance of landing zones sufficient—it seldom was. Infantry commanders routinely overestimated the number of ships that could land in a clearing together. It caused all sorts of havoc when a flight approached a two-ship LZ in groups of four. "It's a two-ship LZ. It's a two-ship LZ," the flight leader would call out. "Space it out. Space it out."

Each flight of four had to break into flights of two, and all had the difficult task of establishing the proper distance from the group it followed. It could be a real zoo toward the back of a flight as the new groups slowed, did S-turns, and swung wide right or left to create the needed spacing, pilots cursing like crazy.

Flight groups dropped off troops in intervals of 30 seconds so that the helicopters in the LZ were taking off as the next group was on short final to land. More time is needed for troops to load, so we allowed 60 seconds between flights when picking them up. We didn't measure the 30 or 60 seconds with a stopwatch. Cruising at the usual 80 knots, you eyeballed the distance between you and the flight ahead.

We usually did not make a full-stop landing when we dropped troops off in an LZ. We would bump the ground with the skids and keep on moving. We were targets: Troops were eager to get away from us. When picking them up, we applied enough power to keep the Huey light on the skids, dancing on the ground as if impatient to fly. The crew chief's "Clear left!" and door gunner's "Clear right!" were the pilot's signal that he was loaded, and away he went.

SIX GIS HAD been captured overnight. We were to put troops on the ground for a rescue operation. It looked pretty simple: We could fly low altitude the entire way, from Bong Son north up the wide An Lao Valley, then turn west into a small, narrow valley to the LZ.

Our favorite pompous major was to lead the mission; accordingly, his call sign would be Gunslinger Yellow One. As so often the case, the flight leader would not be allowed to recon the landing zone. We were informed it was a two-ship LZ. The formation would be "sections trail, heavy left." That meant our 18 Hueys would be in a trail formation, divided into nine groups of two. "Heavy left" meant the second would trail the first by one rotor blade's distance, 45 degrees to the left.

We took off about 8:30 in the morning, nine groups spaced at 30-second intervals. I was Yellow Three, the lead helicopter of the second group, trailing Pompous and Yellow Two. Mac was with me in the right seat that day.

Aviators always prefer to fly over flat terrain, in case of an emergency landing. The floor of the An Lao, perhaps a mile wide, was flat with few trees, while the mountains on both sides of the valley were steep and covered with trees and undergrowth. Our leader did not take us up the An Lao Valley as I expected. From Bong Son we flew west, crossed the An Lao, and turned north, climbing to 1800 feet to fly over the mountains. Clouds hovered low, nearly touching the mountains. We were skipping over the mountaintops to avoid those low-hanging clouds, clearing them by less than 50 feet.

We flitted along in the tight space as we continued north, sandwiched between the clouds and the mountains. As we neared the LZ, the folly of Pompous's chosen route became painfully apparent. The LZ was down in a narrow valley running east to west. The valley was deep, about a thousand feet. Instead of approaching the LZ from the east at low altitude, we would have to descend into it. If we had flown up the An Lao Valley we wouldn't be facing this near-dive.

I had to follow the leader, and I watched Pompous intently as he approached the valley. "Mac, when he hits the edge of that valley, he's gonna disappear from sight as he goes down in there to land. When we start down in, we'll have to watch for him coming out. I don't know how wide that valley is. We'll have to watch it. This could be a little touchy."

Just as Pompous approached the edge of the valley to begin his descent, a cloud rolled in, blocking him.

"Goddamn, Mac, look at that cloud. He can't get in."

Saying nothing on the radio, Pompous began a wide, gentle right turn.

"Boy, is this going to screw things up," I said, with half amusement and half dread.

We followed his flight path, flying to the edge of the valley, then making the same wide right turn behind our boy Pompous. Our leader now had a problem—how to keep his gaggle properly spaced while maintaining airspeed. More importantly, he had to keep us from running in to each other, hemmed in as we were in that crawl space between the clouds and the mountaintops. The long tail of helicopters trailing him could not pull over and park while he figured out what to do.

With the cloud blocking his view, making that turn was all Pompous could have done. However, when his turn reached 180 degrees, he should have continued south until he passed his last pair of helicopters, then followed them back north, forming a sort of racetrack. That would have put him

An Lao Valley near Bong Son. 1967.

in position to make a second approach while keeping everyone properly in trail and out of each other's way.

Instead, he compounded his bad luck with poor judgment: Pompous maintained that wide, gentle right turn to full circle. As he did so, he turned directly into the line of helicopters trailing him. Everyone had to follow standard procedure and follow the group in front of him. Each pilot would have to fly up to the valley edge and make that same 360-degree turn. Our leader had tied a loop in the flight path of his 18-ship gaggle.

"This is going to be a rat fuck, Mac. This is going to be a real rat fuck."

As we turned north to make the full, wide turn, Mac and I had to scramble to avoid colliding with other helicopters. It would have been laughable if it were not so serious. The limited space between the clouds and mountaintops, this neat loop in our flight path, and the blind descent into the valley: The possibility of a mid-air collision was all too real.

"Damn, Mac, I hope that cloud clears and he gets in there this time."

We followed Pompous as he again approached the edge of the mountain leading into the valley. Thankfully the cloud had moved; he and his trailing ship disappeared from sight. We followed, approaching at 80 knots.

What a mess.

Two ships were down in the valley. My two were entering. There were too many helicopters in too little space: Those descending would be coming in on top of those climbing out—after first making that ridiculous loop.

Now Pompous was on our radio. "Gunslinger Flight, this is Gunslinger Yellow One. It's a one-ship LZ. It's a one-ship LZ. Space it out."

Unbelievable.

We would now have to stretch into a single-file trail, 30 seconds between each helicopter. We would have to slow our airspeed. The valley was not wide enough for us to circle and gradually descend. Adding to the difficulty, the landing zone was a B-52 bomb crater, a giant hole in the ground.

It was unnecessary for me to issue instructions to my trailing helicopter. He would automatically drop back into his 30-second spacing, as would all the others.

As we broke over the edge of the valley and started down, I took the controls. "I got it. Holy shit, Mac. Can you believe this? Christ! I'll fly this son-of-a-bitch, Mac—you just make sure we don't run into anybody. Chief, you all make sure we don't hit anybody. Keep your eyes open."

We spiraled down as Pompous climbed out, not a hundred feet away from us. We moved to the valley's northern side to avoid Yellow Two. There were choppers over us, under us, and to the sides of us, some coming up, some going down.

I can't believe this.

Reaching the valley floor, I swung wide of the bomb crater as Yellow Two lifted out. I pulled the nose up high, flaring the helicopter to stop forward speed, and landed rough. The troops were out the doors.

"Clear left!"

"Clear right!"

I told the crew, "Keep your eyes open, now! Keep your eyes open!"

To avoid those coming down, we zipped down the valley a short distance to begin our spiral up and out of the valley.

On the way back to Bong Son, my crew said nothing.

I had only one thing to say. "Mac, that was the biggest rat fuck of all time."

Chapter 24
Company Policy

SOON AFTER THAT last debacle with Pompous, I was moved to Operations again. I enjoyed assigning missions and crews, making sure that aircraft and pilots were where they were supposed to be, and generally supervising the company's flight operations.

Radios were always on in the operations tent, monitoring our missions in progress. One day we heard a comically frantic call over the radio: "I'm hit! I'm hit! Oh, my God! I'm hit!"

It was Pompous. We rolled in laughter. It was so typical of him. It wasn't that we were not concerned. We just couldn't get past his Hollywood cry, which was so funny. We knew if his wound had been serious he would not have been broadcasting it with such theatrics. He suffered a minor leg wound. He would live to amuse us another day.

BOB, CHUCK, BUTCH and I had become the best of friends. When Chuck went home in February and Bob in March, I was happy for them, but it left me feeling a bit empty. Butch would have a few months to do after my time was up in mid-April. I was the "oldest" pilot in the company in terms of time in Vietnam.

As my 12-month tour was drawing to an end, I pushed thoughts of home out of my mind. Thinking of home as anything other than a dream could drive you crazy. Better to stay present mentally and psychologically and simply attend to the business at hand. It was too dangerous to do otherwise. A single moment's inattention could cost your life. Bullets are indiscriminate in their killing power and they have no sense of timing. One of my former classmates, taking just one more flight, was killed the day he was to leave for home.

It was our company's policy to send a pilot to An Khe to command the rear detachment in his final three or four weeks before going home. In effect, his flying time was over. A few days after Bob left, I went to An Khe to run the rear detachment. There I began to feel like a noncombatant. After those many months living on the edge, I felt uncomfortable. I didn't like being grounded.

One night shortly after dark, Operations received a call that a warrant officer aviator replacement was at battalion headquarters. I walked down the hill and across the road to Headquarters Company to bring him back to our company area. He was a heavyset kid, 19 or 20 years old, and fresh from flight school, as almost all the replacements were. After we were introduced, I moved to help him with his bags. He looked at me and proudly blurted, "Well, sir, you've got yourself a genuine honor graduate!"

I wasn't in the mood. And I wasn't impressed that he had finished first in his flight class. That arrogance would kill him for sure and, no doubt, other good men with him.

In the halls of flight school at Fort Rucker, one might feel quite good about himself if he had finished first in his flight class. And rightfully so. But Vietnam was the big leagues and beyond. Vietnam did not care who you were or where you came from. You followed certain rules of behavior, and there wasn't time to figure out the rules on your own. New guys had to be taught, and the sooner their advanced education began, the better.

"You stupid son-of-a-bitch," I said, turning away without a bag. "Pick up your bags and follow me."

There is a certain air that surrounds experienced combat helicopter pilots. It may appear as a slight arrogance or a sort of distant superiority. In reality it is a presence born of experience and skill. It is found in one whose spiritual sword has been tempered by the fire of combat and the presence of death. It is the mark of one who has given his life and, by the grace of God, had it given back to him.

Until that presence, earned over months or years—through hundreds of hours of serious combat flying—one day, uninvited, mysteriously settles onto one's being, any sort of arrogance is an invitation to disaster. Helicopters kill arrogant pilots.

EARLY IN MY tour, before the old guys had gone home, a policy of scattering helicopters at night was adopted. It was called "grasshopping." We would park the helicopters 50 or 100 meters apart overnight to guard against several helicopters being damaged by one enemy artillery or mortar round.

As new and less experienced commanders came in, old procedures, policies and rules were sometimes deemed unimportant or insufficient. Grasshoppering went from scattering a unit's helicopters meters apart to miles apart. When operating out of LZ English at Bong Son, we often sent helicopters all the way to Qui Nhon to spend the night in relative safety. We pilots didn't much like the idea. The evening trip to Qui Nhon added an hour to the end of a crew's day and still another hour to start the next as they had to be up early enough to get the aircraft back to fly its mission.

Another company policy: Two new guys never flew together. The only time I ever saw it happen was when Chuck and I made the chow run from Mang Yang Pass. And it nearly killed us both.

I would hear the story a few weeks after I returned to the states.

Two new and inexperienced young warrant officers were assigned to fly a ship from Bong Son to Qui Nhon to park it for the night. The "genuine honor graduate" and one or two others rode along to have some fun that evening in Qui Nhon. The weather was bad. Clouds rolled in as they made their way toward Qui Nhon and the coast of the South China Sea. The young pilots became disoriented. An Air Force C-130 spotted them on his radar screen, 40 miles at sea.

They were never heard from again.

Chapter 25

Leaving

GOING HOME WAS a surreal proposition. My days in An Khe, though few, had dragged by. With the company operating out of Bong Son, there had been little to do. The division had recently gotten an ice cream machine, and I had eaten all the ice cream and bananas that I could hold. I was bored after living on the edge the past year.

Wesley and I had come over together, and we were going home together. At 5 p.m. we were to catch a flight to Pleiku where we would spend the night, then board a chartered United flight to the States at 7:30 the next morning. We met at the airfield at 2 p.m.—three hours early—in case the flight was running ahead of schedule. We were taking no chances. We sat and talked and joked as we whiled away the afternoon, waiting for our flight to arrive. Our biggest worry at the time was riding to Pleiku in the back of an aircraft that someone else was flying.

Finally it was time to board the plane, and Wesley and I arrived safely in Pleiku before dark. We checked into a newly constructed, two-story frame barracks, housing for those coming in and those going home. We found the second floor was empty, so we took our bags upstairs. Narrow, metal GI bunks lined both sides of the long barracks room. After getting dinner, we returned to our quarters about 7:30 and began the longest 12 hours of our lives. We had hoped that sleep would make the time go faster, but still wide awake at 2:30, we knew that wasn't going to work. Some nights aren't meant for sleeping.

Before going home to Durham, North Carolina, Wes was flying to Georgia to meet his fiancée, who lived in Augusta.

I asked Wesley about his homecoming. "What are you going to do when you get there, Wes? Is Joyce going to meet you in Atlanta?"

"No, she's not coming to Atlanta," he said. "I'll be lucky if she meets the plane in Augusta."

"What? What's that about? Why would you even go to Augusta? I would think you two would meet in Atlanta and take off somewhere. What's up?"

"It's Masters weekend," he said. "She says she has to work."

"Damn," I said. "What's so important?"

"I don't know. You got me."

I left it at that.

Some homecoming. Some fiancée.

It was my first indication that even people we knew perceived us to be different from how we perceived ourselves. I thought of the war protesters and those merely apathetic to us as people on TV. They were all from somewhere else. They weren't our families and loved ones...were they?

Wesley and I were sitting on those narrow beds, willing those last few hours to pass, when new troops—freshly arrived on our United jet—began filing into the barracks. Their clothing was new and unfaded, as were they.

We had four hours to go. They had 365 days, if they survived. Unable to express our mutual feeling in words, Wesley and I looked at each other, then shook our heads and shared a small, sad laugh that only the two of us understood.

On Sunday, April 16, 1967, the sun did rise, daylight did come, and we departed Pleiku at 7:30 a.m. Our first stop was Honolulu.

In the airport lobby we eagerly bought a newspaper to read news of home. The front-page headline read "An Khe Suffers Night Mortar Attack." We started laughing, as if we had cheated death once again. We congratulated each other and moved on to explore the wonders of the Honolulu airport. Of course, underneath our laughter was heartfelt concern for those still there.

Soon we were airborne again, on our way to San Francisco. This business about going home was becoming real. When our plane touched down at Travis Air Base, a huge roar went up. Those cheering were inside the plane.

Wesley and I said goodbye, knowing we would see each other again. As Army aviators we would be going to Vietnam a second time. Helicopter pilots were needed. We would be home 18 months and then return for another year of fun and games.

I rode a bus to the San Francisco airport, arriving in the early evening. My flight home was the next morning, so I stayed at the hotel on the airport grounds. Just being there in that nice hotel—in America—was wonderful to me. The room, the lobby, the streets, the traffic—all were lovely surroundings, but I felt out of place. I felt separated from these people. What was the difference between us? Then I realized: These people had no concern for their safety.

How interesting.

I couldn't wait to catch my flight home to Tulsa. I was at the American Airlines ticket counter well ahead of time to purchase my ticket. I was in dress uniform, wearing my flight wings, jump wings, and decorations. There were several people waiting along with me to buy tickets. There was no organized line; it was just a crowd of people. I stood at the counter for quite some time while the agent waited on the others. He took the person on my left and the person on my right. Soon he had waited on everyone but me. When I was the only one left, he turned away from me. An elderly couple approached the counter, and he moved to wait on them.

I turned to the couple. "Sir? Ma'am? Would you excuse me, please?"

I turned back to the agent and spoke evenly in a low tone. "Look, hot rod, you are going to sell me a ticket and you are going to do it right now—else I'm coming behind that counter and you and I are going to have a little come-to-Jesus right here. Now, what will it be?"

Fortunately, he chose the ticket.

It was evening when I arrived in Tulsa. Seeing Ann and my girls, Pam and Terri, was so exciting. Kenneth, who was only three months old when I left, was in his bed sleeping.

Ann warned me, "Don't be upset. He's afraid of men. He may shy away from you."

She went into the bedroom and brought him out, holding him in her arms. She walked to me, half turned, and spoke. "Kenneth, this is your father."

He leaned from his mother's arms and reached for me with both hands. It was magical. I took him in my arms and held him close. My wife and girls were there. My son knew me. I was home.

Chapter 26

Between Tours

I WAS ASSIGNED to Hunter Army Airfield in Savannah. In December of 1966 the Secretary of Defense had approved the Army's request to increase the number of soldiers training to fly helicopters. The Army Aviation School in Fort Rucker expanded its program to include Hunter, formerly an Air Force base. When I arrived in May of 1967, there was one helicopter on the post and no school structure at all. Soon there were hundreds of helicopters, and warrant officer and commissioned officer flight classes were graduating regularly, just days apart. With few exceptions, graduates went straight to Vietnam.

Several of my closest friends, and a number of officers I knew well, were assigned to Hunter. Bob was there, and Butch came after his tour was finished. Chuck was also assigned to Hunter. Not long after my arrival Chuck was one of the first six pilots in the Army to become instructors of the new AH-1G Cobra, the Army's exciting and dynamic new gunship. He and the others went on temporary duty to Fort Worth, Texas, to the Bell Helicopter plant to train, subsequently returning to Hunter to implement instruction at the school. It was a great job for Chuck and he was really happy about it. Bob and I were a little surprised at the assignment—pleased for him but also concerned. Chuck was our close friend and a good officer with many fine qualities, but we wondered about his ability to handle a powerful and unknown aircraft like the Cobra.

After working a few months in an administrative job assisting the lieutenant colonel in charge of training, I commanded the first

Warrant Officer Candidate company formed at Hunter. We sent the students to the flight line every morning where they trained all day. When they were not on the flight line, they were ours to feed, house, and train in other areas of military life.

My training techniques, learned as a student at OCS, were none too popular with the students or my superiors. But popularity was not an issue for me. I was aware that all my new warrant officer pilots would go to Vietnam as soon as they graduated. I wanted those in my charge to have the discipline to do what had to be done when they were flying, were under extreme pressure, could not see, and were scared out of their wits. In flight school a delicate touch with the flight controls is necessary; in combat, it can determine whether you live or die. How these new pilots handled their aircraft and themselves at critical moments would be highly dependent on personal discipline and confidence. They would need to perform instantly and decisively. I tried to instill those skills to the degree that I could.

My battalion commander informed me on more than one occasion that the Department of the Army was quite capable of writing its training curriculum and that my expertise in that area, such as it was, would be asked for if and when needed. Meanwhile, I was to confine myself to housing, administering, and teaching the benign administrative procedures we had been directed to impart.

I, *of course*, followed instructions....

Most of my students made fine warrant officers. I saw a handful of them in Vietnam on my second tour, and I was quite proud of the way they performed.

Conversely, left to me, I would have booted two of them out of school.

THE NAVAL BASE at Corpus Christi, Texas, rebuilt damaged Army helicopters. One day six of us were sent to Corpus Christi to fly six rebuilt Hueys back to Hunter.

The trip was great fun. We stopped for a night in New Orleans on the way back, the first time some of us had ever been there. We came in to the New Orleans airport at low level in tight formation, flying right up to the terminal. We were showing off a little.

The highlight for me was in Corpus Christi. After spending the night in the city we went to the naval base to find our Hueys. We pre-flighted them and got ready for the trip back to Savannah. I started my Huey. As we were running up the engines, I looked up and there she was, that number 848 on her nose. It was the machine that had carried me through Hill 534, the one I took into the trees at LZ Cat.

I would have loved to have flown her on that trip back, but it was too late for me to switch helicopters. It was enough to know that this warhorse had also made her way back home.

Chapter 27

Tommy Gerald

TOMMY SANDEFUR HAD a great personality and was probably the most handsome man I ever knew. Using his middle name, his sisters often called him Tommy Gerald. His family moved to Jenks when I was 11. We struggled through football practice together, double-dated some in high school, and I married his little sister Ann.

Tommy was favored by mother, father, his four sisters—by almost everyone who knew him. Girls loved Tommy. If you weren't getting any dates, just hang out with Tommy for a while—there were always girls around him. I was aghast when I learned he had married. I didn't think anyone would catch him.

Tommy graduated from high school in 1953 and joined the Army in 1954, eventually becoming a helicopter crew chief. In 1966 he was accepted into the Army's warrant officer program, beginning his flight training at Fort Wolters and completing it at Fort Rucker. After graduating from flight school, he was assigned to the 191st Assault Helicopter Company (AHC) and sent to Fort Bragg where the newly activated company organized and trained. Tommy and the 191st AHC arrived in Vietnam on May 24, 1967. They made their new home 22 miles northeast of Saigon at a place called Bearcat where Tommy flew Huey gunships.

Tommy's tour would be up in May of '68, and I would return to Vietnam the following October. Neva and Terrell Sandefur, Tommy's parents and my in-laws, did not get a long respite between tours.

Neva and Terrell visited us about once a year, wherever we were stationed. They would stay several days, and it was always a good

Tommy at Bearcat. 1967.

time when they were at our house. Neva was a professional pianist, a kind and sweet lady who doted on her four daughters and Tommy. Terrell had a reputation for being stern and gruff, but we got along great, and I always enjoyed his company. I recall sitting outside with him on summer evenings and talking baseball as we listened to the Tulsa Oilers on the radio. After I finished flight school he always called me "Flyboy."

In late January 1968, Neva and Terrell came to Savannah for a week-long visit. From our house they drove to LaGrange, Georgia, where Tommy's wife, Carol, and daughter, Lisa, were living while Tommy was in Vietnam. It had been just a few days since Neva and Terrell had left our house. The kitchen wall phone rang about 6 p.m.

I answered in the manner I always did. "Captain Clark."

"Ray, this is Terrell. Tommy's been killed."

"Are you sure?"

"Yes," he answered. "The officers just left. We're in LaGrange at Carol's house. We're going back to Tulsa in the morning."

"I'll have to get permission to leave," I said. "We'll be up there tonight. I'll let you know when we leave. Bye."

The news hit me hard, but my thoughts were with Ann. I was about to deliver the most devastating shock of her life. There was no way to delay or ease the pain.

Having heard my tone of voice and the cryptic conversation, she was quickly at my side, her hand to her mouth. Fear was all over her and in her voice as she asked, "What is it? What is it?"

"I just talked to your dad. Tommy's been killed."

IT DOESN'T SNOW often in Savannah, but it snowed that night. The flakes were thick and heavy as we drove northwest on I-16. I thought we might have to turn around and wait until morning, but we drove out of it about an hour out of Savannah. We spent the night in LaGrange at the home of Tommy's in-laws, then followed the Sandefurs to Tulsa the next day.

At the Sandefur home I met with an Army captain who was acting as liaison between the Army and Tommy's family. It wasn't known precisely when Tommy's body would arrive in Tulsa for burial. I was told it should be no more than a week and we would be informed when he had reached San Francisco. From there the casket would be transported by train.

I wanted to go to San Francisco and escort Tommy's body home, but Carol had agreed to allow her brother-in-law, a Marine noncommissioned officer stationed at Camp Lejeune, to perform that honorable task. I felt strongly about it but thought it would be improper to burden her further with suggestion of a change.

The casket arrived in Tulsa several days later. I went with Terrell to the funeral home in Brookside to identify Tommy's body. I stood at Terrell's side as the attendant opened the casket.

"That's not Tommy. That's not him."

As gently as I could I said, "Yes, it is, Terrell. It's Tommy."

After a moment he turned, and we walked away.

TOMMY WAS INTERRED at Tulsa's Memorial Cemetery with full military honors. "Taps" was played, a rifle salute was fired, and I presented to Tommy's wife the American flag that had draped his coffin.

Chapter 28

It Never Ends

I COMMANDED THE Warrant Officer Candidate company about six months, then was assigned to be the Student Battalion Operations officer. Scheduling training and administering activities unrelated to flying was okay, but not as satisfying as direct involvement with the troops.

I made a number of trips to the helicopter school at Fort Wolters where I briefed and prepared students for their advanced training at Hunter. I enjoyed the trips, but I was always glad to get back home to Savannah.

I came in one day from a five-day trip to Fort Wolters and walked expectantly into the house to see Ann and the children. Ann met me in the kitchen. She wore a look I didn't like.

"What is it?" I asked. "Is something wrong?"

"Ray," she said, "there's been an accident."

She began to tear up. My senses came alive as if I had heard gunfire. Accident meant aircraft accident. Aircraft accident meant death. That we were talking about it meant it was someone close. I steeled myself.

"It's Chuck," she said. "He was in a Cobra."

I braced against the kitchen countertop and dropped my head.

Oh, no. Not Chuck. Not Chuck. Not now. Goddammit! He had no business flying those fucking Cobras! Is there no end to this shit!

I went to see Bob to find out what had happened.

"He had a student," Bob said. "He was demonstrating a high-speed dive. He was nose-down in a dive at 190 knots. He didn't pull out. Drove it right into a swamp east of town. They don't know why."

"Goddammit," I said. "Fucking new aircraft! He didn't have any business in that damn Cobra. Dammit!"

Bob and I were guests of Chuck's family the day he was buried in the cemetery of his little country church near his hometown of Sylvania, Georgia.

OFFICERS WHO VOLUNTEERED for a second tour in Vietnam were promised their choice of assignment. Because I knew I was going back after 18 months, and because it would allow me to choose my assignment, I volunteered to go a month early. A battalion commander with the 101st Airborne Division had promised me command of a rifle company if I could get assigned there. This would ensure that assignment.

I requested to attend the Army's fixed-wing flight school for helicopter pilots en route to my assignment in Vietnam. I was to leave Hunter, attend the school at Fort Rucker and nearby Fort Stewart, take 30 days' leave, and then depart for Vietnam. At the school I became qualified in twin-engine airplanes and earned a standard instrument rating.

Butch and Bob were not required to go to Vietnam a second time because they were not career officers. They both left the service while at Hunter. Butch went home to Kingsport, Tennessee, and worked for Eastman Chemical Company. Bob eventually settled down in Charlotte, North Carolina, and became a captain for USAir.

Bob would travel to Tulsa to visit Ann and the kids while I was away on my second tour of duty. He would call Ann every month or so to check on them, and to check on me as well. He made sure that Ann always knew how to reach him.

This may seem a caring but otherwise inconsequential act, but I knew what he was doing. He was keeping himself in position to provide support and care for my wife and children should I be killed. I have never forgotten that.

I received Vietnam assignment orders to some obscure fixed-wing unit, but that did not worry me because of my second-tour volunteer status. I would get my choice of assignment once I reached the replacement center at Long Binh. I would choose the 101st, and soon I would have my rifle company.

Ann's mother, Neva, found a nice house for us in Tulsa on Terrace Drive, off of East 15th Street. I rented the place for Ann and the children.

All was set. In mid-January 1969, I was on my way again.

II

Oh, Stranger, Go tell America that here we lie, obedient to her orders.

—Rudy Jaramillo
B 2-12, 1966, a Spartan

Chapter 29

Return to Never-Never Land

I WAS 28. It had been almost three years since the beginning of my first tour. I was calmer, not as anxious as I had been before. By the time we arrived in Saigon the old grim, aggressive combat demeanor had fully returned.

After deplaning, we were standing around on the tarmac waiting for transportation to the replacement center. A major, apparently seeing my shoulder patch denoting a previous tour with the First Cav, came up to me. "What do we do now, Captain? Will someone come pick us up?"

"Somebody will be along directly, sir," I said. "They know we're here."

He knew I had been in Vietnam before. Because of his question, I knew he had not. He was obviously nervous, and I didn't give a damn when transportation came. We would get where we were going soon enough, as far as I was concerned.

While we waited, a U-2 spy plane taxied slowly out on the runway. He broke ground in no time. He pulled the nose of that airplane, with its long, floppy wings, nearly straight up. I had seen Air Force jocks do that, but they always leveled off to some degree pretty quickly. Most airplanes will stall and cease to fly if the takeoff angle is too steep. I was surprised to see this unwieldy-looking airplane take off like that. I watched to see how long he could hold that extreme, near-vertical attitude before leveling off. It was a beautiful, clear day with not one cloud in view. That U-2 flew completely out of sight, going almost straight up without leveling one bit. He just disappeared into the blueness of the sky. Damndest thing I ever saw.

I spent three days at the replacement center in Long Binh. I made my assignment choice the first day. There was nothing to do but sit and wait for my orders to the 101st to be published. On the third day the orders were finally posted on a bulletin board outside. I quickly scanned the list for my name.

There it was: "Ray K. Clark, OF102791, Captain, Infantry, assigned to...Division Artillery, 25th Infantry Division, Cu Chi, Republic of Vietnam."

What? 25th Infantry Division? Division Artillery?

I was shocked, then angry.

How could they do this to me? I volunteered early!

My choice of assignment had been guaranteed. Command of a rifle company was waiting for me in the 101st. I wasn't about to settle for this, but there was another problem: If I were to have any chance to get anything done about this assignment, I would somehow have to gain entrance to the headquarters building, and the doors were locked. Obviously I wasn't the first person to be unhappy about an

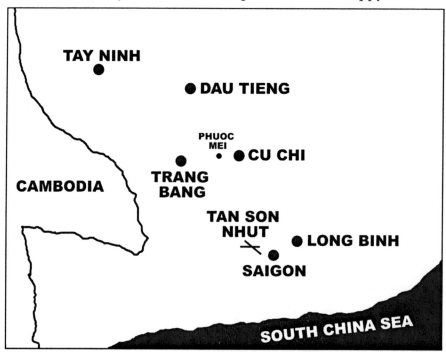

assignment. No one, regardless of rank, was allowed to enter the building where orders were issued. Furthermore, the only phones available were in that building.

I was angry—really hot—and bitterly disappointed. My heart was set on commanding that rifle company. I wanted to be in combat with the storied 101st Airborne Division that had distinguished itself in World War II, and where I had served as an enlisted man and as a second lieutenant. I went to the main entrance of the headquarters building and knocked loudly. The door was opened—and the entryway blocked—by the highest enlisted rank in the Army, a sergeant major. Angry or not, I didn't need to bully this man who was simply doing his job.

I spoke deliberately. "Sergeant Major, I would like to come in. I need to make a phone call."

"Sir, I'm sorry, but you can't come in here," he said. "No one is allowed in except those who work here."

"Sergeant Major, I understand that," I said, "but I have to make a call. Now, I would like you to let me in."

"Sir, I'm sorry, but I can't do that," he said. "I'm not allowed to."

"Sergeant Major, what's my rank?"

"Sir, you're a captain," he said.

"Yes, I am," I said. "What's your rank?"

"Sir, I'm a sergeant major."

"That's right," I said. "Now get the hell out of my way."

The good sergeant major moved aside, and I went in. I didn't feel good about treating him that way, but I had a lot at stake. I was determined to get into that building and call somebody.

I was shown to a telephone and given instructions to reach the headquarters of the 101st. The phone system was quite primitive, and I was unable to get through to the 101st or anyone who could help. After half an hour I gave up. I stalked out, muttering to myself, "Twenty-fifth Infantry Division? Division Artillery? Division Artillery? Hell, I'm an infantry officer!"

I left the next day for Cu Chi. On reaching my assignment as the Division Artillery aviation officer, I learned that even the enlisted men in the aviation section had known my name for six weeks before my arrival. So much for volunteering and guaranteed assignments.

The job at Division Artillery had its moments, but for the most part it was mundane. As a staff officer I gave a short briefing at the daily staff meeting for the colonel who commanded Division Artillery. I commanded the aviation section, which consisted of nine Hughes OH-6A light observation helicopters (LOH), a dozen or so pilots, and about 20 enlisted men, most of whom were helicopter mechanics. I was never happy about being there. As soon as I had my feet on the ground, I began to look for a new job. The division aviation officer made it clear that it would be months before he would entertain my being assigned elsewhere, so I set about making the most of what I had.

Although there's a smile on my face, I wasn't happy with my assignment. LT Bruce Holcomb, one of my best officers, and I are pictured here building a cement patio. Division Artillery, 25th Inf Div. Cu Chi 1969.

The LOH was commonly called the "Loach." This helicopter was new in the Army's inventory; I had never seen one. One of my first tasks was to learn how to fly this little machine. The instructor pilot was CPT Jerry Hicks.

Captain Hicks was a fine helicopter pilot and a real character. A popular guy, his friends missed having him around after his second tour was up. We were sorry to hear that, upon returning to Texas, his wife sued him for divorce. The Texas courts gave her what little he had. Soon after, Jerry reported to his new assignment at Fort Benning. His ex-wife sued him there too.

Jerry was irate. In the Georgia courtroom he jumped to his feet and began berating the judge for the ludicrousness of a second proceeding.

The judge, we were told, did not take kindly to a scolding in his own courtroom. "Captain Hicks, you sit down!"

"Sit down? Why, I haven't even started yet! You—"

"Captain Hicks, that'll be 50 dollars!" said the judge.

"Fifty dollars?" said Captain Hicks. "Fifty dollars! Is that all? Well, hell, judge, I'll just have me another 50 dollars' worth of that!"

And on he went. His attorney was able to seat him before he was carted off to jail. We laughed until we cried over that story.

OUR MISSION WAS mostly flying artillery forward-observers, soldiers responsible for directing artillery fire onto enemy positions. I wouldn't be flying much. Even so, I began learning from the comedian Hicks how to fly the Loach. I took my instruction as time and aircraft became available. I was still a few flight hours away from being qualified. I had three or four hours' flight time but had not yet mastered power-off landings, nor had I learned the starting procedure.

One morning soon after my arrival, I was called to the operations bunker. The firebase at Dau Tieng, about 30 miles away, had been attacked by a large force the previous night. Before they were driven off, the VC had overrun much of the compound. An even bigger attack was expected that night. I was ordered to send a helicopter up there to spend the night. The pilot would wait in the command bunker for the attack to begin. Then he and an artillery observer would dash to the helicopter and get airborne so the observer could direct fire onto the enemy force.

I gathered my young pilots and told them the situation. Because we knew there would be a fight, I asked for a volunteer. "So there it is," I concluded. "One man will have to go up there before dark, about 1700, meet the observer, get briefed, and take the observer up once the attack starts. You will wait in the command bunker until it begins, then jump in your machine, get airborne, and stay there until it's over. Who wants to go?"

There was no response—lot of looking at the floor. I couldn't believe it. I had expected five or six of them, if not all of them, to volunteer. But no one said a word.

"Look, folks, I'd go myself but I'm not checked out yet. Someone has to go, and since I can't, one of you must. Now, who will it be?"

Still not a word.

This was inconceivable to me. "Well, I am goddamn sure glad to know you people. What the hell do you think you were sent over here for? To sit on your ass while somebody else does all the dirty work? Jesus Christ! What the hell's the matter with you?"

Someone had to go up there. Being new, I didn't want to order someone into harm's way when these guys hadn't seen me go myself. It looked like an opportunity to show some leadership and possibly turn my little band of un-warrior-like warriors around.

"Okay, heroes, I'll go. I'm not checked out yet, I haven't done autorotations yet—I don't even know how to start the damn thing, but I will go. And you—all of you—stay here and sleep nice and sound in your sweet little beds!"

I turned to a lieutenant. "You. You get up there to Dau Tieng now in case they need a helicopter before we get up there. You'll be there all day."

I turned to another lieutenant. "And you. You'll fly me up there in another helicopter at 1700. We'll refuel and park it behind the command bunker. Once it is shut down, you set the throttle and all the switches except the battery switch. Fix it so that all I have to do is flick the battery switch on and pull the trigger. Then you two get your little asses back here to Cu Chi so you'll be nice and safe. Got it?"

"Yes, sir."

"Okay, that's all," I said. "Try to stay out of my sight as much as possible the rest of this day."

After the lieutenant and I flew to Dau Tieng late that afternoon, we refueled and set the aircraft down about 50 meters from the command bunker. The lieutenant set the switches and the throttle for start-up. Once the bullets started flying, the observer and I would have to run those 50 meters across a flat, wide-open space to the helicopter. I just hoped we could get airborne before the shooting started.

I went into the command bunker and got my briefing from the operations officer. I met the observer and briefed him. The attack was expected to begin sometime after midnight; I had nothing to do but sit. I was a bit tense and wished the fight would start so we could get on with it.

We waited. And waited. Daylight came, but the attack did not—at least not where I was. The large enemy force had moved past Dau Tieng in the night and hit our main base camp at Cu Chi with a major assault. My boys had experienced their first attack while I was safe in the command bunker all night. I laughed all the way back to Cu Chi.

In fairness to my guys, their reticence was primarily due to a lack of training and leadership. They subsequently proved themselves and became a strong and cohesive group.

WAR ISN'T FUNNY but funny things do happen. There were several young American women in country working for the Red Cross. Because they would stand in chow lines dishing out food, and because many were beauties, the soldiers called them "donut dollies." It often fell to us to transport one or two of these young women between firebases.

One day one of my pilots came in laughing about a donut dolly he had just flown in. He told us that when they had passed over a village west of Cu Chi, she had inquired about it.

"What is the name of that village?" she asked.

"Phuoc Mei," he replied.

"You son-of-a-bitch. You damned aviators are all alike!"

☙

Aviator sunglasses were worth their weight in gold. Nearly impossible to obtain, one new pair could buy a jeep. Somehow our supply officer, a young captain, got a whole case. I had never seen a full case of aviator sunglasses. There were 25 or 30 pairs.

The captain had a crush on a donut dolly and promised her a ride to Dau Tieng. He approached me about this. Right away I'm thinking if I play my cards right, I can get two, maybe even three pairs of sunglasses from him.

I feigned as much seriousness as I could muster in my reply. "Well, I just don't know if I can do that or not. I'm not even sure we are allowed to do that sort of thing."

I paused and studied the floor. He looked real nervous.

"But if we did," I said, "what are you offering?"

He was quiet a moment as he thought this over.

At Charlie Smoot's place. Cu Chi 1969.

Suddenly he blurted: "I'll give you a case of aviator sunglasses!"
Yes…there is a God.

♓

Not long after my arrival in Cu Chi I came face to face with Captain Charles Smoot, one of my best friends from OCS. Smoot was a great guy. He claimed he lived so far up in the mountains of West Virginia that rain running down the eastern side flowed into the Atlantic, and rain going down the western side flowed into the Mississippi.

While most of our OCS classmates became infantry officers, Charlie's background was supply, so he chose the Quartermaster branch. Finding Smoot there in Cu Chi was a stroke of fortune. Imagine owning the only Home Depot and grocery store in your city. That was the position and power my friend had. Smoot's boss, a lieutenant colonel, was in charge of all supply and logistics for the 25th Infantry Division. That meant Smoot effectively owned all the equipment and supplies in the entire division. He was also responsible for the PX—the PX owned all the beer and soft drinks.

Friends wondered how I had mahogany plywood for the inside of my hooch and a huge supply of Pepsi, my favorite soft drink.

Charlie called late one morning. "Hey, Ray, what are you up to?"

"Oh, just on my way up to maintenance to see if I can hustle those boys along," I said. "They've had one of my Loaches for three days."

"Well, look here, the general ordered 16 leather chairs for his conference room. Man, they are beauties. They are low-back captain's chairs made of mahogany and burgundy leather."

"Well, bully for him," I said. "Why the hell does he need stuff like that out here?"

"For his conference room. Guess he must have some big meetings."

"Well, good for him, Charlie. Why are you telling me all this?"

"The general ordered 16 chairs," Charlie said.

"So?"

"Ray," said Charlie, "they sent 17."

"Charles, do not move. I'll be there in five minutes."

TRAGEDY COULD COME from anywhere at any time. I was awakened by a horrendous, whining roar one morning when an enemy rocket came screaming into camp and landed about 50 meters beyond my hooch. Luckily no one was hurt. A few days later one of the enlisted men took an M-16 rifle, rushed into the Headquarters Company orderly room, and shot our first sergeant dead. He then ran into an underground bunker and killed himself.

THE DIVISION BEGAN to employ a tactic that proved tremendously successful in terms of prosecuting the war. The objective in Vietnam was not to take and hold ground, but to kill enemy soldiers until the enemy quit fighting. Score was kept by how many we killed. Thus the infamous term "body count" came about.

The Cambodian border lay fewer than 20 miles west of Cu Chi. American soldiers could not cross that line. The NVA and VC had no such restriction. Early one morning they watched a U.S. infantry company set up a circular defensive position about a kilometer from the border. The terrain there was absolutely flat and nearly devoid of vegetation, leaving our troops in plain sight. A bulldozer was flown in to push up dirt in strategic places. Soldiers placed concertina wire all around and planted mines on the approaches. Two 105mm howitzers were positioned with muzzles lowered, level with the ground. Firebases trained howitzers and powerful eight-inch guns on the area surrounding the position. During the night Air Force fighter jets, C-130 airplanes loaded with firepower, and helicopter gunships gathered, lying in wait for the attack.

After a day of feverish activity, heavy equipment and administrative personnel were pulled out. From across the border our guys appeared utterly vulnerable—sitting ducks even. It may have been the best trap American forces have ever set.

The bad guys couldn't wait. Shortly after midnight they attacked, and the ambush was triggered. From within the position, howitzers fired point-blank, discharging beehive rounds and scattering small, nail-like projectiles like mammoth shotguns. Shells from distant howitzers and the devastating eight-inch guns exploded both on the ground and in air-bursts. Helicopter gunships assaulted with rockets and machine guns. F-4 Phantom jets dropped 500-pound bombs and strafed the area with machine-gun fire. Any enemy soldier unlucky enough to get close to the position was lambasted with mines and small-arms fire.

The enemy force was devastated, some 400 bodies counted on the battlefield the next morning. As I recall, American losses were three. The strategy was used several times and was wildly successful. Hundreds of the enemy were killed in every fight. In some cases not one American life was lost.

Unbelievably, this clever tactic would be abandoned. Word was that some folks in Washington were offended. American boys should not be used as bait, they said.

What the hell were they thinking?

Chapter 30
D Troop

AS THE MONTHS went slowly by, I became good friends with MAJ Eural E. E. Adams, Jr., executive officer of the 25th Infantry Division Aviation Battalion. Major Adams was an armor officer and a good man. One day he told me he was getting command of D Troop, 3rd Squadron, 4th Cavalry. D Troop was a company-size unit of about 225 men. It was the 25th Infantry Division's only air cavalry arm. He asked me to transfer there with him as his executive officer. I was elated. It wasn't command of a company, but it would get me into a real fighting unit.

Cavalry units were commanded by armor officers, that is, those officers specifically trained for the armor branch. Armor command positions were jealously guarded by armor officers, and rightly so. There were very few air cavalry troops in Vietnam and not nearly enough command slots in the Vietnam force for all those career-minded officers who needed combat command time on their records. Command slots calling for majors were particularly hard to come by. An air cavalry troop was to be commanded by a major—more specifically, an armor major, and an experienced one at that.

The air cavalry troop executive officer was intended to be an armor captain. But the executive officer position did not require the specialized training and experience that the command position did, so it did not matter much that I was infantry and not armor. The troop command position definitely required the background and training of an armor officer. Even though I had badly wanted command of a company-sized combat unit, I had given that up. I was happy to be in this dynamic fighting unit where I could learn and experience air cavalry tactics in combat. It was a good situation for me and a huge improvement over my Division Artillery assignment.

I was assigned to D Troop in July 1969. Major Adams was to come later. Soon after I arrived I attended a meeting of officers in the squadron headquarters. As the squadron executive officer was introducing me to the staff officers and leadership of D Troop's parent unit, 3rd Squadron, 4th Cavalry, a captain sitting in the center of the group stood, interrupting the introduction, and stared straight at me.

"You're Ray Clark? You're Ray Clark?"

"Well, yes, I am. Do I know you?"

"No, but I know you. I was a lieutenant in B Company, Second of the Fifth Cav, on Hill 534 in August '66. Everybody in that company knew who you were, man. Everybody knew you."

I had no idea. It was one of my most satisfying moments.

I DIDN'T THINK much of the commander that Major Adams was to replace. Discipline was lax, and it seemed to me he spent too much time flying and not enough time commanding. That was my opinion; as such, I kept it to myself. I was delighted when Major Adams arrived a few weeks later.

My life as executive officer was pretty easy. I was able to fly a few missions, but mostly I looked after the troop when Major Adams was flying. I had enough to keep me busy, but I wasn't directly responsible for anything critical. I did my best to take full advantage of watching the commander run this unique and complex unit. The organization and tactics were unlike anything I had ever seen.

There were 175 enlisted men in the troop, including a rifle platoon for ground reconnaissance. The rifle platoon was sometimes deployed as a unit, but more often fought in 10- to 12-man teams supported by our gunships and other helicopters. There was also a crew that performed extensive maintenance on the helicopters. These enlisted men were highly trained and very competent. I had great respect for them and their abilities.

The troop also had 50 officers and warrant officers, all aviators except for one infantry lieutenant who commanded the rifle platoon.

The most important element in the troop was the unit's 25

helicopters. There were six Hueys for carrying troops, nine Loaches for scouting, and 10 Cobras for blowing hell out of almost anything.

Our job as an air cavalry troop was to find the enemy and start a fight. Most of the time we worked in small groups called "mini-cav" teams and "hunter-killer" teams. A hunter-killer team was one Loach and one Cobra. Add two Hueys and 10 to 12 riflemen and you had a mini-cav team. The Cobra would circle overhead at about 1000 feet altitude. Scout helicopters flew only five or ten feet off the ground, searching for the enemy. In the scout helicopter was one pilot, a man sitting beside him with a machine gun hanging from a bungee cord, and a man in the back seat with a box of grenades. When enemy soldiers were spotted, the man in back would throw out a smoke grenade to mark the spot. He might also throw out a hand grenade or two when close enough to the enemy, which he often was. The scout would dart away and the Cobra would roll in, placing its devastating machine gun and rocket fire on the spot marked by smoke. The Cobra pilot would call for troops. If they were a mini-cav team, the two Hueys would quickly insert our 10 or 12 men at the point of contact. If they were a hunter-killer team, the pilot would call the unit he was working for to put troops on the ground. The troops would kill or capture the enemy force or start a fight and call for more men.

Regular infantry units were able to stand down and rest every few weeks. Not D Troop. Performing reconnaissance for the entire division, we had people in harm's way seven days a week. The troop was never deployed as a cohesive unit. Consequently, it was unwieldy and difficult to manage. Mini-cav and hunter-killer teams were sent in any number of directions every day, making it difficult for the commander simply to decide where he should be.

That major had all he could handle.

ONE DAY IN November, Major Adams called for me. "Ray, I have an emergency. I'm leaving for the states at 1630 today. You will have to run the troop for two or three days until they can get somebody in here to take over. Good luck."

Going home for an emergency was generally not allowed, and I was genuinely sorry for his misfortune. However, I was quickly consumed with thoughts of my own impending problem, namely running the unit for the few days it would take for his replacement to arrive. I knew the job was too big for me. I wasn't looking forward to it, even for a few days.

I was somewhat stressed for the next few days, but I could make it until the new commanding officer arrived. Three days later we held a change-of-command ceremony for our new squadron commander, a lieutenant colonel, and I played host to the visiting high-ranking officers in attendance: four or five full colonels, including some brigade commanders, and the division chief of staff.

After the ceremony, these half dozen or so colonels were standing in a circle with the new squadron commander, congratulating and backslapping and carrying on among themselves. I simply stood there, waiting for them to leave, while I kept one eye peeled for my new commander. Perhaps he had arrived with the new squadron commander.

Unexpectedly one of the colonels—for the life of me I don't know which one—turned to me. With a big smile he loudly exclaimed, "Well, Ray, I have good news for you. We are going to give you the troop. You are the new commanding officer of D Troop!"

He grabbed my hand and began a vigorous, congratulatory handshake. Soon they all began to congratulate me, shake my hand, and pound me on the back. It was there that I had a vivid experience of being two people having simultaneous and very different conversations.

Utterly shocked, I plastered a great big smile on my face and replied in kind. "Thank you, sir. That's great, sir. Thank you, sir. Yes, sir. Yes, sir. That's just great, sir."

Oh, no. Oh, shit. Oh, fuck. Oh, no. Oh, my god. How will I do this?

"It's a great opportunity, Ray!"

"Yes, sir, it is!" I said. "It's just great!"

Oh, shit. Oh, fuck. Oh, no.

I began to know despair, impending doom coursing through my body. It was all I could do to stand straight and keep that fake smile.

"Ray, you'll be great," I heard someone say. "We've been watching you. You really deserve it. You are so lucky. This is such good fortune for you."

"Yes, sir," I said. "Thank you very much, sir. I appreciate that."
Oh, no. Oh, shit. Oh, fuck. Oh, no.

Finally they left. It was over, and I was able to stop the profanity spewing forth in my mind. Never had I considered, for a single moment, I would get permanent command of the troop.

John Wayne won the Academy Award for best actor in 1969, but surely it was I who gave the best performance.

Chapter 31

Taking Over

CAPTAINS DID NOT get command of air cavalry troops, certainly not infantry captains. Perhaps I had become a bit lazy with the artillery aviation job and then the executive officer position. Whatever the reason, I simply was not mentally prepared for the task I faced. But I wasn't about to lie down.

I went back to my little headquarters building, which served as a combination orderly room and troop commander's office, and took stock. The enlisted men wouldn't much care about the change in command. Commanders changed on a regular basis, few holding a command position longer than six months. Furthermore, officers do what officers do. For the most part they live in a world apart from the enlisted men, and they do not mingle socially. The enlisted man's job goes on regardless of who his commander is.

My official troop commander photo. Cu Chi 1969.

I figured there would be grumbling from some of the officers. Most of the commissioned officers were armor branch, and the captains in particular wanted an armor officer as commander. I didn't consider that attitude a serious threat. It was simply a leadership problem that I would have to solve. Being a captain commanding other captains did not concern me. I was senior to all of them—and I was the commander.

The main thing men want is leadership. They demand it. They may not like some of the things they have to do under a good leader, but they always admire and respect good, strong leadership. They feel safer and are more content when they have it. I felt my predecessor's leadership had not been strong enough, and his predecessor's was weak. I could not swear things would be better with me in charge, but they would be different.

In my view the troop had been run improperly. It was getting its job done, but not functioning as I thought it should. My 50 officers and warrant officers were giving far too many directions to the enlisted men, bypassing the NCOs. NCOs run the army. Any unit is as good as its NCOs and no better. My NCOs were not doing their jobs because officers were pushing them out of the way.

Every day we sent recon teams to support combat units in the division, and almost every day teams were late reaching their assignments. Lieutenants were going into enlisted quarters and routing troops out of bed. Often those troops were confrontational—that was not tolerable. The mess hall was poorly run, and the food was below par. While the helicopter mechanics and maintenance personnel were excellent, we did not have a strong maintenance officer.

Nothing stopped because there had been a change of command. We did not get a day off to reorganize, and few knew or cared that I was the new commanding officer. The missions had to go out the next morning, and the war kept right on moving.

I kept moving too, but faster and with a hell of a lot more purpose.

MY FIRST NIGHT as CO I had a meeting with the officers in the operations building. The purpose was to assert my leadership.

"Gentlemen. As all of you know by now, Major Adams is not coming back and a new major is not coming in. I am the CO now. Now, Major Adams was the epitome of a commander. He was always calm, cool, and laid-back. He never got excited. Well, boys, Major Adams is gone. I'm the CO now. And you can bet your sweet ass that I goddamn well get excited! And when I get excited, you had better damn well be excited too!

"Now, let's look at a few things. Every single day one or more mini-cav teams are late reporting to their assignments. Those days are over. Never again will any one of you ever be late reporting to another unit for a mission. For every mission, you are issued a start time, a takeoff time, and a reporting time to your assignment. All you have to do is start up when you are supposed to start up, take off exactly when you are supposed to take off, and that will put you at your assignment on time. I do not want to hear of anyone being late ever again.

"Now, every day, I get a copy of all the missions and all the takeoff times. Starting at 0530 tomorrow morning, I will be standing right outside the maintenance hangar every day as you take off. If you are late taking off, I will see it, and I will know it. 5:30 takeoff means 5:30 takeoff. It does not mean 5:31 or 5:30-and-one-half. It means 5:30. If you are late—ever—you will deal with me when you get in. A professional unit, a good unit, is never late. We are professional, and we are good. And we will not be late again.

"Some of you are going into the EM hooches and routing men out of bed. Do not do that. That's what you have NCOs for. Have them do that sort of thing if it's necessary. Some of these men are about half-mean. You open yourself up to all sorts of problems when you expose yourself that way. Use your NCOs. Stop trying to run privates around. You fly your machines. The NCOs will handle the troops.

"Now, listen, with me you are going to get exactly what you deserve. You do your job and do it to the best of your ability, and you will hear nothing but praise from me. You are going to fuck up from time to time. We all do. It isn't easy out here. If you are doing your job and you are doing your best and you fuck up, don't worry about it. You'll hear nothing from me. But if you are goofing off and you are not doing your job and you fuck up, you can bet your sweet ass we'll talk about that. You and I will deal when you get in. If you go out and you earn the Medal of Honor, I'll damn well bust my ass to get it for you. And if you goof off at your job and you fuck up, I'll be sure you pay the price.

"So you decide how it is going to be for you. I decide nothing. I will just be damn sure you get what you ask for. You are all damn good men. There is no reason there should ever be any trouble between us. You do your job the best you can, and I will be with you 100 percent every day.

"Now, what we do with each other and what we say to each other where problems are concerned stays right here inside this unit. I may be all over your ass about something and maybe I'll give you holy hell. But when it is over, it is over. When I go outside this unit and talk to the colonel or anyone, I'll have nothing but good and positive things to say about you. What we do and say among ourselves in handling our problems is no one else's damn business. When I am outside this unit, everything I say about you and D Troop will be strong and positive. Now, you and I may have a little prayer meeting or two when we get back here at night. But that's our business—no one else's. I will always speak positively about you outside this unit, no matter what is going on here. And I expect the same from you. If you have a heartache with something that is going on here, you come see me and we'll work it out. But outside the unit, I want nothing but good words.

"You work for me and I'll work for you. You remember that when you are out there and you are doing your job as best you can, I will stand up for you no matter what. As long as you are doing your job, do not worry if you fuck up. Just fix it as fast as you can and let me know about it so I can handle it.

"That's all I have. Any questions? Okay. That's all."

I was in a position I thought was beyond my ability. I truly did not know if my best would be good enough. All I could do was give it everything I had. There would be mistakes, some by my officers and men, and some by me. There would be crashes, there would be crises, men would be killed. I knew these things were coming. I *knew* they were coming.

As I thought it through, I began to accept what I knew was to come. Surprisingly, I began to feel calm about having command of this dynamic and difficult unit. It would require all of my strength, all of my attention, and all of my being. The supreme test of my capability as an officer and my character as a man was underway.

FIRST SERGEANT HENRY gathered the noncommissioned officers.

I was brief and to the point. "I'll make this short. I've been around here for a while. I know all of you. You're a damn fine bunch.

And the truth is you haven't been doing your jobs. All these lieutenants have been trying to do them for you. You and I know that doesn't work. Well, that bullshit is over. I have instructed the officers to stay the hell out of the enlisted man business. You and I know that without the NCOs running their units and, for the most part, the troop, nothing works. Hell, without you all, the rest of us are just out here running around whistling Dixie. As I see it, you all have not been allowed to do your jobs. Well, that bullshit's over too. I am holding you to the same standard I hold the officers to. That means you do your job, and do it the very best you can, and I will be on your side like no one you have ever seen before.

"Now, I want you to start running your units like you know how to do. If any of my officers get in your way, you let me know. This troop will never be worth a damn until you all are doing what you are supposed to be doing, and that is running this goddamn unit. You got any problems the first sergeant can't handle, you come to me.

"Any questions? All right, go to work."

Their faces had brightened as I talked. I was sure this was the best thing I could have done. The NCOs' shift in attitude would spread throughout the troop. That would go a long way toward achieving the level of performance that I wanted.

I KNEW THE enlisted men would test me. It didn't take long.

The first sergeant came in the next morning. "Sir, we have three men AWOL."

I couldn't believe it. "What? AWOL? How the hell does anyone go AWOL in Vietnam?"

"Well, sir," he said, "we think they went to Saigon. It's happened before. They'll be back in a day or two."

"They'll be back in a day or two? No shit! You find those young heroes and get them in here."

The next day First Sergeant Henry brought them in. I read them their rights and issued the first three of eleven Article 15s that I would give in my first two weeks as CO. I also handed out three courts-martial in that time. Apparently the boys got the message. After those two weeks, there were no more disciplinary problems.

For minor disciplinary issues, Article 15 was a punitive action that I had authority to issue as I saw fit. The punishment could be two weeks' restriction, two weeks' extra duty, a fine of up to a month's pay, or a combination of the three. Restriction or extra duty in the combat zone didn't have much bite, but there is universal pain in the pocketbook. I used the fine almost exclusively.

Court-martial was another matter. That could put a soldier in jail and/or result in a less-than-honorable discharge—serious stuff. I could bring charges, but the outcome was up to higher authority. The requirements of administration were time-consuming and seemingly nonproductive. It had not occurred to me that I would have to deal with such problems in a combat zone. Even so, they were nothing compared to the frustration I felt from the rules that we were ordered to follow in our conduct of combat. I had so many rules to follow—more specifically, rules for my men to follow—that it got in the way of fighting the war.

Every officer and soldier had to follow the "rules of engagement." This idea was new to us. Basically these rules covered when we could—or could not—fire on the enemy. This might be entirely logical to some politician back in Washington, but to the tough, young Americans out there in the rice paddies and jungles going toe-to-toe with a cunning and well-armed enemy soldier, it was lunacy.

There were times when we were allowed to shoot at our discretion and times when we could not—unless we called higher authority and got permission. *Permission?* I couldn't believe it. The VC wore civilian clothes: It was impossible to know if a Vietnamese man, woman or child was on your side or was planning to kill you. The only way to be certain was to let them try.

I was fundamentally opposed to that option for my boys and me. I followed the rules when I could. When there was a judgment call to be made, I opted for the lesser risk to my young Americans. If you give your enemy the edge in battle, you will die. You *will* die. It was important to me that we not kill or injure a noncombatant. It was more important that none of my boys be killed.

I spent an inordinate amount of time drilling new officers and soldiers on the rules of engagement. It was quite possible for a man to come into the unit, face the terror and risks of combat for months on end, acquit himself in splendid manner, and then face disciplinary action for an incident of firing without permission. I hated that, but it was the reality we faced.

THE VC AND North Vietnamese were smart fighters. They stayed out of sight, fighting only when they thought they'd win. Simply finding them could be a chore. Finding them and starting a fight was what D Troop was all about.

The lead men in that endeavor were the scout pilots. These daredevil jocks were fearsome young fighters. The scout pilots searched for the enemy in camouflaged holes dug in the ground, caves, and other ambush sites. Receiving enemy fire from point-blank range was often how the enemy was found. In D Troop the scout pilots were only 19 or 20 years old. As far as I know, we never had one longer than six months. They either got hit or they just wore out. Theirs was the most dangerous of jobs, and they loved it. They were brave as hell. They seemed oblivious to the extreme danger they faced, but they understood—they were simply up to the challenge.

While the scouts were high-spirited, aggressive, and filled with youthful flamboyance, the gunship pilots were deadly. As a rule, Cobra pilots were a more sober, intense and dangerous bunch, perhaps reflecting their greater age, experience, and the lethal power they wielded. They were like unknown assassins, quietly strolling the sky in their deadly machines. From nowhere they would strike, suddenly and violently, a flurry of rockets and super-rapid machine gun fire obliterating whatever was in the path of their wrath.

I had no time in the Cobra. I flew only a couple of orientation flights to get a feel for the aircraft. I had become proficient in the LOH, but it was not where my experience and expertise lay. I flew the Huey when I flew.

In a Huey I could lead a mission and stay in constant radio contact with Operations. If I were needed elsewhere, I typically could be on my way immediately. The physical presence of a commander is often the difference in the outcome of his troops's endeavors. I tried always to be where I was needed most. Some days I would lead an important mission. Other days I would be in the operations center, monitoring those missions. If aircraft availability were critical, I was in Maintenance. If parts were slow to arrive I worked on that.

Every day the goal was to have four Hueys, seven Loaches, and six Cobras ready to fly. That was not so easy, considering all that could ground an aircraft. For every 25 hours a Huey or Cobra flew, there were mandatory, 2 1/2-hour inspections. For every 100 hours of flying, there was a 24-hour inspection required in which our maintenance men took the engine apart, then put it back together. The LOH inspections were scheduled every 300 flight hours.

In addition to the downtime for routine maintenance, there were accidents, common mechanical problems, and damage from enemy fire. It was a challenge every day to have enough aircraft to fly the missions.

ONE OF MY best warrant officers came to see me the second day of my command. He was 32 years old, married, and the father of three small children. Experienced and dependable, he was a fine pilot. He was an American doing the dirty work his country had bade him do while so many at home were castigating their military men as faceless entities—as if there were no 32-year-old married men with three children fighting this war for America.

I could see that he was upset. "What's on your mind?"

"Sir, read this letter, please."

It was from his wife. My heart fell as I read. She was pregnant. He had not seen her in 10 months. What was he to do? What was *I* to do? Even though it did happen on rare occasion, policy was soldiers were not to be sent home for personal or family problems. The entire force would be sent home if that were allowed. Rules or not, in my judgment this man needed to be sent home.

"That's a tough nut," I said. "I'm sorry. Listen, I have to ground you. I don't want you flying for a few days."

"Okay, sir," he said.

"Have you seen the chaplain?"

He looked down as he spoke. "No, sir, I haven't."

"I would recommend that, but that is up to you. You know that no one is allowed to go home over something like this, do you not?"

"Yes, sir, I know," he said quietly.

"Well, I don't know that I can do anything about it, but I'll see if there's any possibility we can get you out of here. But don't count on it. It isn't likely to happen."

"Okay, sir."

I handed the letter back to him. "You go on back to your hooch, and I'll let you know when I find something out."

OH-6A Light Observation Helicopter, a scout ship, D Troop 3/4 Cav. Cu Chi 1969.

I figured there were two people who could get this done: One was the division commander, and the other was the division chaplain. Going through the chain of command to get to the division commander would take days or weeks and would not likely be successful in the end. But the chaplain: This would be his cup of tea. It would only take more time to consult with the chaplain at squadron level, so I got into my jeep and drove to division headquarters. I found him in his office and told him of this fine warrant officer's plight.

"Sir, if anyone ever needed to go home, this man does. Is there anything we can do to get him out of here?"

The chaplain looked out his window for a moment, then turned to me. "Get him up here to see me right away. We'll have him out of here by noon tomorrow."

"Sir, that is great," I said. "Thank you so much. You don't know how much I appreciate this."

"Just get him up here," the chaplain said.

"Yes, sir!"

Sure enough, he went home the next day. It would not be a joyous homecoming for him, but at least he could face his problem head on. That was all I could do for him.

D Troop, 3/4 Cav AH-1G Cobra gunship and a group of D Troop fighters. Cu Chi, early 1969.

NOT ONE MISSION had been late since I had taken over. The officers and NCOs were responding. They really went to work after I talked to them and told them what I expected. Morale was rising quickly as the unit began to come alive. I was gratified to see it, but it gave me no reason to relax. There was still a long way to go to get the troop where I wanted it.

One Sunday morning I decided to sleep in. The operations officer on duty awakened me a few minutes ahead of schedule. A Cobra flying a routine morning patrol had crashed at 6:50. Both pilots were killed on impact.

I flew to the site right away. The bodies had already been removed by medevac. The aircraft commander was a 25-year-old blond-headed captain. He had just 30 days left on his tour. His gunner/pilot was a young warrant officer. The once-ominous flying machine lay half-buried in the ground. The main rotor shaft had sheared, and they had plummeted to the ground. What a way to die—free-falling from 1500 feet. I could not imagine the terror they must have felt in those last moments.

There had been no enemy action of any type. Accident investigators were unable to determine what caused the blades to shear. All we knew for sure was that we had lost two fine young Americans.

Chapter 32

I Just Love Ammunition

"SIR, WE HAVE a trooper on special duty down at the airfield," First Sergeant Henry told me late one morning. "Been there a few months, I guess. Anyway, they're sending him back to us. Seems he took an M-16 while he was on guard duty the other night and shot up the whole place. Nobody got hurt, but he nearly killed some of our own people."

"He sounds like a nut case," I said. "Do we have to take him?"

"Yes, sir, we do," Henry said. "There is no place for him to go, and they won't keep him. He is a certified nut, sir. They have tried twice to send him out of country for mental reasons, but they keep sending him back."

That didn't make sense. "What do you mean 'they keep sending him back'?"

"It takes two psychiatrists to send a man home for psychiatric reasons," he said. "Our division psychiatrist signed off on him and sent him to Saigon to the psychiatrist there. All he had to do was sign off on him and he would have been shipped out right then, but he sent the crazy son-of-a-bitch back to us—twice! Said he was okay."

"Okay, my ass!" I said. "It doesn't sound like he's okay. When's he coming?"

"He's coming today, sir. Be here in about an hour."

"What's his name?" I asked.

"His name's Delaney, sir," he said. "He's a private."

"Well, that's no damn surprise. Bring him in when he gets here, Top. I want to talk to him."

Later that day First Sergeant Henry brought Private Delaney in to see me. I invited him to sit with me, and we talked for several minutes while I learned as much as I could about him. All the while he held in his hand several rounds of small arms ammunition. That was strange, I thought. He had no reason to have those rounds in his possession.

I tried to keep my tone familiar and non-threatening. "Why are you carrying those bullets?"

He looked down at the rounds in his hand and quietly replied. "Sir, I just love ammunition."

"I see," I said. "Well, I don't want you to have any trouble around here, all right? If anything goes wrong or you start to get upset about something, you come straight here and let me know, okay?"

"Okay, sir, I will," he said.

"Okay, that's all. I'll see you later."

"Okay, sir."

This young man was different. I didn't want him to have access to a firearm. The first sergeant and I decided to keep him around the company area a few days before assigning him a permanent duty. I wanted a better look at this kid.

I GOT TOGETHER with the chaplain and scheduled a memorial service for the two men killed in the Cobra. We had to squeeze it in between missions late in the day. We finished flying about 5 p.m. We had to get dinner and take off at 6:10 to fly to Dau Tieng to conduct a night assault. After chow and about 20 minutes before takeoff time, we gathered in our small chapel to honor those two fine, young Army aviators lost in combat.

Earlier, in my hooch, I had considered and prayed about what I would say. To the extent that I could, I wanted to comfort and encourage the men. As I opened my New Testament, the pages fell to the book of John. I scanned the page, and there was the story of Lazarus. It seemed perfect. I wrote my message in about five minutes.

As we gathered in the chapel, there were two pairs of boots and two flight helmets on a table beside the lectern.

The chaplain said a few words, and then it was my turn. "It is very difficult for us when we lose a comrade to death. We don't understand, in spite of the books we've read and the studies that have been made. It's difficult for us because we lose them to life as we as human beings know life. These were good men; they were good soldiers and fine officers. They achieved the heights during their lives. Yes, I say they achieved the heights. They accomplished their dreams, something not all men do. They were Army aviators, combat aviators. They flew the skies. They were masters of one of the most powerful and most exciting machines on earth. They gave their lives for freedom. And what is more noble, they gave their lives for freedom for people—of another country, for people—of another race, for people—of another color. They were volunteers.

"We mourn our loss, but we do not grieve. No, we do not grieve. And the reason we do not grieve is summed up in one statement made many, many years ago. A man was talking to a woman about the death of her brother who had just recently died. He said to her, 'I myself am the Resurrection and the Life. He who believes in me will live, even though he dies. And he who lives and believes in me will never die at all.' It is for these men, and for this Man, that you and I carry on."

I paused for a long moment. "Start time is in 10 minutes. Let's get moving."

THOSE OF US flying the night mission went directly to the flight line. We flew to Dau Tieng, arriving about a half hour before dark. I went to the infantry battalion command post to be briefed for the night's operation.

The battalion had just completed an operation in the nearby Bo Loi Woods, a haven for the Viet Cong. On my office wall hung a map with red pins marking the location of every D Troop helicopter that had been lost since D Troop had been at Cu Chi. The Bo Loi Woods area was a near-solid sea of red. Although the battalion's operation was complete, there were about 15 men still out there in the woods. The commander wanted them out of there before dark. I was asked to go out, find them, and bring them back in.

I was given map coordinates for their location. The problem was that these people were on the ground under the cover of thick rainforest with no way to mark their location. They had run out of smoke and had no lights. We had to find them and get them to a clearing where we could pick them up, and we were running out of daylight.

A helicopter is a sitting duck for small arms fire at two or three hundred feet altitude. We either got right down on top of the treetops and flew fast, or we climbed to a thousand feet or more. I would have to locate these GIs from several hundred feet up while trying to peer down through the tree cover.

Fortunately an Air Force Forward Air Controller (FAC) flying his fast, little, twin-tailed airplane over the troops knew where they were. I made radio contact with the troops and with the FAC. The troops tried to direct me, but I couldn't see them. The FAC tried as well, but it didn't help. I was just too high to see down into those thick woods. The FAC would make low passes at them to try to show me where they were. We tried and tried but had no success.

Darkness began to fall. I had to make a decision.

I talked to my three trailing helicopters. "Centaur 2-5, this is Centaur 6. I'm going down there and find those guys. You all stay up here until I find them, and then I'll call you, and you can come on down and we'll pick 'em up."

"This is 2-5. Roger."

I flew down to a hundred feet or so, and again following the FAC's directions, began looking for them. After a couple of minutes I saw arms waving. Then I was able to make out three or four men.

"Okay, Rag Man 6, I gotcha," I said. "I'm gonna find a place to land and I'll be right back."

I flew up another a hundred feet or so and spotted a small clearing about 150 meters north of where the men were. "Rag Man 6, this is Centaur 6. There is a clearing about 150 meters straight north of you. You start that way and I'll help you along."

"This is Rag Man 6. Roger. We'll start that way. It's gonna take us a few minutes to get over there. It's gettin' pretty dark down here."

"This is Centaur 6. Roger. We aren't going anywhere."

Moving on foot in jungle terrain or heavy rainforest can be slow-going, especially in darkness. In minutes the darkness would prevent us from giving them any further directions. How was I going to get them into that clearing? I could think of only one way to guide them—show them a light. I didn't want to hover down in that clearing and turn a bright light on, but hovering over the treetops would have been worse. If bad guys were there and I turned a light on, we were shot. Period.

"Rag Man 6, this is Centaur 6. I'm gonna move over there and drop down in that clearing and turn my searchlight on for you. I'll turn it on for a moment and then turn it off again. We don't need any spectators other than you. Over."

"This is 6. Roger. That would really help."

"This is Centaur 6. You just move as quickly as you can and keep talking to us as you get closer. I don't want any surprises. Over."

"This is Rag Man 6. Roger. We will."

I lowered the chopper down into the clearing and turned the searchlight on for a few seconds.

"Rag Man 6, how you coming?"

"I think we're about 50 meters."

"Roger."

I turned the light on again, then turned it right back off. I peered intently into the darkness.

This may be the dumbest thing I have ever done.

"Centaur 6, this is Rag Man 6. We're really close now. Could we see the light one more time? Over."

"Roger, Rag Man 6. You keep talking to me all the way in. Over."

On the UHF frequency, I called my other helicopters. "You all come on down here one at a time and pick up a load as soon as you see me lift out. I'll wait for you up top."

"Roger, 6. We're watching."

"Centaur 6, this is Rag Man 6. We're right on you. We're right on you. We're there."

To my left front, troops stepped into the small clearing. I flashed the light on them briefly to make sure they were GIs. "Get 'em on here, 6. Let's get out of here. Two other choppers will be down just as soon as I lift off."

"Roger, 6, roger!"

I could hear relief in his voice.

Six men loaded and we lifted up out of the clearing. Another chopper landed, loaded, and left, and then another.

They were all safely out. Not a shot had been fired. The next day I learned that the area was a Viet Cong battalion base camp.

We dropped the troops at their unit and I went to see the infantry battalion operations officer who had been listening on the radio as the operation unfolded. I assumed he had more work for us to do.

"That's all we have for you, Captain. You can go on back to Cu Chi. By the way, damn good job you did out there. I'm putting you in for the Distinguished Flying Cross."

"Uh, okay, thank you, sir. Let us know if you need us."

I never knew how to respond to such a statement. I turned and left.

Distinguished Flying Cross, huh? Fat chance of that. His intention seems good, but that is the last I will hear of that.

And so it was. Those guys were busy as hell.

WE FLEW BACK to Cu Chi, arriving about 10 p.m. I checked in at Operations and found the first sergeant waiting for me.

"Sir, we got a problem. That guy Delaney got hold of some mortar rounds somewhere and threw two or three up on top of the NCO hooch. Tried to kill 'em."

"What? Well, goddamn! They didn't go off, did they?"

It would be highly unlikely, if not impossible, that a mortar round could be detonated that way.

"No, sir, they didn't go off," he said, "but it scared the hell out of some people."

"Where is this young hero now?" I asked.

"The MPs came and got him, sir," he said. "They said they would keep him overnight."

"Overnight, my ass! We'll lock his little ass up for good. We can't have people running around here trying to kill NCOs!"

"Sir, we have to go get him in the morning," he said. "The MPs say they won't keep him."

"What? The hell they won't," I said. "We'll see about that."

I went to the MP station the next day to see what I had to do to get this troubled young soldier locked up. As usual, the first sergeant was right: There was no jail and no means for any type of detention. If Delaney were considered a psychiatric case, there were procedures for that. Otherwise, I was to keep him in the unit. There were no other avenues.

Clearly the young man was mentally unbalanced. He was a physical threat to my soldiers and aviators who were fighting the war. I dared not arm him and put him in the field. I had to keep him under direct supervision 24 hours a day to make sure he didn't hurt anyone. This was intolerable. I couldn't afford the wasted manpower or the distraction. We were taking our share of casualties, and there were 225 well-intentioned young men who needed and deserved my attention.

I got the flight surgeon and the division psychiatrist to recommend that he be sent home. They sent him to Saigon to see the psychiatrist there to corroborate their recommendation. Delaney was interviewed and pronounced fit for duty. I was livid, but I could see nothing else to do. I put him under 24-hour direct supervision and went about my work.

Late that afternoon one of the mini-cav teams set off a booby trap while on a sweep in the rice paddies west of Cu Chi. Five of our men were seriously wounded, along with two Kit Carson scouts (former Viet Cong who had come over to our side). Two others suffered minor injuries. By the time I was notified, the wounded were already on their way to the field hospital at Cu Chi. I got in my jeep and beat it down there as quickly as I could.

I entered the emergency room to find five of my boys lying on gurneys, waiting for surgery. Their wounds were not more than 15 minutes old. Understandably, they were agitated and emotional. I stood beside a kid from Miami, Oklahoma. His feet and legs were full of shrapnel. He was cursing repeatedly, excitedly telling me what had happened. A big, beefy female nurse walked over and began giving him hell for cursing in her presence.

I couldn't believe it. "You stupid son-of-a-bitch! Don't you ever talk to my boys like that! You get your overgrown ass out of here!"

She turned and left the room like a scalded dog.

I was shocked at her behavior. The nurses I had encountered were the most compassionate and caring souls imaginable. As for me, I was so livid, so unprepared for her, that "you stupid son-of-a-bitch" was out of my mouth before I knew it.

After surgery the boys were flown to a better equipped and staffed hospital in Japan. As usual, we didn't see them again.

HOVERING HELICOPTERS CAN raise a lot of dust and dirt. I needed the asphalt-like substance we called "pentaprime" to be poured around my hangar and aircraft maintenance area.

"First Sergeant, we need pentaprime out there around that hangar area in the worst way," I said. "Let's write up a request and see how fast we can get it through channels."

"Sir, that request for pentaprime has been in for six months," he said. "Either they don't have it or we are just too far down the list."

"Bullshit, they're pouring the goddamn stuff all over Cu Chi," I said. "They have it. Some goddamn hidebound engineer just won't let loose of it."

Apparently, following established procedure was not going to work. Cu Chi was the size of a small city; there was construction going on all the time. The man in charge of the pentaprime would be an American civilian, a construction man, a man not unlike my dad. I set out to find this person.

It didn't take long. As I walked into the civilian supply and construction area, it was easy to see who was in charge. He was 45 or 50 years old and was obviously a construction hand. He had that gruff, no-nonsense air of I'm-just-too-damn-busy-but-I-can-handle-it attitude common to construction foremen and oilfield superintendents.

I walked up to him. "Sir, are you in charge here?"

He looked at me sternly, probably for calling him "sir."

"Yes, I am," he said. "What can I do for you, Captain?"

"Well, I'm running that unit down there by the airfield, the one on the east side with the big hangar," I said. "It's D Troop, Three Quarter Cav. I need some pentaprime down there around that hangar area real bad. If you've got time, do you think maybe you could get me some pentaprime down there in the next day or two?"

He studied me a moment. Something clicked. Maybe I reminded him of someone, as he reminded me of my dad. "Well, I don't see why not. I think we might be able to get down there tomorrow afternoon sometime."

"Man, I sure would appreciate that," I said. "I can't tell you how much that will help me out. By the way, I got 25 helicopters down there. Anytime you want to go to Saigon or anywhere else, I'm pretty damn sure we can find you a ride."

He grinned and stuck out his hand. "I just might take you up on that."

"Anytime. You just let me know."

As I expected, he kept his word. The next afternoon, about 3 p.m., one of his crews rolled in and did the job.

Some would say that you can't run the Army that way. Established procedure must be followed; otherwise there is no discipline, only chaos. My boys were fighting the war. They were in harm's way seven days a week. I didn't much give a damn about someone else's procedure.

Chapter 33

Sweet Talk

I HAD A cold that was making me dizzy, so I went to see the flight surgeon, who was a captain and my friend.

"Well, Ray, you have a bad cold," he told me. "Here, take these APCs (tablets containing aspirin, phenacetin and caffeine). If it keeps bothering you, come on back."

I walk in with a cold, he tells me I have a cold. Standard treatment—APC and if I die, come back.

"Damn, Doc, I know I got a cold," I said. "I've had the damn thing for three weeks. It's making me dizzy. I need to be out flying. If these damned APCs were going to do anything, I believe it would have happened by now. Don't you have anything that will work?"

"Yeah," he said. "Go get some rest."

"I'm not taking you anywhere else, Doc," I laughed. "You're going to have to walk everywhere you go in Vietnam from now on—everywhere you go. And I am going to find some more crazies for you. Rest, my ass. See you later."

About half an hour before midnight, I walked into my hooch to go to bed. A huge mosquito was buzzing around my head. I aimed a can of GI bug spray at him and he fell from midair like he was shot. Scratch one VC mosquito.

Before I could sit down, a trooper burst through my door.

"Sir, Delaney's right outside! He's got a grenade in each hand and he's talking crazy. He wants to see you, sir."

This nutcase—with a grenade in each hand?

I felt like a tank was bearing down on me at full speed.

"Christ! Where is he?"

"Right around the corner on the walkway, sir," the trooper said.

"Okay," I said. "You stay here."

I walked outside and around the corner of the hooch. There stood Delaney, his arms hanging loosely at his sides. He held a live grenade in

My hooch at D Troop 3/4 Cav. Initial evening conversation with Delaney took place on this walkway. Cu Chi 1969.

each hand. It was dark, but I could see that the pins were pulled from the grenades. If he let go of either of them, it would explode in three to five seconds. I walked up to him casually, stopped about three feet in front of him, and spoke gently. "Delaney, you all right?"

"No sir, I don't think so," he said quietly.

"What's wrong?" I asked.

"I don't like it here, sir."

"Yeah, I know," I said. "I don't like it here either. Maybe we'll all get to leave here one of these days and go home. What are you doing with those grenades?"

"Oh, I'm just holding 'em," he said.

"Well, you know the pins are out of them," I said. "If you drop one, it's going to go off."

"Yes, sir, I know," he said.

"Well, let's be careful. We don't want anybody to get hurt here."

I was getting nowhere. We were right in the middle of the officers' sleeping area; a grenade could do a lot of damage. This was a job for the MPs, but I couldn't instruct anyone to call them without upsetting Delaney. Of all things, I wanted him to stay calm.

"Delaney, you want some gum?"

"Yes, sir, I'll take some," he said.

"Okay," I said, "I have some right inside my hooch. Let me just go in there and I'll get us some. Okay?"

"Okay, sir."

"Now, you stay right here, all right?" I said. "I'll just be a minute. I need you to stay right here, though. Okay?"

"Okay, sir."

"All right," I said. "I'll be right back."

I moved quickly inside, picked up a pack of gum, and called the MPs. "Listen, this nutcase Delaney that you people refuse to lock up is standing right outside my hooch holding two grenades with the pins pulled. He's dangerous as hell. I want you to get somebody down here right now and collect this crazy son-of-a-bitch."

"Okay, we'll get someone there right away."

"Good," I said. "Now, look, don't come racing down here with sirens blazing and make a big show. You've gotta be quiet about this. Come in the back way and come quietly. This guy could hurt a lot of people. I don't want him getting scared or excited. Got it?"

"Got it, sir. We'll be right there."

"Good," I said. "I'll try to keep him right here."

I hung up the phone.

Boom!

Oh shit! That's a goddamn grenade! Jesus, I hope he didn't kill anybody!

I ran for the door. The sound came from the direction of the operations building. I ran as hard as I could go.

As I passed a sandbag bunker, I saw a soldier in the darkness. "Did you see what happened?"

"Yes, sir!" he said. "Delaney walked by the bunker here, sir, with some grenades, and someone tried to take them away from him. He dropped one and it fell in the bunker and went off!"

"No one was hurt?" I asked.

"No, sir! We were lucky as hell, sir!"

A grenade goes off...and it falls into a bunker?

I was so relieved. Seeing there was a big commotion beside the maintenance hangar, I raced past the operations building. A crowd of 40 or 50 men had gathered to the right of the hangar and were standing in a big circle. The area was partially lit from an outdoor light on the hangar. As I came up behind my men, I was initially relieved to see the MPs. As I stopped to assess the situation, I saw that the MPs were doing precisely what I told them not to.

It looked like a movie scene. At the center of the crowd stood Delaney. He must have had a third grenade in his pocket because he'd dropped one and still had one in each hand. Three military police jeeps surrounded him, their lights shining on him. MPs walked around the inside of the circle, watching him, the crowd of soldiers still forming an outer circle around the scene.

He looked like a frightened deer.

Suddenly one of the MPs rushed Delaney from behind and tried to pin his arms. Delaney whirled and, still holding the grenades, bodily threw the man off him. He turned and began striding away toward the helicopters that were parked in two long rows just beyond the hangar.

I was sure that a physical confrontation was absolutely the wrong thing, and clearly the MPs' use of force had failed. My men standing around either did not care or had not considered the danger they were in from the grenades. Delaney himself was in danger. I could not let him walk into the midst of my helicopters, or anywhere else for that matter, carrying those grenades with the pins pulled.

The situation was rapidly careening out of control. I had to do something.

As I moved through the gathering of men and into the center of the crowd, I yelled at him. "Delaney! This is Captain Clark!"

He stopped and turned to face me. "Yes, sir."

I was relieved to see him stop and answer, and was thankful for the time I had spent establishing a relationship with him.

I walked up to him, speaking in a casual tone. "What are you doing?"

"Sir, I'm going to kill myself," he said.

"Why?"

"Because nobody cares about me, sir," he said.

"I care about you," I said.

"No, you don't, sir. Nobody cares about me."

If he released his grip on either of the grenades, I would have those three to five seconds to react before they exploded. If he dropped one I would turn, take two or three steps and hit the ground. If I were facing away from him, perhaps the shrapnel would tear up only my legs.

"Well, now, I wouldn't be standing here beside you, and you with a grenade in each hand ready to go off, if I didn't care about you, would I?" I said. "Of course I care about you."

"Sir, I'm going to kill myself," he repeated.

"Well, now, let's don't do that," I said. "Why don't you let me take you to the doctor? Would you like to get a shot so that you feel better?"

He had been sedated by the flight surgeon after violent episodes in the past.

"Let me have the grenades, and I'll take you to the doctor."

"No, sir," he said. "You can't have the grenades. The MPs will get me."

"No, they won't," I said. "I won't let the MPs get you. I'll take you to the doctor myself. I'll take care of you."

"No, sir."

The conversation went on like that for about 20 minutes. During that time the squadron executive officer, a major, walked out and stood beside us. I didn't want him there. I thought that could be intimidating to the young man and detrimental to the situation. And I didn't know if he would follow my lead. He tried to help, but Delaney would have none of it.

I continued talking gently. "Would you like to have a shot so that you wake up feeling good?"

"Yes, sir, I guess so," he said.

"Let me have the grenades, then, and I'll take you to the doctor."

"No, sir, you can't have the grenades, sir," he said.

"Well, okay," I said, "if you won't let me have the grenades, will you throw them so we get rid of them and no one gets hurt?"

"Yes, sir, I guess so—if you'll take me to the doctor."

"Fine. I'll take you to the doctor," I said.

I was taking a risk, having him throw the grenades with so many people nearby, but it was my first break with him. I decided to take it.

"Why don't you go ahead and throw the one in your right hand down toward the helicopters. Okay? Go ahead."

He turned and made a long throw away from the large crowd and toward the helicopters. The grenade exploded harmlessly, making a huge noise.

"Now, go ahead and throw the other one," I said, "and I'll take you to the doctor."

He threw the second one, and it too exploded harmlessly. I took him gently by the arm, and we walked into the darkness across our small airfield to find the flight surgeon, leaving the lights, the MPs, the crowd, and the surreal scene behind.

The flight surgeon sedated the young man and kept him overnight. As I walked back to the troop area I focused on what might possibly be done to solve this situation. I had to do something about this dilemma, but what, I had no idea. In my judgment and that of the division psychiatrist, the young soldier was mentally unbalanced. He had proven to be dangerous to himself and those around him. It was obvious that the medical authorities were not going to take him off our hands, and higher command had offered no solution.

Perhaps I could have him discharged. A medical discharge seemed appropriate, but I had no idea how that worked. And there was that psychiatrist in Saigon that no doubt would have to be dealt with again. But I was determined to find something. In the Army there is a regulation for every single thing. Usually kept in large, loose-leaf notebooks, Army Regulations (ARs) are in every commander's office. The good first sergeant had them readily available, even there in lovely Vietnam. I would get into those ARs and go to work. If there was any way a rapid discharge from the Army could be accomplished I was going to find it.

I turned on the lights in my little office, selected the book that covered discharges, and began to scan and read. Soon I found a section on "Bad Conduct Discharges." No doubt that process would take forever—but wait! There it was: "In a combat zone a battalion-size commander has authority to administer a Bad Conduct Discharge. He needs no approval from higher authority."

I had no idea.

Damn! I got it. I got it!

I was not a battalion-size unit commander, but my boss was. He was fully apprised of the situation, and I was sure he would do whatever I asked to remedy this problem.

Early the next morning we completed the necessary forms. By noon Delaney had undergone a physical and a psychiatric interview.

I flew the papers to the squadron commander myself for his signature.

Before the afternoon was out, Delaney was out of the Army and on one of my helicopters to Saigon.

Chapter 34

Captain, Are You Any Good?

"MAYDAY! MAYDAY! I've got an engine failure! Oh, goddamn! OhgoddamnOhgoddamnOhgoddamnOhgoddamn!"

It was one of our young warrant officer pilots broadcasting urgently from the Huey he was flying as I was sitting in Operations early one afternoon. I feared the worst.

"OhgoddamnOhgoddamnOhgoddamnOhgoddamn!"

Oh, hell, he's lost it. Listen to that. I hope he hasn't frozen.

"OhgoddamnOhgoddamnOhgoddamnOhgoddamn!"

Then silence. The operations officer and I looked at each other.

He got on the radio. "Did anybody see that engine failure?"

"Roger, this is 2-5. Looks like a perfect landing. He's just outside the perimeter. Nice job."

What a relief.

His verbal reaction had not boded well for the outcome. But, under extreme pressure, he had functioned as he was supposed to as that helicopter fell out from under him. He did a superb job of landing the aircraft without power.

Later I asked him about his soliloquy on the way down.

"What are you talking about, sir?" he said. "I didn't say anything until we got on the ground."

I could only laugh as I congratulated him on the fine job he had done under the most intense and immediate pressure.

Late that afternoon I took a mini-cav team out. I wasn't flying nearly as much as I wanted, and this mission was a special request from one of the infantry battalion commanders, a lieutenant colonel.

I had heard that this particular commander had, on two different occasions, made disparaging remarks about some of my people who had scouted for him. As far as I was able to determine, there was no basis for his attacks. Others told me that he had a reputation for abrasiveness. I had not met him, so this would be an opportunity to find out for myself what kind of man he was.

The lieutenant colonel had his own battalion firebase a few kilometers west of Cu Chi. Every afternoon at precisely 5 p.m., a VC unit would fire three or four mortar rounds into the firebase. This had been going on for about a month, and the battalion had been unable to locate the perpetrators. The VC were masters at going underground and staying hidden. The colonel thought that, with our helicopters, we might be able to do what he and his men had not.

I reported to the firebase about 4 p.m. I left the LOH and Cobra behind so as not to alert the VC to our presence—a Huey landing at the firebase was commonplace; a mini-cav team was not. I went into the operations bunker to meet with the colonel and get briefed on the mission. He was standing and talking with another officer. I waited for a break in the conversation and then introduced myself. He was pleasant enough and started the briefing right away, looking directly at me as he spoke. Not much was known other than the shells came from the northeast, fell every day at 5 p.m., and had for a month. Our job was to find the people firing the rounds and kill or capture them.

Then, his voice heavy with sarcasm, he said, "Well, Captain, most aviators can't read a damn map. Think you can find these little bastards?"

His manner was neither friendly nor joking. I was agitated right away. I didn't like it when someone judged me negatively because I was an aviator, as if flying were the only thing I knew how to do. I had been in the infantry all my military life until I had gone to flight school. One thing I could do well was "read a damn map."

I looked him in the eye and kept my voice low and even. "Well, sir, I found you. I think we'll manage."

He raised his voice slightly. "Well, I haven't seen a goddamn aviator yet who could do a damn thing. Captain, are you any good?"

"Maybe not as good as you, sir," I said, "but then I'm not the one getting my ass shot off at five o'clock every night for the last month, now, am I? You asked for me, sir. I didn't ask for you."

His smug expression did not change, and he did not speak for what seemed like the longest time. He just stood there, looking at me as if he didn't know what to say. I didn't think he expected a lowly captain—an aviator at that—to stand up to him and his demeaning comments. I was not in the habit of debating with senior officers, but this turkey was behaving beneath his rank.

Finally he said, "Well, see what you can do."

"Yes, sir," I said.

I went back and briefed my team. The terrain was flat and open. That would be helpful, but catching a handful of people jumping out, firing off three or four rounds, and then hiding again would be no easy task. We would need some luck, but two things were on our side: My boys were good; and if the bad guys stayed true to form, we knew when they would come out.

We waited until about 10 minutes before 5 p.m. and then got airborne. I put the scout in the quadrant the firing would most likely come from. I scanned a nearby area in my Huey, and, as always, the Cobra circled above.

It was right at 5 when the Cobra called me on the radio.

"Centaur 6, this is 2-5. I got 'em! I got 'em! They're in that house down there. Can I use rockets? Over."

"This is 6. Is it that house down there by itself? Over."

"2-5. Roger. That's the one. Over."

The house sat a hundred meters beyond a small village.

"Did you see them go in there?" I asked. "Over."

"Roger," he said. "There were four or five of them. They just ran inside. Can I use rockets? Over."

"Roger the rockets, 2-5. Take 'em out."

The Cobra rolled in and fired several rockets into the house. There was substantial damage, and I could see smoke rolling out the windows.

"2-5, this is 6. You do good work."

Six of the troops were in my Huey; the other six were in the Huey right behind me. Their job was to move in and kill or capture anyone in the house. We put the troops on the ground about 100 meters behind the house. I got back airborne to watch the operation. As they moved across the open terrain toward the house, there were three houses about 150 meters to their right.

My troop leader on the ground called. "Centaur 6, this is Centaur 1-6. Can we put fire in those last three houses? They're looking right over us. Over."

We were forbidden to fire into any village. If we killed civilians, I would undoubtedly be the author of an "atrocity." Following the rules of engagement, we would find out there were VC in the houses when they fired on my troops. Follow the rules, or put my boys in further jeopardy?

It was an easy decision. "Roger, 1-6. Go ahead. We'll cover them from up here, too. Over."

I called the Cobra. "2-5, this is 6. Keep an eye on those last three houses. If anything moves, blow hell out of it. Over."

"2-5. Roger."

We watched intently for enemy movement as the troops approached the house we had hit. They drew no fire and in moments were inside. There was a good chance that everyone inside was dead or incapacitated from the rocket attack, but you never knew. There could be fighting inside the house.

It was a tense few moments before he called. "6, this is 1-6. We got 'em. They're all dead. There's five of 'em, three women and two men. There's a mortar and ammunition and other weapons. We're pulling it all out now. Over."

"Roger, 1-6," I said. "Good work. We'll be down and get you when you're ready. Over."

"1-6. Roger."

I was pleased that we had run such a successful operation, finding the attackers at the first opportunity. My boys had proved themselves again. I couldn't wait to see that sarcastic colonel.

THE NEXT MORNING I was called to meet with the aviation battalion commander, LTC Robert R. Gosney. Although D Troop was part of the 3rd Squadron, 4th Cavalry, it was attached to the aviation battalion for operational purposes. Therefore, Lieutenant

Colonel Gosney was my immediate superior and the person who wrote my efficiency report. He was a good man, and we got along well.

The colonel and I sat and idly chatted in his office for a few minutes before he turned serious. "Ray, there are a couple of changes we have to make."

"Oh? What's that, sir?"

"We can't call your scouts 'hunter-killer' teams anymore," he said. "They will be simply 'scout teams' from now on."

"What? What the hell is that about, sir? Who gives a damn what we call 'em?"

"Apparently somebody does, son."

"Well, hell's bells, sir, that doesn't make any sense," I said. "They *are* 'hunter-killer' teams. They are out there hunting and killing! These are tough little bastards out there flying these scouts and Cobras, sir. We can't start calling them 'ice cream' teams. Hell, sir, it's a morale thing."

"Well," he said, "they will just have to get over it. That's the way it is from now on. They are 'scout teams.' Period."

"Well, goddamn, sir, I sure don't understand that one," I said. "It has to be those stupid bastards in Washington. I know damn well the general would never do that."

I got up and left. This was so petty. Now they were concerned about the connotation of the names we assigned our smallest fighting teams? We read newspaper accounts every day about the protesters on the streets at home. Our enemy was not about to cease hostilities as long as we were fighting among ourselves at home and publicly condemning our fighting men. It was easy to see that the public protests at home were prolonging the war, not shortening it.

Chapter 35

The General and Me

I **WALKED INTO** my office early one afternoon just as First Sergeant Henry was answering the phone.

"It's for you, sir," he said. "Someone from Squadron."

I picked up the phone and was startled by the cryptic message: "Captain Clark, the division commander wants to see you in his office at 1600."

What? The general wants to see me?

Division commanders—major generals—do not call company-size commanders—captains—to their headquarters. If that company commander has done something to merit the general's attention, it is his boss—a lieutenant colonel, usually, or a full colonel—who hears about it first.

I had seen the general before but had never met him.

What could he possibly want with me?

After inquiring, I was pretty sure I knew. One of my scout teams had killed a Vietnamese man, and apparently there had been a complaint about it from the local Vietnamese government. This would not be a pat on the back.

I went to division headquarters at 4 p.m. and was shown to the general's office.

I knocked on his door, entered, crossed the floor to his desk, then locked my heels and saluted. "Sir, Captain Clark, D Troop, Three Quarter Cav. You wanted to see me, sir?"

He rose and came from behind his desk. He wasn't antagonistic, but his tone wasn't exactly friendly, either. I sensed I was in a little trouble here—maybe a lot. How I handled myself could determine how the future would go for my scout pilot and me. I didn't want to appear defensive, but I felt I had to hold my ground. I tried to match his tone while being absolutely respectful.

"At ease, Captain," he said. "One of your scouts killed a Vietnamese civilian about 1300 hours today. According to the province chief, he was a village official. How did this happen?"

"Sir, my scout came over the top of a hill maybe five feet off the ground," I said. "There was a cart in the open 20 or 30 feet from the tree line. There was a man in the trees. When my boys popped over the hill, he broke and ran toward the cart. When he broke toward the cart, they fired and killed him."

"Why didn't they identify him before shooting?" he asked.

"Sir, my boys are five feet off the ground and closing fast," I said. "If he's a good guy and just scared, he stays hidden in the trees. He doesn't dash out in the open to a cart. If he's a bad guy he comes up out of that cart, point-blank in the face of my boys, with an AK-47. Then we are identifying *them*."

"Captain, we can't be killing people we aren't supposed to kill."

"Sir, I know that," I said, "and we are trying very hard not to. But my boys don't get a second chance, sir. If they wait and they guess wrong, they die. I don't like those odds, sir. My instructions to them are to shoot unless they are satisfied they don't have to."

The general spent the next few minutes lecturing me severely.

He finished by saying, "I know it's tough out there, Captain, but we just can't be killing people we aren't supposed to kill. That's all."

"Yes, sir," I said. "We'll work hard at it, sir."

I turned and left, feeling like a beat-up prizefighter who had just won a decision. There had been no threat of disciplinary action toward my scout pilot, I was still a captain, and I still had my command. I figured it was a win.

A few days later I got a call to see Lieutenant Colonel Gosney. There were no niceties this time, and the conversation was way beyond what names we might use for our scout teams.

Before I could sit down, he got right to the point. "Ray, you all are killing people you aren't supposed to kill. Your scout pilots cannot shoot first anymore. They must get permission to fire or they must be fired on first. Then they can return fire."

It took me a moment to reply. "Sir, you can't be serious. You can't mean that."

"I'm dead serious," he said. "That's the way it is from now on."

"Sir, you have the wrong man for the job," I said. "I can't do that."

"Dammit, Ray, that's the policy. Now get out of here and go put it into effect!"

"Yes, sir," I said.

There was no point in arguing. I got up and left. This was not Lieutenant Colonel Gosney's idea. He would never have done that. Perhaps the general ordered it, but this directive had the mark of Washington on it. Certainly it did not originate with a combat soldier. What were those people thinking? I know what I was thinking. They could go to hell with that one.

I loved the Army. My heroes were Eisenhower, MacArthur, Patton, and a hundred others of lesser name but equal valor and commitment on the battlefield. It was my intention to serve 30 or 40 years.

There was a conversation I had a number of times over the years with officers or men who were leaving the service for some other endeavor. "Hell, Clark, why don't you get out? Why, you would be great in civilian life."

"Somebody has to take care of the country, Ace. That's what I do."

And I meant it. But I was not going to issue that order. They could take my command, they could take my commission; they could do whatever they wanted—I never even considered issuing the directive.

It was the only order I ever disobeyed.

Chapter 36

Buddha

WHEN I FIRST arrived in Cu Chi, I met a first lieutenant at the aviation battalion. He was a big, overweight, redheaded kid with a less-than-exemplary military bearing. Frankly, he looked like hell. But he had a really good personality, and I liked him. I wondered what assignment he would get. Wherever he went I figured he was sure to be discriminated against because of his appearance.

I left for Division Artillery and did not see him again until I arrived at D Troop. There he was, a captain and platoon leader of the Cobras. I had to look at my own prejudice because I was surprised that he was holding such a demanding position. I knew nothing of him except that he was grossly overweight and I liked him. He looked nothing like any fighter I had ever seen or imagined, yet he already had a fearsome reputation in the troop. Because of his size and appearance, his friends called him Buddha. He was simply a killing machine. No matter where we put him in the troop, he managed to increase his personal toll of enemy dead. We could have made him mail clerk and still he would have found enemy soldiers to annihilate.

Buddha's best buddy was a slightly built, dark-headed, dark-eyed, mustachioed young man named White, but to his friends and everyone else in the troop, he was Snidely T. Whiplash. Snidely was always giving Buddha hell about Buddha's increasing body count. He swore to Buddha's face that Buddha was making up half his reported kills. Snidely was not to be overlooked himself. He was a platoon leader for one simple reason—he was good. He was *real* good.

One day, unbeknownst to me, Snidely and Buddha scheduled themselves to ride together in an LOH on a hunter-killer team mission. It was standard operating procedure that two platoon leaders never flew together in the same helicopter. If a helicopter went down, you did not want to lose two of your leaders at the same time. Curiosity and banter between the two friends overrode good judgment.

Their good friend CPT Bill Malinovsky, another fine Cobra pilot and one of my best officers, would fly the Cobra 1000 feet above, watching over them as they flew along the ground looking for the enemy. This hunter-killer team was operating by itself, several kilometers from any assistance. Along with Snidely and Buddha in the scout helicopter was the crew chief, who was sitting in the back with a machine gun and a box of grenades. Malinovsky, of course, had his gunner/pilot with him.

About midafternoon Snidely and Buddha, only a few feet in the air, flew right up on an NVA company and took several rounds of small arms fire. The helicopter crashed to the ground, flopping over on its left side, throwing the giant Buddha on top of the diminutive Snidely T. Whiplash. Buddha and Snidely were shot, Buddha in the calf and Snidely in the ankle. Snidely was trapped under Buddha. Buddha could not move himself off Snidely. The crew chief was unhurt.

Still taking fire, Buddha and Snidely wanted out of that helicopter in the worst way.

"Buddha, you son-of-a-bitch, get off of me!"

"I can't, goddammit," Buddha said, "I'm shot!"

"Well, goddammit, so am I!" yelled Snidely. "Now get the fuck off of me!"

The crew chief pulled his machine gun from the wreckage. Seeing Snidely and Buddha in a heap, he pulled them from the helicopter and dragged them into a small depression in the ground for cover. He set up his machine gun and went to work on the enemy position.

Overhead, Malinovsky called for help and rolled in, firing machine guns and rockets on the enemy position to hold them at bay. He made pass after pass, finally emptying all his rockets and ammunition into the enemy position. Help was still several minutes away. How long could the crew chief hold off the NVA by himself? It seemed inevitable that the three men would be overrun and killed.

For Bill Malinovsky, there was only one thing to do—rescue his friends. But there was no room for them in the Cobra, no room even for a rifle. No matter. Malinovsky landed, placing his Cobra between the enemy position and his friends. His pilot got out and removed the empty ammunition containers from the Cobra while Malinovsky stayed at the controls and fired his .38 pistol at the enemy.

Removal of the ammunition trays left an open space through the narrow body of the Cobra. The pilot and the crew chief dragged Snidely and Buddha to the Cobra and pushed them into the open space. The crew chief climbed in with them. All three were hanging out of the Cobra, feet and legs on one side, heads and shoulders on the other. Malinovsky put his .38 away. The pilot got back in and closed the canopy. They flew off, the Cobra full of bullet holes.

Two days later, I watched in Snidely and Buddha's hospital room as the commanding general awarded five Distinguished Flying Crosses to the cast of the Snidely and Buddha Follies. The crew chief took it all in stride. I took great pleasure in seeing the crew chief decorated along with the officers.

Snidely and Buddha were evacuated to a hospital in Japan, and, sadly, we did not see them again. Before he was shot, Buddha killed 106 enemy soldiers.

Chapter 37

When You Come Back

THE GRENADE LAUNCHER on a Cobra jammed while a mini-cav team was on a mission west of Cu Chi. The aircraft commander reported the problem, stating to expect him in 15 minutes to have it repaired. A crew was waiting for the Cobra when it landed.

The grenade launcher is mounted on the nose of the helicopter. The barrel of the weapon is short and stubby. The grenade it discharges is roughly the size of a person's fist. It looks like a big, fat bullet rather than a hand grenade. The grenade flies about 10 feet before arming itself, and it explodes when it makes contact with a solid object.

A jammed weapon is a serious situation. It might never fire again, or it might fire at any moment. We had specially trained people to repair such weapons.

The crew began working gingerly on the grenade launcher. A few minutes into the job, an 18-year-old crew member walked in front of the helicopter. At that precise moment the grenade launcher went off, firing the large projectile into the young soldier's torso.

The hospital was nearby; they had him there within five minutes. The grenade had severed an artery that couldn't be reached and held by the surgeon's clamp. The young soldier bled to death. He had been with us about two weeks.

I got the news late that afternoon when I returned from flying. I was not allowed to write the young man's family. Form letters from division headquarters were sent instead, by someone who never saw the lad's face, let alone had any idea who he was.

He wasn't the first of our boys to die, nor was he the last. Tragedy could strike at any time and from any direction. The administrators, safe in Washington, had their rules of war. I had 18-year-olds.

The next morning First Sergeant Henry informed me we had a visitor. "Sir, there's a reporter from Life outside. Says he wants to talk to someone who's killed people."

"What kind of a stupid son-of-a-bitch is that?" I said. "Is he real? Are you serious?"

"Yes, sir. That's what he says."

I didn't even want to see this clown. "Well, Top, line the boys up. Tell the silly son-of-a-bitch to take his pick."

MAIL IS A precious thing to a soldier in combat. Everything written in letters from home tends to be magnified. Love is too sweet to contemplate. Disappointments are bitter, even devastating. A soldier yearns for mail. There is an ache in the pit of the stomach when letters and packages are given to others while he is passed by. Letters are a lifeline.

My wife had written almost every day over my two years in Vietnam. But the best letter I ever received was from my four-year-old daughter, Terri.

DEAR DADDY

How Are You.

I Am Fing But I Miss You. How Is Army Prety Good? I Hope So.

You So Good To Me When You Come Back. I Hope You Have A Good Good Time

· Love Terri

Letter from my daughter Terri, barely 4. 1966.

Chapter 38

Ten Cents for My Career

I WAS IN deep trouble this time. It was the kind of trouble that sees one relieved of his command. Nothing is more devastating to a military career than being relieved of a command in combat. You might remain in the service if that happens to you, but your career is over.

I was working harder than I ever had, and positive results were evident in the enhanced performance of the troop. Morale had gone from poor to high and was still climbing. I was drawing praise from my two immediate commanders. We had a long way to go to get to the level of performance I was striving for, but we were well on the way. And then one afternoon....

In the middle of a big fight, one of my mini-cav team leaders, a warrant officer, refused a combat order from a battalion commander. I received a call about 2:30 p.m. informing me of this and directing me to meet the brigade commander, a full colonel, at his helipad at 6 p.m. It was clear that it meant my obituary as troop commander. How could one possibly justify refusal of an order in combat? I could not imagine such a thing. It did not matter that I had not been there. A commander is responsible for everything his people do or fail to do. I was mortified that one of my officers had refused an order, but I had told my officers and men that if they got in trouble while doing their best, I would stand up for them no matter what. I wasn't about to back away from that promise.

I needed to learn exactly what had happened. If I met the colonel with no knowledge of the details of the incident, I would have no chance at all for survival. Even with full knowledge, I could imagine no circumstance that could justify the refusal. Orders cannot be refused—they simply cannot. I figured there was a good chance that when I met the brigade commander I would be relieved on the spot.

The team remained engaged in the fight through the afternoon. It appeared that they would not return before I was to meet the colonel. The afternoon dragged by and I was able to obtain no details at all. Finally, about 5:30 p.m., the team made radio contact with Operations, and I was able to get some sketchy detail.

I knew the battalion commander involved. He was none other than the obnoxious lieutenant colonel we had relieved of the daily mortar attacks a few days earlier. I knew he was a horse's ass. There might be an opening there. My team leader's story, as I heard it, had at least some merit, but I had no justification and no strong or convincing argument. If that colonel wanted me, he had me, and I knew he would be madder than hell. This was a dilemma from which there was no escape. I could see only one thing to do—attack.

I met the colonel as he stepped out of his command-and-control helicopter at the 2nd Brigade helipad. He wasn't just mad—he was bristling. I gathered myself to meet the assault and followed him into his headquarters building. We entered the building, and he stopped and turned to face me as I closed the door.

Still dressed in full combat gear, including steel helmet and rifle, he glared down at me where we stood in a small hallway.

Why are all these senior officers I keep getting in trouble with so damn tall?

I stood at attention and looked him dead in the eye.

"Captain," he said, "why did I get a combat refusal out there!"

"Sir, you didn't get any combat refusal out there! My man was following my instructions, and I was following yours!"

"What do you mean?" the colonel said.

"Sir," I said, "just three days ago your operations officer and your executive officer instructed me personally that under no circumstance, absolutely no circumstance, were any of my people to make insertions west of a certain line at the bottom of the Bo Loi Woods. Where your battalion commander told my team leader to insert his team was well across that line! And when my team flew over that clearing where your colonel said to put my ten men, there were five bodies in the open. When they came back over, there were only four. That means VC in the wood line, sir. That was not a ten-man mission! Your colonel knew that, sir! He should have put his men in there!"

This sounded a little weak to me, but it was the only argument I had, and it was true.

Surprisingly, the colonel lowered his tone a bit. "Well, goddam-mit, Captain, we can't have that kind of thing! I took care of it myself. I put a company in there and we cleaned it up!"

A company! A company? That's 180 men! And they wanted my guy to put in 10?

I knew I had won, so I pressed. "That's what I'm talking about, sir! That colonel knew that was a company-size mission! If my guy puts my 10 men on the ground and there are VC in the tree line, my boys are all dead right now! And further, sir, while we are talking about your battalion commander, I'd like him to quit bad-mouthing my troops, sir. We have done good work for him in the past, sir, and I keep hearing he talks bad about my people.

"Sir," I continued, "I take more casualties than any company-size unit in this division. We don't get two-week stand-downs. We're out there seven days a week in front of every operation this division does. We do damn good work, and I don't want him bad-mouthing my boys, sir."

Luckily I had about run down, because I could see it was past time for me to shut up.

"Well, I didn't realize that," he said. "I'll speak to the colonel. We'll put a stop to that."

"Thank you, sir," I said. "I would appreciate it."

"Captain, you make sure your people follow instructions!" the colonel said.

"Yes, sir. I will," I said. "I'll make damn sure we do!"

"That's all!" said the colonel.

I got out of there fast. When I walked in that door with him, I wouldn't have given 10 cents for my career. I marveled that I got away with it, though everything I had said was true.

Except the part about my troop taking more casualties than any other company-size unit in the division. I made that up.

Chapter 39

Guardians of the Nation

THE TROOP WAS steadily growing more efficient, and morale was soaring. I had begun to feel a real ownership of my charge and I was maturing as a young commander. My responsibility for the mission and well-being of my troops had transformed from the realm of duty to a way of being and living. My purpose was clear and I was devoted to it, yet I could not help but be affected by news from home. I was an American infantry captain, a guardian of the nation. And the nation, to my eternal dismay, seemed not to care.

We continually saw newspaper clips and features of public protests of the war and castigation of the military. The military—that was me. It was those young men out there being killed and maimed and, in unseen ways, scarred for life. To see an American movie starlet in Hanoi wearing an enemy helmet and perched on an enemy artillery piece was devastating. How could this happen? While we knew she did not speak for everyone, where were those who did not agree with her? Since Valley Forge the American soldier in combat has been a committed, driving force, personifying honor. What was going on?

An Army officer, a combat leader, a commander—that's who I was. I started my career as a 17-year-old private, spent three years in the 82nd Airborne Division, then two in the 101st Airborne Division jumping out of airplanes and honing my skills as a small unit leader. I went to more colleges and night schools than I can remember in order to educate myself and get a degree. I went to OCS at Fort Benning, finishing first in my class. I was profoundly proud to be a Regular Army officer. As my tour was coming to a close, I was at the pinnacle of my performance. In sad contrast, I was having severe problems at home.

Over previous weeks I had grown concerned that I might lose my family. I was scheduled to go home in January, only a month away—but that might be too late. The thought of leaving my command early, even three or four weeks, did not sit well with me. I felt a responsibility to every man in the troop. I remembered General MacArthur's ringing words, "Duty, Honor, Country." I thought of the words of an old cavalry first sergeant who, when asked about a pending change of command, replied, "The commanders, they come and they go, but they don't hurt the troop none."

I asked to go home early. I was released and sent home just before Christmas 1969. An armor major came in to replace me the day I left.

With six Hueys at my disposal, I scheduled a 4:30 p.m. departure for Saigon and Tan Son Nhut Airport. I wasn't about to ride in the back of a helicopter while someone else flew the aircraft. I put my bags in the back and crawled into the familiar left seat for my last flight in Vietnam.

What an honor it was to command these men in battle. If Vietnam truly was a "helicopter war," as it has been called, it was not the helicopter but the pilots and crewmen who made it so. Most pilots were right out of flight school; few had wartime flying experience when they entered Vietnam. They learned their craft in combat—and they learned it fast. They had more courage than sense. When needed, they went. When they could not see, they went. When they did not know how they would get out, they went in. They made instant decisions, and lived and died by them. They asked no quarter and gave none.

I thought of Malinovsky landing his Cobra in front of that enemy position, daring them to defeat him and his .38 pistol while his pilot loaded the wounded into the ammo bin; of Wesley and Jerry losing their engine at 6000 feet over mountains in total darkness; of Charlie telling that general on the radio, "Don't worry about the mule, just load the wagon!" I thought of my friend Jesse Chapman, shot between the eyes while flying his scout helicopter, sustaining only a superficial wound and two black eyes; my B/227 crew chief on his last day in country, leaning out the cargo door, watching his tail rotor disappear into the trees. I could see Chuck trying to pull out of that high-speed dive that killed him; I saw my two boys going down in their Cobra after the rotor blades had separated. I thought of my brilliant, young warrant officer candidate, Mark Mitchell, killed just days before I was to assume command of his unit. I thought of how Tommy was respected and loved by his peers of the 191st at Bearcat, and the gut-wrenching news of his death. I remembered my class-mate who, taking just one more flight on his last scheduled day in country, was killed on that flight.

These helicopter pilots and crewmen stand alongside the best in America's history. What a privilege to have been associated with, to *be* one of those American helicopter pilots of the Vietnam Era.

I flew low-level up the taxiway and landed right next to the main terminal building. I got out, said goodbye to my boys in the Huey, took my bags, and walked away.

Afterword

IN EARLY 1997 I was in the Napa Valley of northern California, participating in a personal development course delivered by the Hoffman Institute.

Late one bright and warm morning, I was sitting in a beautiful outdoor setting of flowers, lush spring grass, and the most magnificent trees. As part of a course exercise, I was alone, talking aloud to my father, who had died in 1978. I was thanking him for being the man and father that he was.

When I finished, it occurred to me to ask him a question. "Now, Daddy, is there anything you would like to say to me?"

In my mind, I heard him speak.

"Well, yes. By the way, after 1978 I went back to Vietnam. I took every flight with you—every flight. It was so much fun! You know I had never ridden in a helicopter before. I sat right beside you."

It sounded like time travel to me. I pictured him sitting to my right and slightly behind, between the two pilots' seats, as I sat in the left seat in my Huey.

"It was so exciting!" I heard him say. "I got the rush of the flight as you went in and came out. I saw everything. And what's more, I got to watch you. I got to sit right there and see how you reacted when you got in trouble, and how you acted going into trouble. I saw how you behaved and what you did to save people and to save yourself. It was awesome. I was there on every flight, son—every flight."

I cried, and I laughed, and experienced the most joyful moment of my life.

Who better to know.

Glossary

1/5. 1st Battalion, 5th Cavalry, 1st Cavalry Division (Airmobile).

101st. 101st Airborne Division, storied infantry division renowned for its role in World War II; unit I was assigned as both an enlisted man and second lieutenant. Base is Fort Campbell, Kentucky.

1st Cav. 1st Cavalry Division (Airmobile), commonly referred to as the 1st Air Cavalry Division, an infantry division combat-tested in Vietnam with 434 helicopters and new airmobile tactics.

2/5. 2nd Battalion, 5th Cavalry, 1st Cavalry Division (Airmobile).

227th. 227th Aviation Battalion (Assault Helicopter), 1st Cavalry Division (Airmobile); my assignment during my first tour in 1966. Base camp was in An Khe.

229th. 229th Aviation Battalion (Assault Helicopter), 1st Cavalry Division (Airmobile), sister battalion to the 227th.

3/4 Cav. 3rd Squadron, 4th Cavalry, 25th Infantry Division; where I was assigned with D Troop in 1969 during my second tour.

82nd. 82nd Airborne Division, airborne infantry division specializing in parachute landing operations; my first unit assignment in the Army. Base is Fort Bragg, North Carolina.

6. Unit commander; unit commander's radio call sign.

AHC. Assault helicopter company, as in 191st AHC.

AH-1G. Cobra gunship providing fire support for ground forces; paired with OH-6A scout helicopters to form hunter-killer teams.

airspeed. Speed of the aircraft relative to the air.

altimeter. Aircraft instrument that indicates altitude in feet above sea level.

An Khe. Village in the Central Highlands in Vietnam; home of the 1st Cavalry Division (Airmobile) mid 1965-1968.

APC. 1. A large white tablet containing aspirin, phenacetin and caffeine; used as an analgesic. 2. Armored personnel carrier.

approach. Final part of a flight just before landing.

ARA. Aerial rocket artillery. In 1966 and 1967 they were B or C model Huey helicopters that fired rockets only. Later the Cobra replaced the Huey as ARA.

artillery preparation. Firing of artillery into a landing zone preceding landing of helicopters transporting combat soldiers. The purpose was to kill and disrupt the enemy and thus make it safer for the helicopters to land. The landing area would be saturated with shells from big guns for typically five or six minutes.

autorotate. Fly to the ground and land a helicopter that has lost its engine power. When power is lost, the pilot removes all pitch from the rotor blades; the blades automatically disconnect from the failed engine and, due to air rushing up through the blades, continue to spin as the helicopter falls, allowing flight and a degree of maneuverability as the aircraft descends.

base camp. Field headquarters for a given unit.

bunker. Protective shelter, generally underground.

C-130. Fixed-wing military transport aircraft.

CA. See combat assault.

Central Highlands. Strategically important, prominent geographic region in South Vietnam with elevations ranging from 100 to over 1000 meters.

checked out. Qualified and certified to fly a particular type of aircraft.

Chinook. CH-47, twin-rotor cargo helicopter.

choppers. Helicopters.

close air support. Air strikes against enemy targets.

CO. Commanding officer.

Cobra. See AH-1G.

combat assault. Landing of infantry troops into a hostile area by helicopter with the intention of doing combat.

command-and-control helicopter/ship. Helicopter that transported a senior infantry commander; an airborne platform from which to command and control his unit.

commo check. Check of radio's operating condition.

contact. Active engagement with the enemy.

C-rations. Canned rations issued to GIs for field operations.

crew chief. Helicopter mechanic assigned to a particular helicopter. A Huey crew chief rode in the back of the cargo compartment on the left side. He sat facing outward and operated a mounted .30-caliber machine gun.

Cu Chi. Small city in Vietnam near Saigon; location of 25th Infantry Division base camp.

cyclic. One of three primary controls in the helicopter. Stick-like object that protrudes vertically from the floor between the pilot's knees; provides directional control by tilting the path of the plane of the rotor blades.

dink. Disparaging term for a North Vietnamese soldier or guerilla in Vietnam War.

Distinguished Flying Cross. Medal awarded for heroism or extraordinary achievement while participating in aerial flight.

donut dollies. Young female college graduates sent to Vietnam by the American Red Cross to boost morale of the troops.

door gunner. Helicopter crewman. A Huey door gunner sat in the back of the cargo compartment on the right side. He sat facing outward and operated a mounted .30-caliber machine gun.

Dustoff. Nickname for a medical evacuation helicopter or mission.

executive officer. Second-in-command.

final. Last part of an approach to land.

FAC. See forward air controller.

firebase. Area in a war zone which usually serves as a forward base for a battalion or brigade size unit; may include artillery units.

FM. Frequency modulation; radio frequency band commonly used for ground-to-ground communication, but also used by aircraft to communicate with ground units.

FNG. Fucking new guy, a term used for new arrivals in Vietnam.

forward air controller. Provides guidance to close air support aircraft to ensure attack hits intended target and does not injure friendly troops.

forward observer. One who directs artillery fire onto targets.

Fox Mike. Vernacular for FM radio. See FM. (Fox and Mike are both parts of the military phonetic alphabet.)

FPM. Feet per minute; measure of an aircraft's rate of ascent or descent.

gaggle. A flight of helicopters.

GCA. 1. ground-controlled approach; aircraft landing in bad weather in which the pilot is talked down by ground control using precision approach radar. 2. Ground Control Approach; portable ground-controlled approach radar landing system.

GI. Government issue, vernacular for soldier.

go around. Abort an anticipated landing, typically circling to set up another approach.

Golf Course. Parking area at An Khe (Camp Radcliff) for the 1st Cavalry Division (Airmobile)'s 434 helicopters.

gook. Derogatory germ for a Vietnamese soldier, often civilians too.

GP. General purpose.

grease gun. World War II sub-machine gun.

ground speed. Speed of the aircraft relative to the surface of the earth.

guns. See gunship.

gunship. Typically UH-1B or UH-1C model Hueys or Cobras armed with rocket pods and machine guns, and sometimes a grenade launcher.

gun-target line. Imaginary line from gun to target.

H-hour. In general, the specific starting time of an operation or attack. In a combat assault, the specific time of touchdown in the LZ for the lead helicopter.

heavy left formation. Four helicopters flying in an inverted V formation, the fourth helicopter on the left side.

heavy right formation. Four helicopters flying in an inverted V formation, the fourth helicopter on the right side.

Hill 534. In the southern portion of Chu Pong Massif near the Cambodian border.

hooch. Any house or living quarters that is not a tent.

hot LZ. Landing zone receiving enemy fire.

Huey. Army UH-1 helicopter. This helicopter was the Army's workhorse in the Vietnam War. B and C models were slightly smaller than D models and were configured with machine guns and rocket pods. Accordingly, they were used as gunships. The D model had a larger cargo area and was used as a troop carrier. The H model succeeded the D model. It was essentially the same as the D model except that it had a stronger, more powerful engine.

"I got it." I have control of and am now flying the aircraft. You may release the controls.

instructor pilot. Authorized to certify other pilots as flight-ready.

instrument rating, standard. Authorization to fly in instrument conditions.

instrument rating, tactical. Authorization to fly in instrument conditions only in Vietnam.

instrument takeoff. Using the aircraft instruments rather than outside visual cues to execute a safe takeoff in instrument conditions (limited to no visibility).

IP. See instructor pilot.

ITO. See instrument takeoff.

Jesus Nut. Main rotor retaining nut that holds the main rotor onto the rotor mast.

KIA. Killed in action.

knots. Nautical miles per hour used for stating military aircraft airspeed. (1 knot equals 1.151 miles per hour.)

landing zone. Commonly the landing area for a heliborne combat assault. Any designated place or spot for landing one or more helicopters; sometimes a specific place, such as LZ Cat.

Kit Carson scout. Former Viet Cong soldiers who defected and acted as scouts for U.S. troops.

lift pilot. Pilot who flew lift ships, typically the D or H model Huey.

lift ship. Helicopter, typically a D or H model Huey, used primarily for transporting or "lifting" troops.

Loach. See LOH.

LOH. Light observation helicopter, OH-6A, nicknamed "Loach."

LZ. See landing zone.

Mattel. Reference to the large corporate manufacturer of toys.

medevac. Medical evacuation.

mike. Microphone.

Montagnards. Aboriginal mountain people of Vietnam who wore loin cloths, lived in huts built on stilts, and hunted with bowguns they made from the wild.

mortar. Muzzle-loading, indirect fire weapon. It typically has a shorter range than a howitzer, employs a higher angle of fire.

MP. Military police.

NCO. Noncommissioned officer.

NDB. See non-directional beacon.

non-directional beacon. Radio transmitter at a known location, used as a navigational aid.

NVA. See North Vietnamese Army.

North Vietnamese Army. Army of North Vietnamese regular soldiers, as opposed to guerilla fighters called Viet Cong or VC.

Never-Never Land. Vietnam (my own colloquialism).

OCS. See Officer Candidate School.

Officer Candidate School. Training school that produced second lieutenants (entry-level officers). Not affiliated with any university or service academy; typically six months in duration.

OH-6A. See LOH.

pedal. In a helicopter, refers to the pair of foot-pedal flight controls that control the tail rotor. The purpose of the tail rotor is to counteract the torque effect of the main rotor, to control the heading of the helicopter during hovering flight, and to initiate and control turns while hovering.

pentaprime. Asphalt-like substance used to coat dirt air strips.

Peter Pilot. Pilot whose primary responsibility is to fly the aircraft, as opposed to the aircraft commander who has overall responsibility for the aircraft, crew, and cargo.

pickup zone. Site where troops were to be picked up by helicopter.

pinnacle. Mountain peak.

pitch control. Control lever that adjusts the amount of pitch or angle at which the rotor blades bite into the air as they spin. Increased pitch makes the helicopter go higher; decreased pitch allows the helicopter to go lower.

pull pitch. Increase in pitch angle of rotor blades to take off; typically refers to takeoff from the ground. Analogy would be to step on the gas of a car.

R&R. Military slang for rest and relaxation. During the Vietnam

War, a five-day vacation from the combat zone to a major city in Asia, Australia, or Hawaii. Provided by the military for the serviceman or servicewoman. Family travel was at one's own expense.

rappel. Descend from cliff or helicopter by rope.

ready reaction force. Combat unit held in reserve, its purpose to respond immediately to any combat emergency.

recon. See reconnaissance.

reconnaissance. Scout an area.

rifle company. Company of infantry soldiers, typically around 180 when at full strength.

RPM. Revolutions per minute, typically refers to speed of the helicopter engine and/or rotor blades.

scout pilot. Helicopter pilot who flew light observation helicopters in a scouting role. They typically flew five or ten feet off the ground looking for the enemy.

short final. Final part of an approach just before touching down to land.

six. See 6.

slick. D or H model Huey with two mounted machine guns, one on each side, used to carry troops.

sling load. Load carried beneath a helicopter in a sling.

spider hole. Small hole dug in the ground where enemy soldiers would hide.

stand-down. Relaxation from a state of readiness or alert.

Silver Star. Third highest military decoration in the U.S. Awarded for valor in the face of the enemy.

tail boom. Extension beginning at the rear of a helicopter cabin area. Serves as a mount for the tail rotor.

tail rotor. Small, vertically mounted rotor at the rear-most part of the helicopter. It provides torque or spin control. As the main rotor blades spin to the left, physical law makes the fuselage or body of the helicopter spin in the opposite direction. The tail rotor, operated by two foot pedals in the cockpit, controls that opposite spin. It also provides the ability to turn while at a hover.

Top. Vernacular for the rank of first sergeant, the senior enlisted rank in a company-sized unit.

triple canopy. Thickest jungle with vegetation growing at three levels: ground, intermediate, and high.

troop. Company-sized unit (approximately 200 soldiers) in the cavalry. Also vernacular for trooper or soldier.

UH. Utility helicopter.

UH-1. See Huey.

UHF. Radio frequency band commonly used for air-to-air communication.

VC. See Viet Cong.

Viet Cong. South Vietnamese Communist guerillas.

warrant officer. A skilled technician ranked below commissioned officers and above noncommissioned officers.

XO. See executive officer.

"you got it." You have control of and are now flying the aircraft. I have released the controls.

TAY NINH

TRANG
BANG

CAMBODIA

● DAU TIENG

PHUOC
MEI
● ● CU CHI

TAN SON
NHUT
● LONG BINH
●
SAIGON

SOUTH CHINA SEA

CPSIA information can be obtained at www.ICGtesting.com
Printed in the USA
LVOW130948111112

306541LV00001B/7/P